Edward Felix Mendelssohn Benecke

Antimachus of Colophon and the Position of Women in Greek Poetry

A Fragment Printed for the Use of Scholars

Edward Felix Mendelssohn Benecke

Antimachus of Colophon and the Position of Women in Greek Poetry
A Fragment Printed for the Use of Scholars

ISBN/EAN: 9783337250997

Printed in Europe, USA, Canada, Australia, Japan

Cover: Foto ©Thomas Meinert / pixelio.de

More available books at **www.hansebooks.com**

Antimachus of Colophon

AND THE

Position of Women in Greek Poetry

BY

E. F. M. BENECKE

A Fragment

PRINTED FOR THE USE OF SCHOLARS

LONDON
SWAN SONNENSCHEIN & CO., Lim.
1896

ERRATA AND ADDENDA

Page 22, n. 1, l. 10, for 'xxxix.', read 'xxxvii.'
,, 27, n. 1, for '$βίβλια$,' read '$βιβλία$.'
,, 31, l. 8, after 'dissolute habits,' add: [Bergk, ed. I. (used by the author) reads $μηδένα\ πω\ κ.τ.λ.$ in *Theog.* 547: Bergk, ed. IV., has $παῖ$ for $πω$].
,, 60, for '$ὑβρίζουσ : οὐ$,' read '$ὑβρίζουσ · οὐ$.'
,, 107, n. 3, add: [$Τμώλιον\ αἴζαον$. The author accepts Hermann's reading; see *Opusc.* iv. 245. $αἴζαον = ὄρος\ ὑψηλόν$ (Hesych.)].
,, 108, note, l. 6, for '$ἑταῖραν$,' read '$ἑταίραν$.'
,, 117, n. 1, for '405-336,' read '403-336.'
,, 158, l. 12, for '$ἄνθρωπος$,' read '$ἄνθρωπος$.'
,, 160, l. 23, for '$πείθειν$,' read '$πείσειν$.'
,, 191, note, l. 4, for '*La Rêve*,' read '*Le Rêve.*'
,, 204, n. 1, l. 5, for '$ἡβητὴς$,' read '$ἡβητής$.'

CONTENTS

			PAGE
ESSAY	I. WOMEN IN GREEK POETRY	. . .	1
,,	II. WOMEN IN GREEK COMEDY	. . .	117
EXCURSUS	A. THEOGNIS (l. 261 *seqq.*)	. . .	199
,,	B. THE "PHAEDRA" OF SOPHOCLES	. .	201
,,	C. THE "ANDROMEDA" OF EURIPIDES	. .	203
,,	D. THE "HIPPOLYTUS" OF EURIPIDES (Two Emendations)	. . . .	206
,,	E. THE SECOND BOOK OF THEOGNIS	. .	207
,,	F. WOMEN IN THE MIDDLE COMEDY	. .	210
,,	G. WOMEN IN THE MIDDLE COMEDY FRAGMENTS (Analysis of passages)	. . .	219
,,	H. WOMEN IN THE FRAGMENTS OF THE EARLY NEW COMEDY (Analysis of passages)	.	233
,,	I. "WOMEN'S RIGHTS" IN THE MIDDLE COMEDY		243
,,	K. SOME FURTHER NOTES ON FAMILY RELATIONS AS TREATED IN MIDDLE AND NEW COMEDY		245
INDEX	A. OF AUTHORS AND SUBJECTS REFERRED TO	.	247
INDEX	B. OF PASSAGES EMENDED OR DISCUSSED	. .	252
TABLE OF COMIC FRAGMENTS		. . .	253

INTRODUCTORY NOTE

THE author of the following pages met with his death in Switzerland on July 16th, 1895, in his twenty-sixth year. Had he lived to complete the whole work of which they form part, he might have recast it throughout; and some apology is, perhaps, needed for its appearance in the present form. Several scholars have, however, expressed their opinion that the material contained in the extant fragments might be useful to those engaged in similar studies, and they are accordingly published, in the hope that this may prove to be the case.

From the author's papers it appears that his work was, if completed, to have been entitled "Women in Greek Poetry: being an Enquiry into the Origin of the Romantic Element in Literature." It was to have contained three divisions, dealing respectively with (1) the position occupied by women in the Greek lyric and tragic poets, (2) the part played by women in Greek comedy, (3) the Alexandrian ideal of woman. The former of the two essays contained in this volume ("Women in Greek Poetry") no doubt includes much that would have been incorporated in the first of these three divisions. At the same time, as it was, in all probability, written before the whole scheme was arranged, and was intended to be complete in itself, it contains allusions to certain subjects which would more naturally have fallen into the third, and would have received fuller treatment there, while several points which belong properly to the first division have not been treated on the scale which would finally have belonged to them. The second essay ("Women in Greek Comedy") corresponds more nearly in subject to the author's matured plan, but had still less than the first essay the benefit of his final correction and revision. This much is said, not in order to deprecate criticism (a result which the author would have been the last to desire), but merely in explanation of the occasional repetitions, and possibly also inconsistencies, which are to be found in this volume.

In preparing the work for the Press as few alterations as possible have been introduced, and the essays appear substantially in the form given them by the author. Thus the second essay is divided into nine chief sections, while the first has no such sub-divisions. Again, Excursus F (which was originally written for the first essay) contains much material which is elaborated in the second essay. In several places also, especially towards the close of the volume, reference is made to parts of the work which seem never to have been written. It is believed that the reader will be anxious to possess the author's own words so far as possible, and, accordingly, the changes which have been adopted are only such as the author would probably have made himself when revising his work.

In references to the Greek lyric poets, the numbers are those of Bergk's *Poetae Lyrici Graeci* (4th edition, 1878-82). The fragments of the tragedians are cited from Nauck's *Tragicorum Graecorum Fragmenta* (2nd edition, 1889). For the comic fragments the author used Meineke's *Fragmenta Comicorum Graecorum* (five vols. 1839-57). Meineke's numbering has been kept in the text, but a list will be found on page 253, giving the corresponding references to Kock's *Comicorum Atticorum Fragmenta* (three vols. 1880-88) in all cases where the two editions differ seriously. The references to Theocritus, Plautus, and Terence have been verified from the editions of Ziegler, Ritschl, and Dziatzko, respectively; but where the text is doubtful, the author appears to have adopted what seemed to him the most probable reading, without following any editor exclusively.

Additions by the editor of this volume are enclosed in square brackets. He has to acknowledge most gratefully his indebtedness to several friends for advice and assistance on various points.

WOMEN IN GREEK POETRY

GREEK literature may be divided roughly into two parts, the earlier school which culminated at Athens, and the later school which culminated at Alexandria. The obvious differences between these two schools of art have often been described, and there is no need to dwell on them here; but the great, the essential difference between them has been too generally ignored.

The chief inspiring element of all art is love; and it is in their inspiration—that is to say, in their view of love—that the real difference between the two schools consists. The love of the later poetry is the love of man for woman; the love of the earlier poetry is the love of man for man.

By "love" I mean here love in the modern sense. A man of the Alexandrian Age might say "I love you" to a woman, and mean by that what a man may mean if he says as much to-day; before that time a man could only have said "I love you" in this sense to a friend of his own sex. There is no trace in literature of what we now understand by the word "love" earlier than the end of the fourth century.

This phenomenon has been noticed before—indeed, it is one that could not very well escape notice—though its true importance has not always been appreciated; and the general consensus of opinion has agreed to ascribe this great change, the greatest change perhaps that has ever come over art, to the influence of two men, Euripides and Menander. My object in writing now is to endeavour to show, firstly, that this general view is a mistaken one, arising from an insufficient appreciation of the true nature of the change; and secondly, that the real originator of that new feeling which we encounter in Alexandrian literature,—in other words, the first man who had the courage to say that a woman is worth loving,—was Antimachus of Colophon.

The commonly accepted view as to the origin of that "romantic" feeling (for so, for briefness' sake, it will be convenient to call it)[1] which meets us in Alexandrian literature, would seem to be due to a confusion, arising from a misunderstanding of what that feeling really is. This confusion takes two distinct forms. Thus, in the case of some writers, the improved tone with regard to women which appears in Greek erotic literature from the fourth century onwards, has been confounded with that improvement in their social and intellectual position which was so marked a feature of the latest period of the history

---

[1] The expression is, of course, an awkward one, for the word "romance," like "chivalry," embodies the old superstition that such feelings were a product of the Christian Middle Ages; but this and similar expressions are so generally used in this connection, that there is little real risk of misunderstanding, and I cannot think of anything better.

of classical Greece. In other words, romantic feelings have been spoken of as if they were identical with feelings of social and intellectual respect. That they are not, scarcely requires even to be stated. Others again, while perceiving the distinction between these two entirely different things, have yet argued as if the one were the natural and inevitable outcome of the other, and inseparably connected therewith; as if, in fact, all that was necessary to purify and elevate the feelings of men towards women had been the social emancipation of the latter. This view is of course possible, and as such is entitled to consideration rather than the previous one; but not only is it improbable in itself, but it is also in direct opposition to the teaching of history: for while no one would deny that this emancipation, if more or less simultaneous with the appearance of the romantic feeling, would serve at once to disseminate and to dignify it, how entirely independent the one is of the other is sufficiently proved by the conditions prevailing in the Middle Ages. It is surely a fact which cannot well be ignored in discussing this question, that just during that period of history when "chivalry" and "romance" were at their height, the social and intellectual position of women, both absolutely and relatively, was perhaps lower than at any time before since the creation of the world.[1]

---

[1] Among the many arguments in favour of the social emancipation of women at the present day, I have never heard it suggested that such an emancipation would inevitably lead to an increase of chivalrous feelings on the part of men; the general view seems to be that it would have just the contrary effect.

When once the romantic element is cut clear from all extraneous entanglements, so that it is possible to recognise what it really is, it becomes, I think, immediately evident that neither Euripides nor Menander can have much to do with its origin. The leading motive of romance is the idea that pure love for a woman may justifiably form the chief interest in a man's life. But this idea, as I hope to be able to show clearly, does not appear in literature until after the time of Euripides, while it is already to be found fully developed before the time of Menander. This being so, it seems impossible to regard either of these writers as the originators of it.

In the course of the following pages, I shall therefore endeavour to show, by a detailed examination of such parts of the contemporary literature as bear upon the subject, that low as was the social position of woman in most parts of Greece during the so-called classical period, the place which she occupied in the minds of men and in their art was even lower, and that her subsequent social emancipation did not by any means immediately lead to her being regarded with any more real respect. In the course of this argument, I purpose to dwell especially on the influence of Euripides, and hope to succeed in making it clear that though he, as judged by his works, was strongly in favour of giving women larger liberties, and firmly convinced that their capacities both for good and evil were far greater than the more old-fashioned among his contemporaries supposed, there is yet nowhere in his plays any real love-element as between man and woman, nor is it anywhere suggested that love for a woman may be a determining factor in a man's life.

Secondly, I purpose by a similar process to show that that place which in later Greek art and in modern times is occupied by the love of man for woman, was occupied among the earlier Greeks by the love of man for man—a fact which, though it may at first sight appear foreign to the immediate subject of our enquiry, is yet of such extreme importance for a true understanding of the history of the origin of the romantic feeling, that a consideration of it can on no account be omitted from any work professing in any way to deal with that question. For it cannot be too strongly emphasised that those who wish to study the development of love, as we now know it, must commence their studies with an examination of this essentially primitive emotion. It cannot be too strongly emphasised that love, as it now exists, has been evolved, not from the sexual instinct, but from the companionship of the battle-field, that the first real lovers the world ever knew were comrades in arms. The *Iliad* of Homer is a love story, its heroes Achilles and Patroclus; the *Ajax* of Sophocles is a love story, its heroes Ajax and Teucer. To ignore such facts as these is wilfully to misunderstand the meaning of Greek poetry and the meaning of Greece in the history of the world.

Having thus cleared the ground, I hope finally to show that it was Antimachus who first taught that that love which was possible between man and man was possible also between man and woman.

Antimachus stands at the junction of the two great

tendencies of his time. The influence of Sparta and of Euripides was gradually re-emancipating women, and showing that their powers and their passions were at least equal to those of men; the steady growth and development of that relation between man and man which found its highest exponent in Plato had made it clear, even to the blindest, that love was possible as distinct from lust. It was left to Antimachus to unite the two streams of thought in one, and to show that woman, with her newly-awakened capabilities, was a worthy object of pure and chivalrous devotion.

The works of Antimachus are lost, and none of the few fragments which survive are of any importance. All discussion with reference to them must therefore be based on suppositions and an examination of relative probabilities. The risks of error in entering on such doubtful ground are manifestly infinite, and conclusions can be reached only through the accumulation of a mass of evidence, the separate particles of which are often in themselves of very little weight; the veil of darkness covering all such Greek literature as does not bear the hall-mark of Athens is so thick that it is perhaps no longer possible for the real truth about it ever to be known. *Ceterum, fiat justitia.* It is a bold claim, I know, that I am making for Antimachus; it is a claim which, if established, would give him right to rank among the greatest poets of the world: it would give him right to rank as the founder of modern literature. How great a poet he really was we do not know. Perhaps my estimation of his importance is altogether exaggerated. His contemporaries, we know, preferred Choerilus; perhaps they were right; for myself, *Malo cum Platone errare.*

It is generally agreed that in prehistoric times the position of women among the Greeks was a much higher one than was the case subsequently. There seems every reason to believe that the social conditions of the Lesbians and the Dorians and the other nations which did not come under the influence of the history-writing Ionians, were but the survivals of what was originally a more or less general state. It is of considerable assistance for a proper comprehension of the earliest literature, if one remembers that at the time of its production the enslavement of women had only comparatively recently taken place.

The reason of the influence of primitive woman over primitive man is probably not very far to seek. In early times women were regarded with superstitious reverence[1]—one need only watch a woman making lace, say, to be able nowadays still to quite appreciate the feeling—and with natural woman's wit for a time kept up the illusion, the hard head of man taking some time to come to maturity. But when man did at last wake to the fact that he was physically, and therefore, for practical purposes, generally superior, an inevitable reaction set in, and the history of early Greece shows women as occupying on the whole a very low position—a position, too, which became lower still with advancing civilisation.[2]

---

[1] Very noticeable is the preponderance of goddesses in the Greek Pantheon. The powers of nature, whether of sea, mountain, river, or forest, were almost invariably incarnated in the form of women.

[2] This change, retrograde or not, according to taste, may be exactly paralleled from the social history of the Arabs.

That the original state of women was not one of slavery is clearly shown by the early epics. The *Iliad* and the *Odyssey* are pictures of an earlier state of society than that of the poet who describes them. A man living in a society in which women were despised, had to deal with legends belonging to an earlier social condition, in which women played a prominent part. Traces of this anomaly are easy to find in both poems. The Trojan war was the work of a woman, but how very little that woman appears in the *Iliad!* A woman has been managing the affairs of Odysseus for twenty years in an exemplary fashion; but the hero of the *Odyssey* on his return prefers to associate with the swineherd. It is by this contradiction between the actual experiences of the poet and the social conditions which he was called upon to depict, that the many inconsistencies in the treatment of the Epic woman must be explained.

Another excellent illustration of this conflict between the primitive and the subsequent views of the nature and importance of women is furnished by the elaborate treatment of the Pandora legend in the *Opera et Dies* of Hesiod. On the one hand is the early conviction of the power of women's influence— it is only by the help of a woman that Zeus can outwit man: on the other the later conviction that this influence must be for evil—before Pandora came

ζώεσκεν ἐπὶ χθονὶ φῦλ' ἀνθρώπων
νόσφιν ἄτερ τε κακῶν καὶ ἄτερ χαλεποῖο πόνοιο. (l. 90)

And a like contradiction runs through all the details of the description. Woman will be man's ruin, but he cannot fail to love her all the same—

τοῖς δ'ἐγὼ ἀντὶ πυρὸς δώσω κακὸν ᾧ κεν ἅπαντες
τέρπωνται κατὰ θυμὸν ἑὸν κακὸν ἀμφαγαπῶντες. (l. 57)

Woman will gain man's heart by her beauty, which is like that of the immortals—

ἀθανάταις δὲ θεαῖς εἰς ὦπα ἐΐσκειν
παρθενικῆς καλὸν εἶδος ἐπήρατον (l. 62),

by her skill and by her charm; it is but as an afterthought that the poet adds—

ἐν δὲ θέμεν κύνεόν τε νόον καὶ ἐπίκλοπον ἦθος
Ἑρμείαν ἤνωγε διάκτορον ἀργειφόντην. (l. 67)

And, lastly, it is through a woman that trouble comes into the world; but it is this same woman's doing that Hope at least is left. It was Pandora herself that shut down the lid of the casket before Hope had flown; it was she that preserved this "dream of waking hours" for mankind.[1]

But if we pass from the general condition of women, as depicted in Homer or Hesiod, and come to our own more immediate subject, it must be admitted that neither in the prehistoric legends, nor in their subsequent development, is there any trace whatever of a romantic sentiment existing between men and women to be found. Considering the important position occupied by women in these poems, the absence of the love element is most remarkable.

The insignificant part played by Briseis has always

---

[1] It is both instructive and amusing to compare this primitive ideal woman with the contemporary Greek woman, as Hesiod himself knew and described her. A striking passage is *Op.* 693 *seqq.*, and others will be mentioned in the next few pages.

struck those who have wished to regard the *Iliad* as an Achilleis, of which she is the heroine; nor can Agamemnon's love for the daughter of Chryses be said to go very deep. He is distressed at losing her, no doubt, but the loss is far from irremediable. He evidently agrees with Antigone, πόσις ἄν μοι κατθανόντος ἄλλος ἦν.

Paris again had originally been a celebrated warrior, and it was to this that he owed his position and his name. But his love for Helen, instead of inspiring him, seems to have had the very opposite effect. One exception there is, no doubt, to all this—the relation between Hector and Andromache. But the relation between Hector and Andromache (as illustrated by *Iliad* vi. 392, *seqq*.) is unparalleled in all Greek literature, and it is not, perhaps, without significance that they are Trojans and not Greeks. How great was the impression that they made is visible in the way in which the later literature cites Andromache rather than any Greek woman as the ideal of a wife. At the same time, how little really sympathetic to the Greek of the period was this wonderful and unique passage is sufficiently shown by this very fact, that no attempt was ever made to imitate or develop it. It may sound strange to say so, but in all probability we to-day understand Andromache better than did the Greeks for whom she was created; better, too, perhaps than did her creator himself.

In the *Odyssey*, well nigh the entire action is in the hands of women. What with Athene and Leucothea, Circe and Calypso, Nausicaa and Penelope, Odysseus himself hardly comes to the fore at all; and yet it cannot be said that anywhere from beginning to end is there so much as a suggestion of a love-motive.

Nausicaa is always regarded as a charming type of woman, but, after all, how one naturally thinks of her is as a charming type of washerwoman. Penelope again is merely the ideal housekeeper: she longs for the return of her husband, no doubt, but what really grieves her about the suitors is not their suggestions as to his death, but the quantity of pork they eat.

As for any idea that her devotion requires similar constancy on the part of Odysseus, it is not so much as suggested. The *Odyssey* opens, it is true, with its hero longing to see even the smoke of his home rising in the air; but it must be remembered that he has been spending seven years alone with Calypso on a desert island, which for a man of his tastes was doubtless exceedingly tedious. There is no reason to suppose that he did not enjoy the first year or so of his stay quite as much as his visit to Circe or Aeolus.

An examination of other Greek myths and legends that have any claim to antiquity will furnish a very similar result. Whether in those myths of gods and heroes which found their way into literature from its beginning, or in those local legends which, though first appearing in the Alexandrian writers, are evidently in reality much older, wherever the antiquity of the story can be proved, two characteristics are very noticeable. The first is the importance of women as the originators of the action; the second is the absence of the romantic element. The capabilities of women are thoroughly recognised, though the tendency of the time is to describe their influence as for evil rather than as for good; their importance is everywhere admitted: but that a man should be really or seriously in love with a woman is a thing unknown.

This is certainly at first sight a strange anomaly, and yet it is, perhaps, capable of explanation. The developer of the myth could not fail to be confronted by a great contradiction—the traditional importance of women and their actual condition of repression. He saw in the stories the women, like Medea or Ariadne, profoundly influencing the career of their lovers, while the men, like Jason or Theseus, stood helplessly and more or less apathetically on one side. The converse of such positions he naturally did not find. His surroundings forbade his drawing the true deduction, that the stories were intended to illustrate the helplessness of men without a woman to direct them; he drew therefore the contrary deduction, that the dignity and superiority of man prevented him from taking an active interest in any matter where a woman was concerned. From this deduction, combined with all that was known of the emotional and passionate character of feminine nature, there followed that view of the relation between man and woman which is so noticeable in all the myths and legends as we find them in literature. A woman may be desperately in love with a man, but the converse is impossible.[1] Love may lead

---

[1] That this was the general character of the erotic legends introduced into the celebrated "Catalogus" ascribed to Hesiod, seems shown by the remark in Serv. *ad. Aen.* vii. 268: "Hesiodus etiam περὶ τῶν

women to humiliation, to treachery, to crime, and to suicide, but never, except under the most extraordinary circumstances, men.[2]

The most cursory examination of the ordinary and most familiar Greek legends will sufficiently illustrate this.

Ἐκ Διὸς ἀρχώμεσθα. Of the many amours of Zeus, the only one of at all a permanent character, the only one which he thought it worth his while to legalise, was that for Ganymede.[3] His treatment of Minos, again, was very different from that which any of his female friends received.[4]

The goddesses suffer for their indiscretions, never the gods. Aphrodite's pathetic confession to Anchises,[5] or her agony for Adonis, the helpless devotion of Luna to Endymion, or of Aurora to Tithonus, can find no parallels among the stories of the gods. Love may drive Apollo to tend cattle, but it is love for Admetus.

In the lower stratum of humanity, the treachery of

γυναικῶν inducit multas heroidas optasse nuptias virorum fortium"; cp. the whole note.

[2] The parallel view, that if a man wished to really love anyone, the only worthy object he could find would be another man, was doubtless, in part, the result of a similar line of argument, though its true origin must of course be sought in something more inspiring than mere contempt for women. A further examination of this side of the question will be made later on.

[3] Zeus pays ἄποινα to Tros for his son (cp. *Hymn. Hom.* iv. 210); that the golden shower in which he visited Danae means as much, is hardly a primitive notion. The argument in Ach. Tat. ii. 37 is ingenious, but scarcely convincing.

[4] This version of the relations between Zeus and Minos is at least as old as the *Odyssey*. Cp. *Odyss.* xix. 179; Athen. xiii. 601 E.

[5] *Hymn. Hom.* iv. 247 *seqq.*

Medea or Ariadne, the story of Scylla[1] with its dozen variants, the guilt of Stheneboea, of Myrrha, of Pasiphae, the deaths of Byblis or Phyllis,[2] are but a few of the more obvious examples.

The idea that a man could be subject to such passions is not to be found till much later in the history of the legends. The original version of the story makes Eriphanis follow Menalcas through the forest and die for his disdain;[3] that Menalcas should afterwards die of love for Euhippe is an addition by Hermesianax.[4] In the old legend, Daphnis is the companion of Artemis, and the nymph who loves him seeks him in vain by every fountain and by every grove;[5] it is Sositheus who tells of his search for his lost Pimplea,[6] and Alexander Aetolus, or whoever Tityrus may be, who sets him wandering over the mountains after Xenea.[7]

A good commentary on all this is furnished by the stories selected, apparently more or less at random, by Parthenius in his Περὶ Ἐρωτικῶν Παθημάτων, and an examination of this work (dedicated to the Roman Cornelius Gallus) may serve to show how

---

[1] The general view that the erotic version of this story is not the original seems to rest on the sole authority of Aesch. *Cho.* 613 *seqq.* Probably one version is as old as the other, the one being perhaps Dorian, the other Ionian. Aeschylus' treatment of Dorian erotic legends will be touched upon later. (*Infra*, p. 42.)

[2] A man may sometimes commit suicide after the death of his lady; but that is a very different thing to dying because she declines to have anything more to do with him. Stories like that of Iphis and Anaxarete only appear at a very late period.

[3] Athen. xiv. 619C.   [4] Hermes. *Leont.* i. *Fr.* 3. (Ed. Bach.)
[5] Theocr. i. 82 *seqq.* Cp. Reitzenstein, *Epigramm und Skolion*, p. 212 *seqq.*
[6] Serv. *ad Ecl.* viii. 68.   [7] Theocr. vii. 72.

tenaciously the original idea of the relative positions of men and women retained its hold even among the "romantic" Alexandrians.

The stories narrated by Parthenius number 36 in all.

In three cases, those of Leucophrye (5), Peisidice (21), and Nanis (22), love induces women to betray their country to the enemy; in each case the suggestion of treachery is made by them. In one case a man, Diognetus (9), is guilty of similar treachery, but here he is trapped into it by an oath to his lady to do whatever she asks him—an oath which he swears without thinking what it may imply; and, besides, he betrays, not his own countrymen, but merely his allies.

Of other sorts of treachery there is enough and to spare, and always attributed to the woman. Penelope (3), out of jealousy, induces Odysseus to kill his son Euryalus; Erippe (8), owing to her love for a barbarian, plots against her husband's life; Cleoboea (14) tries to seduce Antheus, and, failing, murders him.

Where a man is led by love to any unnatural crime, it is invariably excused as being the result of temporary insanity or the vengeance of some deity. Leucippus (5) falls in love with his sister κατὰ μῆνιν Ἀφροδίτης; for Byblis (11) no such excuse is alleged. Clymenus (13) violates Harpalyce διὰ τὸ ἔκφρων εἶναι; Orion, Hero (20) ὑπὸ μέθης ἔκφρων; Assaon's love for his daughter Niobe (33) is a punishment from Leto; Dimoetes' love for a corpse (31) is brought on by a curse. The sins of Neaera (18) and Periander's mother (17) have no such palliative. The unique case in which Alcinoe (27) is driven κατὰ μῆνιν Ἀθήνης to elope with a stranger (as a punishment for sweating her sempstress) is derived from Moero, who would naturally regard women from a peculiar point of view.

Lastly, Rhesus (36) and Leucippus (15) are, it is true, induced, like Eriphanis, to follow the objects of their affection into the hunting-field, but in each case their devotion is very promptly rewarded.

The foregoing examination of the myths and legends of early Greece has led to certain definite results; but the importance of these results has been in many cases discounted by the impossibility of assigning any even approximate date to the myth or legend from which they have been drawn. Even if, in the case of any given legend, one could determine with certainty the occasion of its first appearance in literature, one would in reality be very little nearer determining the date of the legend itself. To the stories in Homer everyone is willing to allow a respectable antiquity; but who can say how long the story of Phaedra had been current at Troezen before Sophocles adopted it? It is satisfactory therefore to be able to leave this doubtful ground, and come to something more definite, in the shape of the actual words of the subjective lyric writers, who belong to the second stage of Greek literature.

It is, perhaps, generally agreed that romantic love-poetry was not produced by the early Greek lyric writers. What is less generally appreciated is the fact that these writers, at any rate before the time of

Anacreon, wrote practically no love-poetry (addressed to women) at all.[1] So little indeed has this fact or its meaning been understood, that not a few passages in the fragments of these writers have been misinterpreted or strained; but really, if one comes to think of it, this absence of love-poetry is quite capable of explanation. The subjective lyric literature of early Greece, which extends roughly over the seventh and sixth centuries, and lasts on, in a desultory sort of way, into the fifth, is chiefly Ionian, and introduces one to a very different state of society from that of the heroic age. The actual social and intellectual position of women is, in the main, a very low one; and in other respects also the place which they occupy in the interests of men is very insignificant. But this is not all. The ideal woman of the time is not one to whom love-poetry could be addressed. The Greek of this period looked upon a woman as an instrument of pleasure, and as a means of creating a family, nothing more. The comparison of marriage to cattle-breeding sounds quite natural.[2] Now such feelings as these can neither of them provide the material for love-poetry of even the most rudimentary kind.[3]

---

[1] The only real exceptions to this rule are, perhaps, Sappho and her followers!

[2] Theognis, 183; cp. Pseudo-Phocylides, 189. Very similar in spirit is Hesiod's advice to the farmer to get

οἶκον μὲν πρώτιστα γυναῖκά τε βοῦν τ' ἀροτῆρα. *Op.* 403.

[3] That is to say, these feelings by themselves. As regards the first, no one, of course, would wish to deny that the sexual instinct, in its most sensual form, has often played a prominent part in what is unquestionably love-poetry; but the sexual instinct can never of itself supply the fundamental basis of the feeling necessary for the production of such poetry. Woman, regarded *merely* as a source of pleasure or convenience, can no more be an object of love than a bottle of brandy or a railway train.

The former of these two ideals we shall have frequent opportunities of encountering in the next few pages. A striking commentary on the latter, and, of course, more general one, is furnished by that important document for the early history of women in Greece, the "satire" of Simonides. If one examines the types of women that Simonides describes, and the objections that he urges against them, and compares these with the types one encounters in Juvenal, for instance, a noteworthy fact at once becomes apparent. The faults which Simonides blames, as well as the virtues he somewhat grudgingly commends, are simply those which concern woman as a housekeeper; those faults and vices which provoke the indignation of Juvenal are but lightly touched upon, or not mentioned at all. One woman is slovenly, another talks her husband's head off, another is always eating, another is a thief, another is too fine a lady to do any cooking or sweeping; and the only three definite virtues of the woman "like a bee" are, that her husband's income increases, that her children are satisfactory, and that she does not waste her time gossiping with the neighbours.

Indeed, the famous lines (*Fr.* 6)—

γυναικὸς οὐδὲν χρῆμ' ἀνὴρ ληΐζεται
ἐσθλῆς ἄμεινον οὐδὲ ῥίγιον κακῆς,

might almost be translated, "There is nothing better in the world than a good cook, and nothing worse than a bad one."[1]

[1] Cf. Hes. *Op.* 700, *seqq*. A comparison of that passage with the types mentioned in Simonides, *i.e.* the γυνὴ γηΐνη and the γυνὴ ἐξ ὄνου,

Simonides grumbles a great deal, and thinks most women a great nuisance; that a woman could be more than a nuisance, or, if God were good, possibly a convenience, does not enter his head.

A century and a half later we find little change. Phocylides divides woman into four types: three bad—the flirt, the slattern, and the shrew; one good, the efficient housekeeper.[1] Another hundred years later the ideal of a wife is still unchanged.[2]

There was little reason, then, for these Greeks to address love-poetry to their women, or, indeed, to sing of "love," otherwise than in its purely animal aspect, at all. It remains to convince oneself, by an examination of what remains of their works, that they actually did not. It is, of course, a very general opinion that Archilochus, the earliest lyric poet about

would seem to show that the sense of δειπνόλοχος is not so much 'fishing for invitations to dinner,' *i.e.* fond of going out (so L. and S.), as 'waylaying dinners,' *i.e.* making havoc of the food, like Plautus' 'pernae pestis.' Wastefulness in household matters was much more likely to 'burn up' a Greek husband, and bring him to a 'cruel old age,' than any amount of frivolity or flirtation. For the idea cp. Aristoph. *Eccl.* 226.

[1]
ἡ δὲ μελίσσης
οἰκονομός τ' ἀγαθὴ καὶ ἐπίσταται ἐργάζεσθαι·
ἧς εὔχου, φίλ' ἑταῖρε, λαχεῖν γάμον ἱμερόεντα.
[Phoc. *Fr.* 3.]

ἱμερόεντα sounds to a modern ear almost like bitter irony.

[2] Nor, for that matter, is the Hetaera, whom later writers manage so to idealise, treated with any more respect or courtesy than the wife. Cp. Archil. *Fr.* 142, 184; Hippon. *Fr.* 110, 111. In curious contrast to what may be called the 'wife-poetry' of the early Greeks is the pretty picture in Hesiod (*Op.* 517, *seqq.*) of the unmarried girl, sitting at home, in every sense of the words κακῶν ἄπειρος. But strangest of all is the touch where, falling unconsciously into a manner of speech that dated from a very different social state, he calls her

οὔπω ἔργ' εἰδυῖα πολυχρύσου (!) 'Αφροδίτης.

whom we know anything of moment, addressed love-poetry to a woman, Neobule.

This view rests mainly on two fragments (*Fr.* 84, 103), which it is customary to consider as having been addressed by the poet to his lady at an early stage of their acquaintance, or as being, perhaps, recollections of this happy state.[1] Where all is uncertain, one does not like to speak with confidence, but there really seems to be no adequate reason for supposing that they are anything of the kind. There is nothing whatever in *Fr.* 84

δύστηνος ἔγκειμαι πόθῳ
ἄψυχος, χαλεπῇσι θεῶν ὀδύνῃσιν ἕκητι
πεπαρμένος δι' ὀστέων,

to prove that it was addressed to a woman, or, indeed, referred to one at all. It is at least as probable that it was addressed to the same person as *Fr.* 85

ἀλλά μ' ὁ λυσιμελής, ὦ 'ταῖρε, δάμναται πόθος,

or someone similar.[2] *Fr.* 103 again must be taken in conjunction with those that go before and those that follow it. The whole scene described in these fragments[3] is very suggestive of the story in Proverbs

---

[1] "But even these are as nothing compared to the real gush of feeling when he describes his youthful passions, his love for Neobule, passing the Homeric love of women. Here he has anticipated Sappho and Alcaeus, &c."—Mahaffy, *Class. Gr. Lit.* i. p. 160.

[2] Perhaps Glaucus, for there is at least as much reason for supposing that Glaucus was the object of Archilochus' affection as that he was the object of his scorn. To see in him a prototype of the Egnatius of Catullus, as, for instance, Lafaye does (*Catulle et ses Modèles*, p. 29), is quite unwarranted by any evidence; for the epithet κεροπλάστης of *Fr.* 57 is not necessarily derogatory, while the tone of such passages as *Fr.* 54, 70, is certainly not that of invective.

[3] *Fr.* 100-3, 106-7, 109-10, 116.

vii. 6 *seqq.* A lady of mature charms (100) and somewhat doubtful character (101, 102) receives a youthful visitor, whose feelings are described in *Fr.* 103

τοῖος γὰρ φιλότητος ἔρως ὑπὸ καρδίην ἐλυσθείς
πολλὴν κατ' ἀχλὺν ὀμμάτων ἔχευεν
κλέψας ἐκ στηθέων ἀταλὰς φρένας.

The subsequent fragments deal with the arrival of the husband, and the change to the more rapid metre must have been very effective. This context, of course, makes it clear that φιλότητος ἔρως means simply *coitus cupido*, and there is no reason to suppose that this fragment ever formed part of what could properly be called an erotic passage.[1]

As a matter of fact, all that we know of Archilochus tends to make it extremely improbable that he addressed love-poetry in any sense of the word to women. There is no evidence that he addressed any poems to Neobule (or for that matter to any other woman) except satires. In these satires we know that he referred to Neobule in terms of the vilest abuse. There is no evidence in his fragments that he ever referred to her otherwise. What reason, then, is there to suppose that he did? His love for her, such as it was, was confessedly purely animal.[2] This is not the kind of love that finds consolation in reminiscences and regrets. His pride was hurt, and he determined to take vengeance on the persons who

---

[1] It may further be observed that the passage is to all appearances descriptive of the emotions of some person other than the writer himself, and there is certainly no reason to suppose that it was addressed to the woman in question. The difference between describing such an emotion generally, and describing it as one's own, to the person who causes it, need hardly be dwelt upon. [2] Cp. *Fr.* 71, 72.

had offended him. If one of these persons happened to be a woman, that was just as much a matter of chance as the fact that one of the enemies of Hipponax was a sculptor. The woman, like the sculptor, had tried to make the poet ridiculous, and the poet proceeded to have his revenge by satirising her. The fact that she was a woman may have given the satires a certain peculiar colouring, but it certainly did not make them love-poems. Under the circumstances it was not to be expected that Archilochus should express his feelings in erotic poetry, and, as a matter of fact, on the present evidence there is no reason to believe that he did.[1]

The claims of Alcman in this respect seem at first sight somewhat stronger.[2] He has been described as ἡγεμὼν ἐρωτικῶν μελῶν;[3] this has been supposed to mean that he was the first poet who wrote love-poems, and it has been assumed that these poems

---

[1] To endeavour, as some have done, to reconstruct the satires of Archilochus from those of Catullus, is simply labour thrown away, because between the periods in which the two poets lived, the whole way of regarding women had been revolutionised, and ideas which seemed obvious to the Latin writer would have been unintelligible to the Greek. To Catullus thwarted love was an agony; to Archilochus it was an insult, and no man of his time would, or could, have regarded it otherwise. Thus, to suppose, as Lafaye (*op. cit.* l. c.) does, that the satires of Archilochus were interspersed with erotic passages, like Catull. xxxix. (a poem he considers to be imitated from Archilochus), is to suppose an anachronism.

[2] His date, and the general character of his poems, make it more convenient to consider him here, than among the other choral lyric writers, of whom we shall speak later.

[3] Ἀρχύτας δὲ ὁ ἁρμονικός, ὥς φησι Χαμαιλέων, Ἀλκμᾶνα γεγονέναι τῶν ἐρωτικῶν μελῶν ἡγεμόνα, καὶ ἐκδοῦναι πρῶτον μέλος ἀκόλαστον, (ἀκόλαστον) ὄντα καὶ περὶ τὰς γυναῖκας, καὶ τὴν τοιαύτην μοῦσαν (εἰσαγαγεῖν) εἰς τὰς διατριβάς.
Athen. xiii. 600 F. (The reading is uncertain.)

were addressed to women. This is not, however, all so certain as one might at first be inclined to suppose.

It has been said that Alcman was ἡγεμὼν ἐρωτικῶν μελῶν; but in how far were these μέλη ἀκόλαστα love-poems as we now understand them? All that the words of Archytas imply is that Alcman wrote melic poems, of which "love" was the chief subject. There is nothing whatever to prove that these μέλη were personal, or addressed to any particular woman; it is a misuse of words to call them "love-poems," and then think of them as if they were what modern love-poems are. As soon as subjective poetry came to be written at all, it is obvious that the sexual passions must have appeared in it in some form. This no one would wish to deny. But there is a great gap between singing of "love" in general, of the pleasures of

κρυπταδίη φιλότης καὶ μείλιχα δῶρα καὶ εὐνή,

and singing of love as existing between two particular persons. It is a commonplace that every new lover loves as no one has ever done before. Until a poet speaks of himself in this way, until he emphasises the individuality of his own particular passion, he cannot be said to write real love-poetry. And certainly the fragments, at any rate, do not supply any proof that Alcman ever wrote such love-poetry. He may have been in love with Megalostrate; as far as we know, he never said so.[1]

---

[1] It is noteworthy that Archytas (*ap.* Athen. *l.c.*), when wishing to illustrate Alcman's love for this lady, can quote nothing more pointed than the lines
τοῦθ' ἀδεᾶν Μωσᾶν ἔδειξεν
δῶρον μάκαιρα παρσένων
ἁ ξανθὰ Μεγαλοστράτα. [*Fr.* 37.]

Again, it must not be forgotten that Alcman also wrote poems addressed to boys, and it is at least possible that some of those erotic fragments which are preserved may have belonged to these.[1]

As for the *Parthenia*, they are not love-poems in any sense of the word. The poet is merely ὁ τῶν παρθένων ἐπαινέτης τε καὶ σύμβουλος,[2] which was possible in the happy condition of Spartan society, quite without anything further being implied.

"Multa tuae, Sparte, miramur iura palaestrae."

One of these poems was written in old age;[3] perhaps all of them were.[4] Besides, they celebrate a number of girls indifferently; love-poems would not do that.[5]

Till Egypt renders up some more Alcman, it will

---

[1] The fragments which may with some confidence be assigned to these, probably early, poems, are 29 and 94. Besides this, the mention of Tantalus (87, to which belongs 100) may well have been introduced by the story of Ganymede; that of Niobe's children (109) by the story of those loves of theirs of which Sophocles afterwards wrote. The expression ἐν Θεσσαλίῳ κλείτει (85) might well in such a poem have had reference to Apollo and Admetus, whose love is held up as a model, like that of the lovers in Theocritus xii. But most striking of all, perhaps, to the modern reader, is the feeling that prompts Alcman to speak of the Spartan girls as his "female boy-friends." (καὶ Ἀλκμὰν τὰς ἐπεράστους κόρας αὐτὰς λέγει. Hypoth. *ad Theocr.* xii.)

[2] Aristides ii. p. 40, Dind. [3] Cp. *Fr.* 26.

[4] Alcman seems somehow to speak of girls like an old man. To think of him so, renders far more natural the charming gallantry of his lines on Agido, or the ὑποκορισμός with which his maidens speak, or his confessions of how he likes his dinner served. One can think of those Spartan girls laughing at their old Lydian dancing-master, as they ran away down to the "baths of Eurotas," while he went slowly home and made them immortal.

[5] Anyhow, not in primitive times. One must go a long way down the history of erotic poetry to find a "love-poet" who praises two ladies with such impartiality as Alcman does Agido and Agesichora.

be impossible to prove that he ever addressed a love-poem to a woman.

Strange as it may perhaps seem, it is almost an equal misuse of words to call Mimnermus a love-poet. It has so long been customary to regard him as such, that it is at first hard to realise that, in all probability, he was never anything of the kind. As a matter of fact, it seems naturally reasonable to suppose, and there is at any rate nothing in the fragments to contradict this view, that Mimnermus was, like the other elegiac writers of his age, purely didactic.[1] The philosophy which he inculcated differed from that of Tyrtaeus or Solon, no doubt, but it was none the less a philosophy. Mimnermus argued that, considering the shortness of life, and especially of youth, it was advisable to devote one's self immediately and strenuously to sensual pleasures, before the power of enjoying them was lost. The argument was quite general. "What is life without love?" he says; he does not say, "What is life without your love?"[2] This enunciation of general principles is not love-poetry. As has already been remarked, no poetry can properly be so described until the personal element has entered into it, and

---

[1] Cp. Reitzenstein, *Epigramm und Skolion*, p. 47 *seqq.*

[2] That the love thus generally recommended was purely sensual, goes without saying; the first two or three lines of the first fragment are proof enough of this.

In *Fr.* 1, l. 3, μείλιχα δῶρα is not very satisfactory, somehow. The passage in *Hymn. Hom.* x. 2, where the expression occurs again, is not quite parallel. In a less primitive poet, one would write without hesitation μείλιχ' ἄδωρα. For this use of μείλιχα cp. Pind. *Olymp.* i. 49, and for the thought *Anth. Pal.* v. 29, &c., &c. Line 4 again might begin ἄνθε' ἐπεί γ' ἥβης.

of this personal element there is no evidence in the case of Mimnermus.

As for the actual poems themselves, there is no evidence that any of them were, as is generally tacitly assumed, addressed to Nanno or any other woman; and indeed, if one considers their nature, one will see that there is really no reason why they should have been. It is worthy of note, in the first place, that the only definite evidence of the existence of such a person as Nanno is that furnished by Hermesianax,[1] and that this writer's information as to the early poets was not always very accurate, is sufficiently shown by what he says of Homer, Sappho, Anacreon, and others.[2] But granted that the story of the poet's love for Nanno was true, that is very far from proving the fact that he addressed his poems to her. What seemed only natural in the fourth century, was by no means so in the seventh. But besides this (as it ought to be superfluous to remark, and probably is not), Hermesianax never states that Mimnermus did so; he does not even go so far as to say that the latter alluded to Nanno in his elegies. Hermesianax makes three definite statements about Mimnermus:—(1) that he invented or utilised the pentameter; (2) that he was in love with Nanno, and used often (in consequence?) to attend entertainments; (3) that he suffered from the enmity of Hermobius and Pherecles. More than this is not to be found in the passage, however one may emend

---

[1] *Leont.* iii. 37, of which passage Poseidippus was doubtless thinking in his epigram *Anth. Pal.* xii. 168.

[2] *Leont.* iii. 27 *seqq.* 47 *seqq.* &c.

or explain it. As for the supposition that Mimnermus gave to his collected elegies the title of Nanno, there is no evidence of a collection so entitled before the time of Strabo, by which time, of course, the influence of writers like Hermesianax had long been at work.[1] In short, there is no evidence whatever to lead one to suppose that the elegies of Mimnermus were anything but purely impersonal didactic moralisings on the shortness of youth, and the consequent advisability of making the best possible use of it.[2] Mimnermus was a philosopher;[3] to call him a love-poet is a misuse of words. He wrote exquisite poetry, and his service in developing the forms of art was unquestionably very valuable, but he brings us very little farther in the history of the treatment of women in literature.

It is in Anacreon that we find for the first time love-poetry addressed to women;[4] though one must never forget, as some modern writers seem inclined to do, that this writer also addressed a number of love-poems to boys, and that, in fact, these formed

---

[1] Suidas, it may be remarked, flatly contradicts one half of this view when he says of Mimnermus ἔγραψε βιβλία πολλά.

[2] It is hardly justifiable to infer from the passage of Alexander Aetolus *ap*. Athen. xv. 699 C, that Mimnermus addressed love-poems to boys.

[3] It is as a philosopher that Horace (*Ep*. i. 6, 65) cites his opinion:
   si, Mimnermus uti censet, sine amore iocisque
   nil est iucundum ;
"censet," the regular word for a philosopher. It is further worth noticing that the Roman poets, when they mention Mimnermus, speak of him as the inventor of the elegiac metre, not as an erotic poet. Cp. *e.g.* Prop. i. 9, 11.

[4] That the ancients already recognised the importance of this particular feature in Anacreon is shown *inter alia* by the emphasis laid upon it by Critias (*ap*. Athen. xiii. 600 D).

the bulk of his work.[1] The poems addressed to women were many of them, perhaps all, the work of the poet's old age,[2] and their general tone is sufficiently indicated by such fragments as 55, 59, 161, etc.:[3] these two features serve, of course, to connect Anacreon with his predecessors; at the same time, the individualisation of this particular emotion, which we find here for the first time clearly indicated, was obviously a great advance in the art of the subject. Purely animal emotions, however highly developed or refined, could never lead to that feeling which we have called the romantic, and hence the direct importance of Anacreon for our immediate subject is but small; but the individualisation of these animal emotions was obviously of inexpressible importance for the development of the literature that dealt with them. The first essential of art is accurate observation, and the essence of accurate observation is attention to a definite object. By appreciating this fact, and concentrating upon a definite object the general emotions described by Mimnermus and the like, Anacreon created love-poetry as between man and woman, and thereby created that form of art in which the romantic feeling, when it arose, found the readiest means of expression. Thus, though in no sense of the word a romantic writer, or one who would have been likely to sympathise

---

[1] Vide *e.g.* Athen. xii. 540 E.

[2] Striking instances of this are to be found in *Fr.* 13. 76, etc.

[3] That this tone was specially characteristic of the poems addressed to women, if not actually confined to these, is shown by the contrast which the ancient critics made between Anacreon's two styles of poetry. Cp. Plut. *Amor.* 4, and *infra* p. 86.

with romantic ideas, Anacreon was yet, unconsciously and indirectly, doing an unquestionable service in preparing the way for the dissemination, if not for the evolution, of this later feeling; and in so far this γυναικῶν ἠπερόπευμα deserves, at least, recognition, if not respect.

The last of the personal lyric writers on whom it will be necessary to dwell is Theognis.

On the general theory that the book of Theognis is a collection of poems by a number of writers of various dates, scholars have agreed to agree; on the details of the theory, they seem to have agreed to differ. For the present purpose, however, these details are unimportant, and it will be sufficient to assume that, while some of the poems are doubtless earlier, and others again later, the great bulk of the first book of the "Theognis" poetry belongs to the first half of the fifth century, while the second book is considerably later.[1]

It is equally indifferent for us how this heterogeneous collection arose; whether it was a chrestomathy "for the use of schools," or whether, as has been argued with great force, it is in reality a volume of songs to be sung at social gatherings, and the forerunner of the later collections of epigrams.[2]

What is of importance for us is that, in any case, whatever theory as to its origin may be adopted, this book may be taken as presenting on the whole[3] a

---

[1] The arguments of Reitzenstein, *Epig. u. Skol.* p. 81 *seqq.*, to prove that its date is not later than *circa* 400, are not very convincing.

[2] Vide Reitzenstein, *op. cit.* p. 52 *seqq.*

[3] The exceptions would be the late "sophistical" pieces, such as that in praise of wealth, 699 *seqq.* etc.

collection of those opinions and views of life which were generally held and generally accepted during the fifth century or thereabouts; for neither the schoolroom nor the dinner table is exactly the place where new and startling theories are welcomed.

Looking at this volume, then, as containing a collection of the ordinary and more or less commonplace views of the time, it is interesting, though, of course, not really surprising, to find that, while boy-love is universally acknowledged and forms the subject of not a few of the poems, women's love is well-nigh entirely ignored;[1] and where the latter is mentioned, its sensual side merely is touched upon.[2]

Indeed, all the allusions of any importance to women can be very briefly dismissed.

In l. 183 *seqq.* marriage is compared to cattle-breeding, the folly of marrying for money being deprecated as spoiling the breed.

Ll. 257 *seqq.* are possibly the complaint of a woman with an unsuitable husband, though what is the nature of the objection to him, and indeed the whole allusion, is not clear.

Ll. 261 *seqq.* appear to deal with the behaviour of a man towards a woman on some occasion; but,

---

[1] It may be argued that in a work intended "for the use of schools" the erotic passages would naturally be cut out. But even granted that this collection was made for the use of schools, the system of expurgation, which, while striking out the passages dealing with women, has left what would nowadays be considered so much more objectionable, is in itself sufficiently noteworthy. The next schoolmaster who undertakes a school edition of Theocritus may lay this to heart.

[2] How different is the treatment of boy-love both in Book I. and also in Book II., which is specially devoted to it, will be dwelt upon later. [p. 88.]

what with the doubtfulness of the reading and the uncertainty as to whether the lines belong to one poem or two, the exact sense has never yet been ascertained.[1]

In l. 457 *seqq.* the infidelity of a young wife to an old man is tacitly assumed. "Girls will have boys."

Ll. 547 *seq.* express vague disapprobation of dissolute habits.

Ll. 1063 *seqq.* are merely a reiteration of the philosophy of Mimnermus, the value of which philosophy for the development of love we have already discussed.

Ll. 1225 *seq.*, "Nothing is sweeter ἀγαθῆς γυναικός." So said also Simonides, and what he meant we know.

And this is all. The result is truly remarkable in its barrenness. Perhaps in no other literature would it be possible to find a collection of short poems on general subjects, of equal length, in which the relations of men to women are so utterly ignored.

Nor is there anything peculiar or exceptional in this. In the somewhat similar *Scolia*, absolutely the same is the case. The democrat sings of Harmodius, the aristocrat of Admetus;[2] the rare allusions that there are to women are regularly trivial or coarse.[3]

In the choral lyric writers, with whom it will now be necessary to deal, the character of the evidence to be examined is widely different from that of the

---

[1] Vide Excursus A. [2] Cp. Aristoph. *Vesp.* 1217 *seqq.*

[3] The only exception, rather an interesting one, is *Scol.* 20, which, evidently modelled on the one that precedes it, is the answer of a woman-lover. But here again the vagueness (merely καλὴ γυνή, any-one will do) shows what the singer means.

evidence which we have hitherto been considering. The Greek choral poets were (with one notable exception) hardly ever subjective in their treatment of erotic matter. The erotic element, such as it is, consists in these writers almost entirely of erotic legends or myths, which would seem to have been recounted without special comment on the part of the poet and, in most cases, without elaborate analysis of the emotions of the characters introduced. The stories therefore that these writers tell, rather than the actual words in which they tell them, will require consideration in the present connection. The subjective lyric writers were, as we have seen, in the main Ionian. The choral writers, on the other hand, are in the main Dorian; consequently, one would naturally expect to find women occupying a more prominent place in their works. And this is, in fact, also the case. From the very beginning, already we find stories about women repeated with an interest and an appreciation which would have startled what one is generally taught to regard as orthodox Greece. At the same time, however, the true nature of this feature of choral poetry must not be overlooked. Though the efforts of these writers to re-awaken interest in women were unquestionably of importance for the ultimate development of the romantic element in literature, it is unjustifiable to suppose, as is too commonly done, that these writers were in themselves "romantic," or, indeed, that they had any idea of what romantic feelings are. An examination of their works, as far as we know them, will show with sufficient clearness that in its essence their view of women differed little, if at all, from that of their Ionian predecessors and contemporaries. They thought more about women, perhaps; they did not think more of them.

A case in point is Stesichorus. In spite of the important part that female characters play in his poems, a result, no doubt, of his Boeotian connections and his freedom from Ionian influences, the poet's way of regarding women is practically identical with that which we have already encountered among the Ionians. In the first place, Stesichorus appears always, professedly at least, as a misogynist. The legends in which he delights are those which relate the ruin caused by women's influence. Besides the famous *Ilii Persis*, one need but mention the stories of Scylla, of Eriphyle, of Clytemnestra (in the *Oresteia*).[1] Even in the story of Artemis and Actaeon, he will not admit that the vengeance of the goddess was due to those feelings of outraged propriety to which it was generally ascribed.[2] As for his palinode of Helen, composed late in life, he was evidently induced to write it by strong private pressure of some kind, perhaps on the part of "Helen of Himera";[3] but how isolated an expression of

---

[1] Perhaps, too, those of Althaea (in the *Syotherae*) and Medea (*Fr.* 54). [2] *Fr.* 68; to the same poem evidently belongs *Fr.* 85.

[3] There is really no adequate reason for disbelieving the story in Ptol. Hephaest. iv. (Gale, *Hist. poet. script. ant.* p. 320); cf. Bergk. *ad Stesich. Fr.* 26.) What that story seems to imply is that Helen of Himera deserted the poet, who was thereby induced to moralise on the innate faithlessness of Helens in general. A subsequent reconciliation with the lady in question then led to the celebrated apology. The greater influence which women seem to have had over old men than over young, will already have been noticed in the cases of Alcman and Anacreon. The phenomenon could easily be explained, if it were necessary to explain it.—Vide *e.g.* Eur. *Suppl.* 1098 *seqq.*

opinion this was, and how very unusual were the whole circumstances of the case, is shown by the great interest which the poem excited in antiquity.

In the more purely erotic legends again, it is striking how he conforms to those views as to the relative positions of men and women which, as has been already pointed out, were current in all Greek erotic stories of early date; the woman falls in love with the man, never, apparently, the reverse. Striking examples are the stories of Calyce, and probably also of Scylla; another, perhaps, that of Daphnis;[1] that of Rhadina seems at first sight a contradiction, but it must be noticed that Strabo (viii. 347) gives no information as to how the intrigue first began.[2]

That in addition to these poems concerned with women, Stesichorus interested himself also in the treatment of love in its more characteristically Greek aspect, may be gathered from Athenaeus xiii. 601 A, though, perhaps, no fragment dealing with this subject is preserved.[3] This side is, however, very

---

[1] That in the original form of the legend Daphnis refuses to yield to love, and dies sooner than submit, has been shown by Reitzenstein, *Epig. u. Skol.* p. 193 *seqq*.

But the passage from Aelian (*Var. Hist.* x. 18) never says that Stesichorus told the story of Daphnis. It says he wrote bucolic poetry, which is not necessarily the same thing. If only Theocritus, who wrote bucolic poetry, had told some more of the story of Daphnis, the necessity of reading a great quantity of literature on the subject would have been spared us.

[2] It is rather tempting to think of this story as a Greek version of Tristan and Isolde. Rhadina is going from Samos to be married to the King of Corinth, and travels out with her cousin Leontichus on the same ship. There the fatal mischief is done; they separate for a while, but the charm is irresistible, and her lover hurries from Delphi to meet his death at the hands of the Corinthian "King Marc."

[3] The name of Cycnus seems at first sight suggestive, but the story as related in the Scholiast on Pindar unfortunately proves nothing.

strongly developed in his fellow-countryman Ibycus, who is again a most interesting figure in the history of the artistic development of Greek love.

Ibycus would seem to have been the first of the choral lyric poets who made use of this form of art for the expression of personal emotion. All the important fragments of him that remain seem to have belonged to passages of this kind. Two at least we know of as being addressed to particular individuals. Those who have been following the development of Greek feeling on this matter will not be surprised to find that these poems were addressed exclusively, as far as we know, to boys. It was a bold thing to introduce personal feelings at all into these choral odes, for a certain odour of sanctity was still hanging about them, and the Greeks had a natural aversion to the public expression of all violent emotions; but to have introduced anything so entirely sensual as woman's love was then felt to be would not have been allowed. If love was to be tolerated at all, it must be that form of love which was generally recognised as dignified and ennobling. This amalgamation of ceremonial and personal poetry does not seem to have been popular or to have found imitators. The Greeks probably felt, what the modern glee-singer does not, the absurdity of a whole chorus expressing their undying devotion to one and the same person; but it is at least a very characteristic fact, and, for those that will not learn, a very instructive one, that boy-love was the only form of the passion which it was considered possible to attempt to treat in this way.

Of Ibycus' views on women we know little.[1] That he followed the tendencies of Stesichorus, sometimes rather wildly,[2] and gave considerable prominence to love stories between women and men, is clear enough; but there is no evidence to show that these stories of his were any different in their essential characteristics to those of his predecessor.

The other choral lyric poets have remarkably little to say on this subject.

Myrtis' story of Ochne is but one of the usual type, showing to what *spretae iniuria formae* may lead a woman. If Corinna tells of the heroism of the daughters of Orion, it is, after all, only what one would expect occasionally from a poetess.

Neither Pindar nor Simonides has anything of interest to say about women. For Bacchylides the climax of the charms of peace is

$$\pi\alpha\iota\delta\iota\kappa o\iota\ \theta'\ \tilde{\upsilon}\mu\nu o\iota\ \phi\lambda\acute{\epsilon}\gamma o\nu\tau\alpha\iota.$$ [3]

Among the dithyrambic writers, Licymnius tells the story of the treachery of Nanis, but the sort of legends which seem to interest him more are those of Hypnus and Endymion, Hymenæus and Argynnus, and the like. The same was perhaps true of Cydias. But one interesting figure these writers do supply; that is the Cyclops of Philoxenus.

---

[1] He seems to have discussed or commented on the habits of the Spartan ladies (*Fr.* 61), but whether to praise or blame we do not know.

[2] *e.g. Fr.* 37, where he makes Achilles marry Medea; or *Fr.* 38, where Hermione becomes the wife of Diomed.

[3] *Fr.* 13, *ad fin.* The Ἐρωτικά of Bacchylides are not very elevated in character, but they are interesting as furnishing what is, perhaps, the first complimentary notice of the ἑταίρα in literature. (*Fr.* 24.)

A good deal has been written about this "romantic" conception, and it has been generally considered as a proof of how strongly the romantic feeling must have been already developed that it was possible to represent Polyphemus as in love with Galatea. Those who have considered what has already been said may perhaps be tempted to come to a somewhat different conclusion. The barbarous and boorish Polyphemus spends his time in singing of his love to Galatea, because no one who was not a barbarian and a boor would be such a fool as to waste so much time about a woman. This view spoils the idyllic charm of the picture rather, perhaps, but it may be the true one for all that.[1]

In the foregoing examination of the remains of the lyric writers, it was always necessary to regard, not only the date of each writer, but also the country to which he belonged; for, as we have already had occasion to notice, the social position of women differed widely in different parts of Greece, and this fact could not fail to be, to a certain extent, reflected in such literature as dealt with them.

In examining the work of the tragedians, this necessity will no longer be present. Early Greek tragedy is entirely under the influence of Athens. The only tragedians whose works have been to any

[1] The Sicilian Telestes makes rather an interesting remark about Athene when she throws away the flute because it spoils her looks:

τί γάρ νιν εὐηράτοιο κάλλεος
ὀξὺς ἔρως ἔτειρεν,
ᾇ παρθενίαν ἄγαμον καὶ ἄπαιδ᾽ ἀπένειμε Κλωθώ;

But, as we have already seen, men took more interest in women in Magna Græcia than in Greece itself.

considerable extent preserved were Athenians; and such fragments of the non-Athenian dramatists as have survived do not in any way lead one to suppose that their work was in any essential characteristic different from that of their Athenian contemporaries.

At Athens the social position of women was, on the whole, a very low one, and consequently the relations between men and women were not on a particularly high level. The men cared very little either for or about the women, and there is nothing therefore surprising in the generally admitted fact that the love-element as between the sexes plays but a very unimportant part in the early tragedians. Aeschylus seems well-nigh to have ignored it; in Sophocles it played a prominent part in but two, or at most three tragedies;[1] even in Euripides the proportion of plays in which love of any sort supplies the main interest is very small.[2]

But one question may very naturally be asked. Assuming that the way of regarding women at Athens rendered it difficult or impossible to interest

[1] The *Phaedra*, *Oenomaus*, and perhaps the *Colchides*.

[2] Among the extant plays there is only the *Hippolytus*, and even in this, probably to the Greek mind a great part of the interest centred in the relations between Hippolytus and Theseus, and in their argument, where both start from the assumption that it would be absurd to suppose that the former could possibly have been in love with Phaedra. Of the lost plays it is hard to speak with confidence, but certainly the *Andromeda*, *Phoenix*, and *Aeolus*, seem to have been the only three in which the love element was at all the leading motive. The heroine of the *Meleager* was probably Althaea, not Atalanta. The *Stheneboea* merely describes the vengeance of Bellerophon for the treachery of his hosts. In the *Antigone* the "love-story" has all taken place before the action begins. Of the *Alcestis* and the *Protesilaus* we shall speak elsewhere, pp. 57, 99.

an Athenian audience with a love-story, as between man and woman, why should not the tragedians have made more use of the many stories that told of the love of men for men? If, it may be argued, this form of love was really so important an element in the life of the time, if it really occupied that place in the hearts of men as a whole that is now occupied by the love of women, why did Aeschylus and Sophocles only devote a couple of plays between them to its treatment?[1] Sophocles, at any rate, ought to have understood all about it.

The answer is probably to be found in the fact that the passion of love, in any shape or form, is foreign to the true spirit of Greek tragedy. The taste of the Greeks, refined in this as in most other things, considered love as essentially unfitted for the stage. That two people should stand up and make love to one another with a crowd looking on was, to the Greek mind, essentially unfitting. Love was an emotion which concerned individuals; it was an emotion which ought to be controlled in public, and only find expression in private.

The whole history of Greek poetry is so much commentary on this one fact. The love-poems of Sappho or Anacreon, just like the later love-poems of Asclepiades or Poseidippus, were meant to be sung by a single singer to a small and select audience. In the choral poetry, which required a number of performers, and was listened to by a large audience,

[1] That is to say, two only in which it furnished the main interest. That it lent a peculiar character to various other tragedies will be shown further on.

the personal love-element is well-nigh non-existent. The attempt of Ibycus to introduce it, and his failure to find imitators, we have already noticed.

And in the choral poetry sung in honour of Dionysus, from which tragedy had its rise, it is obvious, when one considers the intimate connection between the rites of Dionysus and Artemis, and the ascetic principle underlying their worship, how especially out of place a love-element would have been.

The fact, therefore, that love as between man and man does not play any very prominent part in the early tragedies, must simply be explained by the Greek dislike to the public display of violent private emotions. It took a long time to overcome this old-fashioned prejudice, and establish the love-element as an integral part of tragedy; and it is not uninstructive to observe how the movement began. The earliest love-story admitted on the Greek stage was the story of Achilles and Patroclus.[1]

But before entering upon the more detailed examination of the relations between the sexes, as illustrated by the Attic tragedians, it is necessary once more to call attention to, and warn against, a very fertile source of confusion.

It is above all things necessary that the reader should carefully distinguish between two very different things, two very different ways of regarding women, which are not uncommonly confused—woman as an object of interest, and woman as an object of love. As objects of interest, we find the

---

[1] Cp. what has been said above (p. 35) in the case of Ibycus; the parallel is a remarkable and important one.

female characters of the tragedians steadily developing throughout the fifth century; as objects of love, we do not find them develop at all. The relations between women and men are, in reality, as far from the modern in the last plays of Euripides as in the first of Aeschylus. Towards the close of the century, a very considerable proportion of the tragedies concern themselves with studies of female character in its various phases; the power of women for good and evil (especially the latter) is very generally acknowledged; their passions and their emotions are carefully analysed and elaborately discussed; and yet in all this analysis and discussion the love-element, in any modern sense of the word, plays no part whatever. By this time, woman at Athens held an important place in the mind of man; as yet she held no place in his heart at all. From end to end of the three great tragedians, there can hardly a single passage be quoted which so much as suggests the possibility of an unselfish and unsensual attachment between man and woman, playing at all an important part in the life of either; and this important fact it will be the object of the following pages to make clear.

Aeschylus, as has been said often enough, never brought on the stage a woman "in love."[1] That he should never have brought on the stage a man in such a condition went of course without saying;

---

[1] The statement to this effect in Aristoph. *Ran.* 1044, is so definite that it seems necessary to infer from it that, in spite of the words in Schol. *ad Apoll. Rhod.* i. 773, the erotic incident in the *Hypsipyle* was very little emphasised.

even Euripides was never accused of that. Indeed, Aeschylus' characters do not think much of women at all. That girls should not misbehave, if left to themselves, even their own father finds it hard to believe;[1] that in any sort of difficulty they should be a hindrance rather than a help, is only what one would expect.[2] Women are certainly not worth fighting about;[3] what really acquits Orestes is the fact that, after all, it was only a woman he killed.[4]

An apparent exception to all this is of course Clytemnestra. Why should Aeschylus, having so poor an opinion of women, have given so prominent a place to Clytemnestra in the murder of Agamemnon? The answer is doubtless to be found in the very significant fact that between Homer and Aeschylus the story had been treated by Stesichorus, to whom the prominence of Clytemnestra was beyond all reasonable doubt due.[5]

---

[1] *Suppl.* 996 *seqq.* [2] *Theb.* 182 *seqq.*

[3] πῶς οὐχὶ τἀνάλωμα γίγνεται πικρόν,
ἄνδρας γυναικῶν οὕνεχ' αἱμάξαι πέδον;
Suppl. 476.

καὶ γυναικὸς οὕνεκα
πόλιν διημάθυνεν Ἀργεῖον δάκος.
Agam. 823.

[4] οὕτω γυναικὸς οὐ προτιμήσω μόρον
ἄνδρα κτανούσης. *Eum.* 739.

To his views as to the physical unimportance of the mother, as compared with the father (*e.g. Eum.* 657 *seqq.*), I shall have occasion to refer later. See Excursus. [This Excursus does not seem to have been written.]

[5] How far Aeschylus has followed the *Oresteia* of Stesichorus, and how far he has modified it, cannot now be known; but it seems reasonable to suppose that, in all probability, the Clytemnestra of the latter poet was a good deal more in love with Aegisthus than is the Clytemnestra of the former. This would explain some incon-

Aeschylus, then, has little enough to say about women; but in Sophocles there is fortunately somewhat more to be found; indeed, it is probably the female characters of Sophocles that are most generally appreciated by modern readers. And yet, for all the great part played by women in the Sophoclean drama, the part played by women's love is wonderfully small.

Take a woman like Deianira; the man who can listen to her without feeling a positive shock must be more in sympathy with Athens than I ever wish to be.

She guesses the truth from Lichas about Heracles and Iole (*Trach.* 436), and begs him to tell her all, for she is no coward, nor yet is she the sort of woman who would refuse to admit a husband's right to an occasional infidelity.

> οὐ γὰρ γυναικὶ τοὺς λόγους ἐρεῖς κακῇ,
> οὐδ' ἥτις οὐ κάτοιδε τἀνθρώπων, ὅτι
> χαίρειν πέφυκεν οὐχὶ τοῖς αὐτοῖς ἀεί.

"Love is irresistible," she says; "if I were to blame my husband or this woman for falling victims to it, I should be a fool. Do not be afraid to tell me all. Has not Heracles often done this sort of thing before without making me jealous? Why should he make me jealous now? And as for the woman, why, I

---

gruities in the Aeschylean character, such as her sudden protestations of affection for Aegisthus when dead, after her apparent indifference to him when living. (*Cho.* 893, etc.) That she should kill Agamemnon out of revenge for the death of Iphigeneia and through jealousy of Cassandra, are perhaps additions of Aeschylus, to whose Athenian mind it seemed impossible that a woman should murder her husband merely because she was fond of another man.

can only pity her, when I see how her beauty has made her lose her home and her home comforts, for which, *expertae crede*, the love of Heracles is hardly a sufficient compensation."

ᾤκτειρα δὴ μάλιστα προσβλέψασ' ὅτι
τὸ κάλλος αὐτῆς τὸν βίον διώλεσεν.[1]

When this is Sophocles' ideal wife, one can hardly wonder that Haemon owes the only word of sympathy he gets from his Antigone to the editors.[2]

But even Deianira has her human moments, and in one of these she utters that wonderful lament of hers for the joys of her lost maidenhood, and the sorrows of her married life (*Trach.* 144 *seqq.*), a passage which may well be compared with one from the *Tereus*. (*Fr.* 524, Nauck). Both these dwell sym-

---

[1] One may say, of course, if one likes, that this is all ironical, that she does not mean it, and that in reality she is as jealous as anyone else could be, as her subsequent actions show. Personally, I do not believe that the passage is meant to be in the least ironical; the absence of jealousy is always a feature of the model wife (*cp.* Eur. *And.* 222, and numerous similar passages); but even if this be granted, it makes no difference to the point at all. Whatever the audience are to think, the characters on the stage are supposed to take her seriously; and this fact throws a sufficient light on what was then thought to be the duty of a loving wife.

It is satisfactory to notice that neither does Heracles attach any undue importance to Iole. In his last words to Hyllus, after elaborate instructions as to how his funeral-pyre is to be built, he adds casually—

ἀλλ' ἀρκέσει καὶ ταῦτα· πρόσνειμαι δέ μοι
χάριν βραχεῖαν πρὸς μακροῖς ἄλλοις διδούς.

"Just marry Iole for me, will you?" (l. 1216.)

[2] In this same play, the reader must be careful not to misunderstand the motives of Haemon's suicide. He does not kill himself out of grief for Antigone, but out of shame (αὑτῷ χολωθείς) at having attacked his father. That love for a woman should have made him so far forget himself was a disgrace not to be borne.

pathetically on the slavery of married life, and almost make one think at first sight that the poet must have felt what a mockery his "ideal wife" really was. But a little further examination will show clearly enough that Sophocles is not expressing his own views in either of these two passages. The protest in the *Tereus* is merely the direct outcome of the decidedly exceptional circumstances in which Procne finds herself—a woman who has just cooked her only son is hardly likely to have unprejudiced views on matrimony—and as such it is not meant to be more than one of those outcries against irresistible destiny, which one may pity if one likes, or even pardon, but which one cannot pretend to treat seriously. For a girl to complain of having to marry was as reasonable as for a man to complain of having to die. τί ταῦτα δεῖ στένειν, ἅπερ δεῖ κατὰ φύσιν διεκπερᾶν;

As for the passage from the *Trachiniae*, that seems to be simply an echo from Sappho, and Sappho's views on marriage were naturally different from those of Sophocles.[1]

To suppose from these passages that Sophocles saw anything inappropriate in the existing conditions

[1] The words of l. 144 *seqq.* at once suggest Catullus lxii. esp. 39 *seqq.* But this poem of Catullus is generally admitted to be, if not an actual translation, at least a paraphrase of Sappho; hence it is far more probable that Sophocles copied Sappho here, than that Catullus copied Sophocles there.

Another instance in which a tragedian copied an *Epithalamium* of Sappho is furnished by Aesch. *Suppl.* 998. *Cp.* Sappho *Fr.* 91, Longus *Past.* 3, 33, and my *Apospasmata Critica* (Oxford, Blackwell, 1892), p. 5.

of married life, or that he would have welcomed any change in them, is an unjustifiable inference.[1]

But the one play of Sophocles which is generally considered to be of supreme importance for this particular subject is the *Phaedra*. This play, which is supposed to have been the model for the *Hippolytus* of Euripides, is generally looked upon as the first "love-tragedy" of the Greeks. But was it a "love-tragedy" at all, in any sense in which the words are now understood? To judge by analogy, there is every reason to suppose that it was not.

The fragments unfortunately prove little, for no very important ones are preserved, and the one or two of them that do speak of love, merely speak of it in the regular Sophoclean way, not as a human passion, but as an unavoidable kind of disease, something like measles or distemper.[2]

But in spite of the paucity of the fragments, the main principle on which the legend (of which we have already spoken)[3] was treated, is sufficiently clear; and this principle is such as is, I venture to

---

[1] A great deal of light would be thrown on all this intricate subject if only one could find out how far, if at all, Sophocles was influenced by Euripides. Euripides, as we shall see later, was always ready to sympathise with women who suffered from the unreasonable treatment of the time, but it does not seem *prima facie* probable that this particular trait should have had influence on anyone so Athenian as Sophocles. Anyhow, these two passages prove nothing.

[2] This is exactly the idea of the well-known Ἔρως chorus in the *Antigone*. (l. 781). There, too, love is unavoidable (καί σ'οὔτ' ἀθανάτων φύξιμος οὐδείς, οὔθ' ἀμερίων σέ γ' ἀνθρώπων), it results in madness (ὁ δ' ἔχων μέμηνεν, "the stricken one is mad," as the Romans said "habet" of their gladiators), and the chief damage it does is to property (ὃs ἐν κτήμασι πίπτεις). Like Eresichthon's father, what the Chorus most object to is the expense. [3] [p. 38.]

submit, incompatible with the presence in the play of any real love-element.

Phaedra's love is not passion but madness, it is not an emotion but a disease. Aphrodite treats her in exactly the same way as Athene treats Ajax. Her love is so entirely outside her control, it is so entirely the result of external influences, that while one can perhaps pity her, one certainly cannot sympathise with her, for the simple reason that her misfortune is entirely outside human experience. She loves Hippolytus, as Oedipus kills Laius, for no earthly reason except that the story said the god made her do so. The Phaedra of Sophocles, like the Clytemnestra of Aeschylus, is made an instrument of divine vengeance for reasons which do not concern her personally in the least; one pities her, not as an unhappy lover, but as the victim of fate. She is no longer a human being influenced by human emotions; she is simply a tool in the hands of a relentless deity. In other words, she is never in love with Hippolytus at all, in any commonly-accepted sense of the term.

And thus it must be sufficiently clear to anyone who is able to get rid of preconceived ideas on the matter, that the *Phaedra* was in reality no more "romantic" than the *Trachiniae* or the *Antigone*. Like the rest of the plays of Sophocles, it merely drew the usual picture of the gods playing shove-halfpenny with human souls; the fact that Aphrodite for once took a hand in the game gave it on this occasion a peculiar character of its own, but of anything in any way resembling a modern love-element there is no more trace here than there is anywhere else.[1]

But what really affords a more conclusive proof than any other of how utterly anything of the nature of modern love between man and woman was unknown to Sophocles, is the remarkable prominence given in his plays to the affection between brother and sister.[2] The relations between Electra and Orestes, or Antigone and Polynices, are absolutely those of modern lovers; but Sophocles could not conceive of such relations as existing between people whom he would have called "lovers," and, therefore, he had to think of the parties to them as brother and sister. He wished to draw a picture of pure, noble, and unselfish devotion existing between man and woman; the only conditions under which such a thing seemed to him possible were that the man and the woman should be close blood relations.

There are those who complain of the indifference of Electra to Pylades, or of Antigone to Haemon, and think that a little love infused into these heroines would make them more human. These people have overlooked the fact that Electra and Antigone are in reality quite as much in love as ever woman was;

---

[1] Vide Excursus B.

[2] This feature is of course by no means peculiar to Sophocles; it is prominent both in Aeschylus and Euripides (*e.g.* the pathetic passage in *Orest.* 1041 *seqq.*), and doubtless for the same reason. In Sophocles, however, perhaps owing merely to the chance which has preserved certain plays while others have been lost, it plays a particularly important part. Not only are the *Antigone* and the *Electra* almost entirely devoted to it, but the one ray of light in the 1800 lines of the *Oedipus Coloneus* is the farewell of Polynices to his sister. (l. 1414 *seqq.*)

but they are in love with their brothers. They did not know it perhaps; Sophocles did not know it; but the fact remains. Antigone despises love—what she and her audience thought was love. Between Polynices and Haemon there is never a moment's hesitation; almost her last words are an exclamation of the bitterest contempt for marriage: "If my husband had died, I could have married another; if he had failed to get me children, I could have committed adultery; but — my brother is dead!"[1]

And yet, Antigone comes far nearer to a modern lover than Phaedra ever does.

This is a fact of the greatest importance in the present connection, and one that cannot be too much emphasised. The relation of the sexes was such among the early Greeks that a pure love between man and woman seemed to them a sheer impossibility, and yet their instinct told them that pure love was not really an impossible thing. The ways in which the difficulty was surmounted were various. Of the love of man for man and of woman for woman we have already spoken; in Sophocles a third alternative is suggested. The lovers are made man and woman, but the possibility of sensuality is first removed by making them brother and sister. A woman who loves a man may love him purely,

---

[1] Soph. *Ant.* 909 *seqq*. This seems the natural and obvious way of taking these words, but whichever way one takes them they do not imply any very great respect for matrimony.

Whether the lines are Sophocles' or not is of course indifferent in this connection, as everyone is agreed that, if an interpolation, they are a very early one.

says Sophocles, if she is in such a position that she cannot love him otherwise.[1]

In the first two of the Athenian dramatists there are then, as we have seen, practically no traces whatever to be found of a love-element in any real sense of the term. But this, it may be said, is nothing wonderful. This everyone will admit. For the love-element one looks to Euripides. In the following examination of Euripides, I hope to show that not only is love, in any modern sense, quite unknown to his characters, but also that the whole "romantic" element of his plays, on which it is the custom to lay such stress, is much less pronounced than is generally supposed; in other words, that his men take really very little interest in his women.

But before discussing what Euripides did not do, it is well to have a clear conception of what he did do; for he did do a great deal. The great service of Euripides to art was that he emphasised unmistakably the importance of women. He seems to have been the first emphatically to enunciate that doctrine of *cherchez la femme*, which has been the groundwork of all modern art. He was not the first man to discover it; the men who made the story of Troy knew it as well as he did; but he was the first, as far as we know, consciously to adopt it as an artistic canon. He was the first deliberately to maintain that the highest artistic effects were to be

[1] This is not, I think, saying too much. A story like that of Canace, however powerfully it might affect its audience, was, after all, even in later times, looked upon as something quite exceptional in Greece. (Cp. the later Athenian view on the subject as illustrated by Plaut. *Epid.* v. i. 45, *seqq.*)

obtained by the contrast of the sexes. The women of the earlier tragedians, as far as they are of any interest, are merely women, as it were by accident; they are men in everything but their dress. The women of Euripides, however unpleasant they may be, are always intensely feminine. The emphasis which Euripides laid on the feminine as opposed to the masculine element is at once his chief characteristic and his chief merit.

The ways in which he emphasises the importance of women are various. Everyone knows the stress he lays on their power of doing harm; the "misogyny" of Euripides need hardly be illustrated here.[1] At the same time, he is fully aware of their power for good.[2] He dwells on their cleverness repeatedly: "If supremacy were a matter of brains, and not of brute force, men would not have a chance."[3] He is convinced of their heroism: Iphigeneia goes to her death with far more dignity than Antigone. He is even convinced, in a way that not all his successors have been, of their reasonableness: there are few men who could discuss their own deaths as calmly and clearly as Phaedra[4] or Polyxena.[5] It would be easy to multiply instances if there were any need to do so.

All this Euripides did. He made his women powerful, intelligent, heroic, reasonable. He did not

---

[1] It is worth while, however, to notice that even the women themselves in Aristophanes are made to confess that this so-called misogyny is, in truth, merely realism. Cp. *e.g.* Aristoph. *Thesm.* 389 *seqq.*, *Eccl.* 214 *seqq.*   [2] *e.g. Fr.* 822, etc.   [3] *Fr.* 321.
[4] *Hipp.* 373 *seqq.* Tempting as it is to take this passage as ironical, it would almost certainly be wrong to do so.   [5] *Hec.* 342 *seqq.*

make them loved or loveable. In this Euripides is well-nigh as old-fashioned as any of his predecessors. In all the extant plays there is not a single instance of a man in love with a woman; there is no evidence, except perhaps in one isolated case,[1] of such a character in any of the plays that have been lost. So far from Euripides being the poet of love between man and woman, there are numerous situations in his plays where it seems simply extraordinary to the modern reader how such obvious opportunities for the introduction of such love can have been missed or ignored.[2]

A detailed examination of some of the plays will bring this out clearly; but before proceeding to this, it would be well to observe certain of the more general features of the Euripidean conception of the relations, other than social and intellectual, existing between men and women.

The first point to be noticed is that Euripides, too, just like Sophocles, speaks of love as a sort of irresistible madness or disease,[3] which seizes on

---

[1] See Excursus C. It is true that in the intrigue of Macareus and Canace there is some reason to believe that the former was, contrary to the usual habit of these legends, the leading spirit; but in the *Aeolus* of Euripides this beginning of the story seems to have only been alluded to in the prologue, and not to have formed part of the action.—Cp. Antiphanes, *Aeol. Fr.* 1.

[2] The most striking example is perhaps the *Iphigeneia in Aulis*, but there are plenty of others.

Instances in which women are represented as in love with men are somewhat commoner, as they were commoner in the legends; but the part they play in Euripides, as a whole, has been greatly exaggerated. Cp. p. 38.

[3] ἡρῶν· τὸ μαίνεσθαι δ' ἄρ' ἦν ἔρως βροτοῖς.—*Fr.* 161 (*Antigone*). Cp. *Hipp.* 443 *sqq.*

its victims without any particular reason, and can only be cured or borne by being allowed to have free course. It is, as I have said before, exactly like measles; the only proper treatment is to help it as much as you can to "come out," as then it is less painful at the time, and less likely to have serious consequences. Instances of this view are sufficiently numerous. It forms the chief framework of the *Hippolytus*, and all attempts to interpret the emotions of that play in accordance with more modern notions, are without success. The same was still more the case in the *Phœnix*, as Suidas distinctly implies by his use of the words τῷ υἱῷ ἐπέμηνε τὴν παλλακήν in this connection.[1] It is enunciated by Jason to Medea in the *Medea* (526 *seqq.*) as a proof that he owes nothing to her, as she was not responsible for her actions in saving him; by Helen to Menelaus in the *Troades* (945 *seqq.*) as a perfect excuse for her conduct with Paris.

Now it is just here, one may as well notice at once, that the difference between Euripides and modern writers, with the Alexandrians at their head, is so striking. The lovers in Euripides, as far as they are lovers at all, are carried along by a forcible external impulse, the direction of which is entirely sensual and entirely selfish. If, or as soon as, they fail in achieving the gratification of their sensual desires, their "love" immediately turns to hate. The idea of devotion or self-sacrifice for the

---

[1] Suidas (s.v. Ἀναγυράσιος) τούτου δὲ (τοῦ θεοῦ) ἐξέκοψέ τις τὸ ἄλσος· ὁ δὲ τῷ υἱῷ αὐτοῦ ἐπέμηνε τὴν παλλακήν ... ἱστορεῖ δὲ Ἱερώνυμος ἐν τῷ περὶ τραγῳδοποιῶν, ἀπεικάζων τούτοις τὸν Εὐριπίδου Φοίνικα. Cp. id. s.v. ἐναύειν. Vide Nauck, *Trag. Graec. Frag.* p. 621.

good of the loved person, as distinct from one's own, is absolutely unknown. "Love is irresistible," they say, and, in obedience to its commands, they sit down to reckon how they can satisfy themselves, at no matter what cost to the objects of their passion.

Love is irresistible still, one knows, as irresistible now as ever it was in Greece, but the impulse it gives has a different direction. To put it perfectly crudely, the Euripidean woman who "falls in love" (it is of women we are speaking now) thinks first of all, "How can I seduce the man I love?" The modern woman thinks, "How can I die for him?" This is the difference between ancient and modern love, and in Euripides the old is still untouched by the new.[1]

[1] The difference is described with wonderful force by Maximus Tyrius (xxv. 4): ὁ μὲν ἐφ' ἡδονὴν οἰστρεῖ, ὁ δὲ κάλλους ἐρᾷ· ὁ μὲν ἄκων νοσεῖ, ὁ δὲ ἑκὼν ἐρᾷ· ὁ μὲν ἐπ' ἀγαθῷ ἐρᾷ τοῦ ἐρωμένου, ὁ δὲ ἐπ' ὀλέθρῳ ἀμφοῖν.—I have spoken here merely of women because we have so little absolute evidence as to men, but what little we have all goes to prove that their view of "love" was at least as sensual as that of the women, and if anything even more brutal; and, anyhow, there is no evidence of the contrary. It is very hard satisfactorily to compare Euripides with people like Asclepiades, who are the earliest representatives we know of the modern spirit, for this very reason, that while the former nearly always discusses the matter from the point of view of the woman, the latter do so with almost equal regularity, as far as we can now judge, from the point of view of the man. One thing, however, is clear enough at the very outset. While Euripides regards the relation between man and woman as entirely based on the sexual instinct, the Alexandrians have from the first imported into it that further feeling of comradeship and mutual self-sacrifice which had before been peculiar to the relation between man and man. For obvious reasons this great change first became noticeable on the side of the man (for the influence of Sappho's school had probably by this time become inappreciable), but its effects are evident enough as soon as the Alexandrians begin to talk of a woman's love. The difference between, say, the Medea of Apollonius and the most refined heroine of the Attic drama is one, not of degree, but of kind.

It is this sensual, this well-nigh mechanical view of love which makes possible that conception of the ideal wife, of which we have already spoken in the case of Sophocles' Deianira, and which is so strongly insisted upon in the Andromache of Euripides.

Andromache regularly appears as the model wife, not only in the play which bears her name, but also in the *Troades*. Her views on married life have, therefore, a peculiar weight of their own.

οὐ τὸ κάλλος, ὦ γύναι,
ἀλλ' ἀρεταὶ τέρπουσι τοὺς ξυνευνέτας,

she explains to the youthful Hermione.[1] "Now the greatest of these virtues is, to be content with your husband and not to be jealous. You are jealous of me. What would you do, supposing you were married to a Thracian king with twenty wives instead of only two? You would murder them all, I suppose, in your jealousy, *showing thereby how utterly unbridled was your lust.* I was never jealous; *I used to act as foster-mother to Hector's illegitimate children.*

καὶ ταῦτα δρῶσα τἀρετῇ προσηγόμην πόσιν.

"But you, you are afraid to let a drop of rain fall on your husband's head.

μὴ τὴν τεκοῦσαν τῇ φιλανδρίᾳ, γύναι,
ζήτει παρελθεῖν."

φιλανδρία![2]

This is not irony; it is just sober earnest, the

---

[1] *Andr.* 205 *seqq.*

[2] The early Greek view of "love" is put here with almost revolting crudeness. Hermione's devotion to her husband and Helen's desertion of hers, are due to one and the same cause—sensual passion.

sober earnest morality of respectable Athens. The view is by no means confined to Andromache. It is deliberately propounded by Electra to her mother,[1] and Jason twice taunts Medea with her failure to live up to its level.[2] Indeed, it may be said to colour, to a certain extent, the whole conception of married life. For a woman to wish to keep her husband to herself was a sign that she was at once unreasonable and lascivious.

This doctrine of the absolute subjection of the wife[3] is emphasised in various ways. That a really respectable wife not only always stays at home, but also never sees visitors, is more or less of an axiom.[4] To give a woman her head is dangerous in the last degree, and if you do, you will probably get murdered for your pains.[5] Suicide for a husband's

---

[1] γυναῖκα γὰρ χρὴ πάντα συγχωρεῖν πόσει,
ἥτις φρενήρης.   (*Elect.* 1052.)

[2] ἀλλ' ἐς τοσοῦτον ἧκεθ' ὥστ' ὀρθουμένης
εὐνῆς γυναῖκες πάντ' ἔχειν νομίζετε,
ἢν δ' αὖ γένηται ξυμφορά τις ἐς λέχος κ.τ.λ.
(*Med.* 569).

IA. λέχους σφε κἠξίωσας οὕνεκα κτανεῖν;
MH. σμικρὸν γυναικὶ πῆμα τοῦτ' εἶναι δοκεῖς;
IA. ἥτις γε σώφρων.   (*ibid.* 1367.)

[3] πᾶσα γὰρ δούλη πέφυκεν ἀνδρὸς ἡ σώφρων γυνή.—*Fr.* 545 (*Oedipus*).

[4] Cp. Andromache in *Tro.* 642 *seqq.* Other instances are numerous. This view and that as to jealousy evidently hang together, for it must be admitted that if a wife considers it her duty to become so supremely uninteresting and stupid as such a method of life must inevitably make her, it is also her duty to be lenient to her husband if he occasionally seeks for entertainment outside the domestic circle.

[5] οὐ γάρ ποτ' ἄνδρα τὸν σοφὸν γυναικὶ χρὴ
δοῦναι χαλινούς.
Fr. 463 (*Cressae*); cp. *Fr.* 464.

sake is only respectable on the part of a woman,[1] for her husband is her life.[2]

But where is one to find such a model wife? for marriage is such a lottery that one ought really to be allowed, if one can afford it, to have several tickets, in case the first doesn't turn out well.[3] The only chance is to marry a woman of good family; in other words, the only thing worth marrying for is rank.[4] To prefer to marry for love is not only foolish, but unfair on one's children.[5]

It is this view of married life, this devotion to an ideal of drudgery on the part of the woman, and the calm acceptance of such devotion as a matter of course on the part of the man, which explains such a play as the *Alcestis*.[6] The woman is devoted to the man, not because he is himself, but because he is her husband. For the man she does not care in the least, but for the husband—for the ideal of the family—she is perfectly ready to die. It is this which at once makes the story of Alcestis possible,

---

[1] *Tro.* 1012 *seqq.*; cp. *Hipp.* 419 *seqq.*

[2] *i.e.* her means of livelihood.

τὰ μὲν γὰρ ἄλλα δεύτερ' ἂν πάσχοι γυνή·
ἀνδρὸς δ' ἁμαρτάνουσ' ἁμαρτάνει βίου.
(*Andr.* 372; cp. *ibid.* 904.)

[3] *Fr.* 402 (*Ino*).   [4] Cp. *Andr.* 1279 *seqq.*; *Fr.* 215 (*Antiope*), &c.

[5] οὐκ ἔστι τοῦδε παισὶ κάλλιον γέρας,
ἢ πατρὸς ἐσθλοῦ κἀγαθοῦ πεφυκέναι,
γαμεῖν τ' ἀπ' ἐσθλῶν· ὃς δὲ νικηθεὶς πόθῳ
κακοῖς ἐκοινώνησεν, οὐκ ἐπαινέσω,
τέκνοις ὄνειδος οὕνεχ' ἡδονῆς λιπεῖν.
(*Heracl.* 297.)

[6] To what extent it also figured in that strange play, the *Protesilaus*, cannot now be known, but it is only probable that it was prominent there also.

and robs it of half its pathos. Had Alcestis loved Admetus as a man, she could not but have felt the bitterest disappointment at his accepting her offer. As it is, she seems to regard his conduct almost as much as a matter of course as he does.[1]

The brief examination of one further point in the Euripidean view of women may serve as introduction to the more detailed discussion of the romantic element in his plays, or, rather, of its absence. Euripides speaks frequently as if there were a sort of freemasonry existing among women, which makes one woman always ready to side with another as against a man. Instances of this are common, especially in the relations between the heroine and the Chorus, when the latter, as mostly in Euripides, consists of women.

Thus Medea, when asking the Chorus not to reveal her plans, says—

λέξῃς δὲ μηδὲν τῶν ἐμοὶ δεδογμένων,
εἴπερ φρονεῖς εὖ δεσπόταις γυνή τ' ἔφυς.
(*Med.* 822.)

Similar in spirit is a line from the *Alope* (*Fr.* 108):

γυνὴ γυναικὶ σύμμαχος πέφυκέ πως,

or l. 329 of the *Helen:*

γυναῖκα γὰρ δὴ συμπονεῖν γυναικὶ χρή.

---

[1] Here again one almost marvels at the way in which Euripides misses an opportunity. The contrast between the joy of Alcestis at saving Admetus' life, and her grief for her ruined ideal, would have furnished as splendid a conflict of emotions as any dramatist could desire. Athenian taste, however, preferred that she should die congratulating him on having had such a wife, while he stands by expressing his deep regret that he cannot accompany her, as Charon does not issue return tickets. For a further examination of the motives of Admetus, however, see p. 101.

In this same play, too, Menelaus decides that *his wife* is the proper person to go and ask help of Theonoe:

σὸν ἔργον, ὡς γυναικὶ πρόσφορον γυνή.
(*Hel.* 830.)

A "romantic" writer might have thought that the prayers of Menelaus himself would have been more effectual with a lady.[1]

The most important of the extant plays of Euripides is, for the student of the development of the romantic tendency, undoubtedly the *Hippolytus*. But, in thinking of this play, the reader must first of all guard against a very common and, for a modern, very natural mistake. He must remember that the interest of the piece is intended to centre, not on Phaedra, but on Hippolytus. The main interest of the plot is the struggle between asceticism and self-gratification, as personified in the maiden Artemis and the sensual Aphrodite.[2] Phaedra is only made to fall in love with Hippolytus in order that he may reject her advances, and thereby irritate her into working his ruin. As has already been pointed out, she is dragged into a quarrel which does not concern her, for a purpose which does not interest her personally in the least.[3]

---

[1] It must be admitted that Jason has a higher opinion of his own influence (*Med.* 942 *seqq.*), if, indeed, this be the right way to take the passage.

[2] This seems to have been still more the case in the first version of the play, where Hippolytus appears actually as a βουκόλος, or ascetic worshipper of Artemis, and where he is promised immortality as the reward of his constancy. See Reitzenstein, *Epig. u. Skol.* p. 210 *seqq.* and Excursus D.

[3] οἱ σώφρονες γὰρ οὐχ ἑκόντες, ἀλλ' ὅμως κακῶν ἐρῶσι. (*Hipp.* 358.)

Bearing this in mind, the reader will be able to understand that combination of passionate desire and cold-blooded reasoning which marks the utterances of Phaedra. She has come to the conclusion, she says at last (l. 391 *seqq.*), that love is an irresistible disease; and since her position as a married woman makes impossible the only means of cure with which she is acquainted, she decides that, *for the sake of her husband and children*, she had better die. She will never dishonour her children, for, next to money, there is nothing so valuable as a good name.

To this the Nurse replies (l. 433 *seqq.*) that of course love is irresistible, and there is only one way to cure it; but she points out that this way may perfectly well be adopted. The fact that Phaedra is married need not be any obstacle, for husbands are used to seeing more than they say.

"ἀλλ', ὦ φίλη παῖ, λῆγε μὲν κακῶν φρενῶν,
λῆξον δ' ὑβρίζουσ': οὐ γὰρ ἄλλο πλὴν ὕβρις
τάδ' ἐστί, κρείσσω δαιμόνων εἶναι θέλειν,
τόλμα δ'ἐρῶσα· θεὸς ἐβουλήθη τάδε.

"Leave the matter to me, and if women can't effect a cure, perhaps men can."

Phaedra protests. The Nurse answers with a little very natural impatience (l. 490)

"τί σεμνομυθεῖς; οὐ λόγων εὐσχημόνων
δεῖ σ', ἀλλὰ τἀνδρός."

Phaedra admits this, but insists that it would be more respectable to die. The Nurse, however, persuades her to try a love-potion first, and with this excuse leaves her to look for Hippolytus. Hippolytus, as one knows, rejects the Nurse's proposals, and Phaedra takes refuge in suicide, making, as she dies, one last desperate attempt to save her own good name at the expense of the man she is supposed to love (l. 715).

This, then, is the story of Phaedra. Where in all this is there a trace of what we now call love? Where is there a single expression of affection for Hippolytus, a single expression to show that she thinks of him otherwise than of one who has done her a great and irretrievable injury? She seems to think of him as one would think of a man from whom one had caught the cholera. "Love is all bitterness," she says (l. 349); "and he is the cause." The catastrophe comes, and she walks off quietly to murder him,

"ὥστ' εὐκλεᾶ μὲν παισὶ προσθεῖναι βίον,
αὐτή τ' ὄνασθαι πρὸς τὰ νῦν πεπτωκότα."

If this is love, the world must be a poorer place than I gave it credit for.

Then follows the great argument between Hippolytus and his father, which to the Athenians was doubtless the chief point of the play. On the speech of Theseus we need not dwell, though it is perhaps just worth noticing the way in which he enunciates, as a sort of great discovery which his own experience and observation have enabled him to make, the theory that it is possible for the initiative in a criminal liaison to come from the side of the man (l. 966 *seqq.*).

The answer of Hippolytus, however, is well worth

study. For the first 24 of his 52 lines he describes in general terms his own blameless character, and it is only at the 25th that he condescends to discuss the particular incident. "But you do not perhaps believe all this about my chastity," he says (l. 1007); "but do tell me, then, what was the temptation in this particular instance? Was this woman's body so especially beautiful? (1½ lines.) Or did I wish by my conduct to become your heir? (2½ lines.) Or to become king? (3 lines.) Surely you know my only interest is in athletics." (5 lines.) Then, having finished the arguments which he is able to bring forward, he proceeds to swear, and so concludes. In other words, in a speech of 52 lines, the suggestion that he might have been in love with Phaedra, even in the most rudimentary sense of the words, is contemptuously dismissed in a line and a half, and no one seems to think that this part of the subject ought to have been treated at greater length. Now this one fact seems to me in itself almost a sufficient proof that "romantic" ideas, even as they were understood at the end of the fourth century, were utterly foreign to Euripides.[1]

[1] One may argue, of course, that Hippolytus, as a devotee of Orpheus, etc., would be naturally more prone to ignore the "love-element" than a person of more human passions, and that this strange disproportion in his speech is a mark of his character. Personally I doubt this, as, firstly, the characters of the Athenian drama, when making their set speeches, generally quite forget who they are —indeed, the wonder is they don't sometimes slip into an ἄνδρες δικασταί—and, secondly, if Hippolytus had been meant to slur over an important part of his subject, his reasons for so doing would have been more definitely explained. The conclusion seems to me inevitable, that neither Hippolytus nor Theseus thought the possibility of the former's having been in love with Phaedra worthy of serious discussion.

To come to another play. There are probably few things in all literature so strange, not to say comic, to modern ideas, as the relations between Achilles and Iphigeneia in the *Iphigeneia in Aulis.*

Clytemnestra has been trapped into bringing her daughter to Aulis, on promise of marriage with Achilles, and when, in the scene which begins at l. 801, she discovers the truth, she appeals to him for protection. Achilles, "the nearest approach to a modern gentleman of all the Greek tragic characters,"[1] replies as follows (l. 919 *seqq.*) :

"I am a person of the highest breeding, and therefore you may trust me to give you the correct answer under the circumstances. Your daughter, having been betrothed to me, shall not be killed; it would reflect discredit on me if she were, and that I cannot permit. No one shall so much as touch the hem of her garment. *It is not, of course, for her sake that I undertake to do this,* but because I consider that Agamemnon has treated me shamefully. He used my name to trap you into coming here without asking my consent; *of course I should have allowed him to use it if he had asked me,* for I always put patriotism before everything; but he did not ask me. I feel grossly insulted, and he will touch Iphigeneia at his peril."

"Your sentiments, Achilles," remarks the Chorus, "are worthy alike of you and of your divine descent."

"How can I thank you enough," replies Clytemnestra, "for all the trouble you have promised to

[1] Mahaffy, *Class. Gr. Lit.* vol. i. p. 370.

take in this matter, which cannot interest you personally in the least?"

There is a moment's pause; then she suggests timidly, "But would you like the girl to come to you herself?"

"God forbid!" exclaims Achilles with horror. "How can you suggest anything so improper?" Then after a little he adds, "You must first of all go and argue the case with Agamemnon."

"Why that?" asks Clytemnestra. "There is no chance there."

"Perhaps not," he answers, "but still I wish you to try; *for I should very much prefer, if possible, that my name should be kept out of the business altogether.*"

"What you say does you credit," she answers. "I will do my best to obey you."

For the modern reader who studies this scene, and then leans back and thinks a little what he would have done or thought in Achilles' place, comment is, I imagine, superfluous.[1]

Or look at Andromache's speech in the *Andromache*. (l. 184 *seqq.*) She is accused of occupying too high a place in the favour of Neoptolemus. "Tell

---

[1] It is true that, later on, the magnificent heroism of Iphigeneia extorts from Achilles what is perhaps one of the earliest declarations of love from a man to a woman that we know:

Ἀγαμέμνονος παῖ, μακάριόν μέ τις θεῶν
ἔμελλε θήσειν, εἰ τύχοιμι σῶν γάμων·
ζηλῶ δὲ σοῦ μὲν Ἑλλάδ', Ἑλλάδος δὲ σέ.

(l. 1405.)

But this utterance, made under such exceptional circumstances, cannot counteract the effect of what has gone before; and, anyhow, it is a curiously isolated expression, and rather a qualified one.

me," she answers to Hermione, "what reason could I possibly have for wishing to stand well with your husband? Do I wish to reign in your place, or to have more children, or to make my children kings? Or what reason could he possibly have for preferring me? Is my native city so powerful? Have I such influential friends?" &c. &c. As in the *Hippolytus*, the idea that there may be love on either side is dismissed without discussion.

Or look at the character of the Autourgos in the *Electra*. He has married Electra, but refuses to touch her, and why?

αἰσχύνομαι γὰρ ὀλβίων ἀνδρῶν τέκνα
λαβὼν ὑβρίζειν, οὐ κατάξιος γεγώς. (l. 45.)

He is distressed that the daughter of such wealthy parents should have made so poor a match. It is pity for the house of Agamemnon that affects him, not pity for Electra.[1]

Hecuba again, in the play that bears her name, does not think that it is much use to appeal to the "romantic" feelings of Agamemnon.

καὶ μὴν ἴσως μὲν τοῦ λόγου κενὸν τόδε,
Κύπριν προβάλλειν κ.τ.λ. (l. 824.)

In the *Phoenissae* there is not much love lost between Antigone and Haemon (cp. l. 1672 *seqq.*). In the *Orestes* the only incident which causes Pylades to take the slightest interest in Electra is her suggestion

[1] Worthy of notice is the excellent touch which makes this man, though poor, yet a member of a good family. (l. 37.) As Euripides knew well enough, a son of the soil would have been incapable of even this much refinement of feeling. We may observe, by the way, that Orestes expresses himself as very sceptical of the whole story—anyhow as far as motives go. (l. 253 *seqq*.)

that they should murder Hermione. (l. 1191 *seqq.*) In the *Helena* the first exclamation of Menelaus, when his wife assures him that she has really been faithful to him all the time, is, "How can you prove it?"[1] In the *Medea* again the absence of the love-element is a distinct loss. No one can doubt that the character of Medea would have gained at once in probability and in pathos, if she had been allowed to recur, if only for a moment, to the memory of her early love for Jason.

If more plays had been preserved, it would, doubtless, have been easy still further to multiply instances; but what has been said already is perhaps enough to show that the romantic element in Euripides is really most conspicuous by its absence. And this cannot be a surprise to anyone who cares to go to the root of the matter. That relation between men and women which we call the "romantic" is founded upon sentiments and ideas which are entirely distinct from the sexual emotions. Euripides, as we have had occasion to notice again and again, though he had carefully studied the sexual instinct in all its workings, had never been able to conceive of a relation between man and woman which had not this for its basis.[2] Without pure—I had almost said Platonic—love for its fundamental principle, romance is an impossibility. The romantic Alexandrian writers may not have themselves loved purely, but they knew what pure love

---

[1] *Hel.* 566 *seqq*. Still more offensive, of course, are the suggestions of Ion to his mother (*Ion* 1523 *seqq.*); but there the offence is against decency, not against romance.

[2] Except occasionally, as already noticed, in the case of close blood-relations.

was, and such love was their ideal. With Euripides it was not so, and this one fact is enough to show that he belongs to the old literature and not to the new. That Euripides, by the emphasis which he laid on the female character, contributed largely towards preparing men's minds for the growth of romance and what we now call love, cannot be denied; but that he himself had more than the very faintest glimmerings of what such love really was, cannot be maintained by anyone who has ever read his works.

And here we may close this first part of our enquiry. The foregoing examination of the Greek writers, though it has made no mention of various well-known names, has yet been for our present purpose a practically complete one. Pindar was prevented by the nature of his works from dealing to any large extent with the position of women or their relations with men;[1] and even where he has an opportunity of so

[1] Such erotic legends as he does introduce are treated with strangely little sympathy. The best (in the extant odes) is that of Pelops and Hippodameia (*Olymp.* 1), where the writer has, perhaps, been roused to a little warmth by the story of Pelops and Poseidon that has immediately preceded. The legend of Peleus and Hippolyte (*Nem.* 5) is noticeable as being, strangely enough, the only one in which the woman is represented as taking the initiative; but this is doubtless to be explained by the fact that nearly all these stories are descriptive of the amours of *gods*. The story of Jason and Medea is utterly spoiled in *Pyth.* 4. In that of Apollo and Coronis (*Pyth.* 3) only the unfaithfulness of the nymph and her punishment are dwelt upon. The other erotic stories told—*i.e.* those of Apollo and Euadne (*Olymp.* 6), Apollo and Cyrene (*Pyth.* 9), Zeus and the daughter of Opoeis (*Olymp.* 9), Ixion and Hera (*Pyth.* 2), are merely concerned with seductions of the most commonplace kind. The story of Rhoecus and the Hamadryad (*Fr.* 165) is the only one of importance alluded to in the fragments; but here it is uncertain how far Pindar told the story, and how far he merely alluded to it.

doing (as, *e.g., Fr.* 122), the result is very disappointing, especially in view of his Boeotian origin. The fragments of the early tragedians, other than the three discussed, are strangely deficient in references to women. Nor need the old Attic Comedy detain us. The general spirit of this thoroughly Athenian product is sufficiently summed up in what profess to be the earliest words of it extant, the fragment of Susario,

ἀκούετε λεῴ· Σουσαρίων λέγει τάδε,
υἱὸς Φιλίνου Μεγαρόθεν Τριποδίσκιος·
κακὸν γυναῖκες,

while it may be doubted whether in the whole course of this literature a female character was ever introduced on the stage, except with the view of leading up to some form of indecency.[1]

The net results of this examination, though chiefly negative, are yet fairly clear. It has, I hope, been shown that—

(1) That relation between men and women which is now called "love" was, as far as can be gathered from literature, non-existent among the Greeks down to the end of the fifth century.

(2) The position occupied by women in the consideration of men was so unimportant, that even the sensual relation of the sexes was but little treated of in literature till a comparatively late period, and was always, down to the end of the fifth century, looked upon by a considerable section of society as unfitted for public discussion and representation. In other

---

[1] [On the position occupied by women in the Old Comedy compare *Women in Greek Comedy*, § 3, 4.]

words, love-poetry in the modern sense is non-existent in classical Greek literature; while love-poetry in any sense, addressed to women, is a far more insignificant element in that literature than is commonly supposed.

That what has just been said does not hold good of the "Alexandrian" poets is so obvious that it hardly needs to be stated. Equally true, however, and not equally obvious, is the fact that, from the very first, these writers talk of women and women's love in an entirely different tone to that adopted by those of whom we have hitherto been speaking. The line of cleavage between, say, Asclepiades and Euripides, is in reality quite as marked as that between Euripides and Apollonius. On this subject, therefore, it is perhaps worth while to say a few words, though the terribly mutilated condition in which the works of the earlier Alexandrians especially have come down to us, makes it very difficult to point to striking examples of what has been said.

The first representatives of the "Alexandrian" school of poets—that is, of the school of women-lovers—are Asclepiades and Philetas;[1] and in both cases the mere nature of their works (quite apart from their tone) is sufficiently striking when compared with the literature that had gone before.

Whether Philetas actually gave the title of Battis to a collection of his poems is difficult to say—it is, perhaps, on the whole, not improbable that he did—but in any case there can be no doubt that a

[1] Cp. Theocr. vii. 39.

considerable number of his elegies were either actually addressed to Battis, or else treated of her. The erudite and elaborate style of these poems is equally indisputable. Now, whatever may have been the actual tone of address in these elegies—the fragments unfortunately tell us nothing, and such other evidence as there is on the subject is of the scantiest description[1]—the two facts above-mentioned form of themselves a combination quite without parallel in the Greek literature of which we have hitherto been speaking. That anyone should have taken the trouble to devote erudition and elaboration to the praise of a woman, would have been an unheard-of thing in early Greece.

Asclepiades is an equally striking figure in the early Alexandrian literature; for it was he who was

[1] One or two points are perhaps worth noticing in this connection. It is usual to assume that the Battis of Philetas was an Hetæra; but the evidence seems rather to suggest that she was his wife. The way in which she is spoken of in Ovid, *Trist.* i. 6, 2, *Pont.* iii. 1, 57, (in the former place coupled with the Lyde of Antimachus,) seems to support this view; and, at any rate, there does not appear to be any evidence to the contrary. The personal character of Philetas, as we learn it from various notices of him, seems also rather to point in the same direction; though this is not, of course, an argument that can be pressed. (It would be interesting to know whether the fact that Philetas is apparently never alluded to under a nickname, like so many others of the Alexandrian writers, was due to this austerity of character.)

Whether these elegies were as sober and as little sensual in tone as those of Antimachus (cp. *infra.* p. 110), it is impossible now to say; though the two passages cited from Ovid both seem indirectly to imply that they were, and there is certainly nothing in the fragments of Philetas which would lead one to infer that they were not. It need hardly be added that the passage in Ovid, *Ars Amat.* iii. 329 *seqq.* proves nothing, for the "lascivia" there ascribed to Sappho is obviously not meant to apply to all the other poets mentioned in the list, or Vergil's name would hardly appear in it.

the first to introduce woman-love into the epigram—the first, in fact, to give it that social recognition which we have seen already accorded to boy-love, well-nigh two centuries before.[1]

But what renders Asclepiades particularly important for us just now—far more so than Philetas—is the fact that some forty of his epigrams have been preserved, and that it will therefore be possible, by examining these, to study at close quarters the points in which the tone of this new love-poetry differs from that of the old.

In the epigrams of Asclepiades we find, for the first time, love for a woman spoken of as a matter of life and death:—

οἴχομ', ἔρωτες, ὄλωλα, διοίχομαι· εἰς γὰρ ἑταίραν
νυστάζων ἐπέβην, ἠδ' ἔθιγόν τ' 'Αΐδα.[2]
Anth. Pal. v. 162, 3-4.

Here, for the first time, such love appears as an end in life—as an object for which a man may well brave death:—

νῖφε, χαλαζοβόλει, ποίει σκότος, αἶθε, κεραύνου,
πάντα τὰ πορφύροντ' ἐν χθονὶ σεῖε νέφη.
ἢν γάρ με κτείνῃς, τότε παύσομαι· ἢν δὲ μ' ἀφῇς ζῆν,
καὶ διαθεὶς τούτων χείρονα, κωμάσομαι.
Anth. Pal. v. 64, 1-4.

[1] In the poems of Theognis, which are practically epigrams, in the later sense of the word. The epigrams of Plato, if genuine, would be another even more striking instance.

[2] Whether the words are to be taken as really seriously meant is, of course, doubtful, though one's instinctive distrust of their sincerity is perhaps misplaced; for, after all, this is very primitive poetry of its kind. That such words should have been written at all is the remarkable point about them.

Similar in spirit to this is the epigram in *Anth. Pal.* xii. 166:—

> τοῦθ' ὅ τι μοι λοιπὸν ψυχῆς, ὅ τι δή ποτ', Ἔρωτες,
> τοῦτό γ' ἔχειν, πρὸς θεῶν, ἡσυχίην ἄφετε.
> εἰ μή, ναὶ τόξοις μὴ βάλλετέ μ', ἀλλὰ κεραυνοῖς·
> ναὶ πάντως τέφρην θέσθε με κἀνθρακίην.
> ναί, ναί, βάλλετ' Ἔρωτες· ἐνεσκληκὼς γὰρ ἀνίαις,
> ὀξύτερον τούτων εἴ γ' ἔτι, βούλομ' ἔχειν.

or another—perhaps the most beautiful of all his poems that we know—so like, and yet so utterly unlike, the elegies of Mimnermus:—

> πῖν', Ἀσκληπιάδη· τί τὰ δάκρυα ταῦτα; τί πάσχεις;
> οὐ σὲ μόνον χαλεπὴ Κύπρις ἐληΐσατο,
> οὐδ' ἐπὶ σοὶ μούνῳ κατεθήξατο τόξα καὶ ἰοὺς
> πικρὸς Ἔρως· τί ζῶν ἐν σποδιῇ τίθεσαι;
> πίνωμεν Βάκχου ζωρὸν πόμα· δάκτυλος ἀώς·
> ἦ πάλι κοιμιστὰν λύχνον ἰδεῖν μένομεν;
> πίνωμεν γαλερῶς· μετά τοι χρόνον οὐκέτι πουλὺν,
> σχέτλιε, τὴν μακρὰν νύκτ' ἀναπαυσόμεθα.
> *Anth. Pal.* xii. 50.[1]

The love of Mimnermus was hardly of a kind to bring tears to the eyes!

Yet, though this love has reached to such a passionate height, it does not forget to be gallant and courteous;[2] and there is a striking absence of that jealousy and that savage spirit of revenge which may almost be said to be the one motive of the "lovers" in Euripides. A remarkable instance of this most un-Greek willingness to forgive, is the epigram in *Anth. Pal.* v. 150:—

---

[1] [Cp. p. 81, n. 1.] [2] Vide *e.g. Anth. Pal.* v. 158.

ὡμολόγησ' ἥξειν εἰς νύκτα μοι ἡ 'πιβόητος
Νικώ, καὶ σεμνὴν ὤμοσε Θεσμοφόρον·
κοὐχ ἥκει, φυλακὴ δὲ παροίχεται· ἆρ' ἐπιορκεῖν
ἤθελε; τὸν λύχνον, παῖδες, ἀποσβέσατε.

while the sudden bathos of *Anth. Pal.* v. 7, is quite in the same spirit. Even where a more real punishment is suggested, its execution is put off into a very vague and distant future :—

ταὐτὰ παθοῦσα
σοὶ μέμψαιτ' ἐπ' ἐμοῖς στᾶσά ποτε προθύροις.[1]
Anth. Pal. v. 164, 3–4.

Striking, too, is the note of resignation that marks poems like *Anth. Pal.* v. 189, xii. 153.[2] Still more striking, to those who remember the brutality of Epicrates' attack upon Lais,[3] is the tone in which the aged courtesan is spoken of in *Anth. Pal.* vii. 217. The two little pictures of happy lovers, so suggestive of the Acme and Septimius of Catullus, in *Anth. Pal.* v. 153, xii. 105, are also very far indeed away from anything of the kind that had ever gone before.[4]

We are thus confronted by a very remarkable fact. That way of regarding women which we may call

[1] The reading ποτέ is certainly happier than παρά. Cp. Theocr. xxix. 39; vide *infra* p. 84.

[2] xii. 153 is further interesting as one of the very few of the earlier epigrams, which profess to describe the woman's feelings.

[3] In the *Antilais*; vide Meineke, *Com. Fr.* iii. p. 365.

[4] The above instances may serve to give some idea of the prevailing character of Asclepiades' epigrams; on the wonderful grace and charm of this new love-poetry, it is needless to dwell. The best and truest description of Asclepiades and his followers ever given, is that of Meleager, when he calls them the wild-flowers in his Garland.

ἐν δὲ Ποσείδιππόν τε καὶ Ἡδύλον, ἄγρι' ἀρούρης,
Σικελίδεώ τ' ἀνέμοις ἄνθεα φυόμενα.
Anth. Pal. iv. 1, 45.

the romantic feeling—a feeling which we have noticed to be conspicuous by its absence in Euripides—appears suddenly developed to a high degree, in what is practically the first poetry extant after him. The full meaning of this fact we shall come to consider later; but before it is possible to do this, it will be necessary to institute some further preliminary enquiries.

Attention has already been sufficiently drawn to the almost entire absence from the early Greek literature of love-poetry of any kind addressed to women; at the same time, it has been briefly pointed out more than once that love-poetry addressed to boys or men is a very common phenomenon in this literature. This mere fact in itself would be one requiring some investigation, in an examination of this kind; but when the nature of this love-poetry comes to be considered, it will be seen how particularly important, in the present connection, is this phase of the Greek mind. For it is a fact which becomes immediately apparent, and grows more and more evident, the more the matter is looked into, that while such little love-poetry as does exist, addressed by men to women, is entirely concerned with the purely sensual aspect of the matter, in the very considerable volume of poetry addressed by men to men, this aspect is well-nigh entirely ignored. But obvious though this fact must be to everyone who reads the early Greek poetry with open eyes, the influence of our present methods of thought and training has been so strong, that not only has its importance been strangely ignored by modern writers, but even the fact itself has been questioned or denied. Under these circumstances, it will not be superfluous to go into the matter at some length, for reasons which will appear more clearly when the truth has been established.[1]

The story of the *Iliad* is a story without a heroine, a feature which makes it well-nigh unique among national legends. This fact has struck various people, and has been accounted for in various ways, the favourite explanation, perhaps, being that the Greek imagination was severer and more self-controlled, more statuesque, one may almost say, than that of other primitive peoples, and was therefore content with a hero whose sole inspiration lay in love of glory and love of battle, apart from any gentler emotion whatever.[2] This estimate of the Greek imagination is no doubt a just one, but there is none the less a strong objection to seeking in it an explanation of the peculiarities of the *Iliad*. To regard the Achilles of Homer as a person animated solely by ambition and military enthusiasm, is, in face of the facts of the case, impossible. As is well known, Achilles sulks because deprived of Briseis, and is only roused again by the death of Patroclus; that is to say, his two main actions are influenced entirely by motives outside of those which are looked upon as his chief characteristics.[3] In other words, Achilles

---

[1] Those who do not care to read the proof of this really self-evident fact, can skip the next 28 pages, and pick up the thread again on p. 103.

[2] *Vide* Rohde, *Der griech. Roman*, p. 42.

[3] His sorrow for Briseis does not, of course, as already observed, go very deep, as is sufficiently shown by the little effect which her restoration has on him; and his indignation at her loss is doubtless due to wounded self-love, more than to love of any other description. But, none the less, the introduction of such an incident shows clearly how little the purely military hero was in sympathy with Greek ideas.

is not a military hero at all; the interest one feels in him is due almost entirely to the emotional side of his character. But while this much is clear, the question still remains: Why has this emotional hero no corresponding heroine? for, of course, one cannot regard Briseis as such.

The answer to this is one that will not please a certain class of modern minds, but that is no proof that it is not true. There is a heroine in the *Iliad*, and that heroine is Patroclus. The Achilleis is a story of which the main motive is the love of Achilles for Patroclus.[1] This solution is astoundingly simple, and yet it took me so long to bring myself to accept it, that I am quite ready to forgive anyone who feels a similar hesitation. But those who do accept it, cannot fail to observe, on further consideration, how thoroughly suitable a motive of this kind would be in a national Greek epic. For this is the motive running through the whole of Greek life, till that life was transmuted by the influence of Macedonia. The lover-warriors Achilles and Patroclus are the direct spiritual ancestors

---

[1] There is an elaborate analysis of this erotic element in Max. Tyr. xxiv. 8: καὶ τὸν ἀνδρεῖον (ἔρωτα) ἐπὶ τῷ Πατρόκλῳ, τὸν πόνῳ κτητὸν καὶ χρόνῳ, καὶ μέχρι θανάτου προερχόμενον, νεῶν καὶ καλῶν ἀμφοτέρων, καὶ σωφρόνων, τοῦ μὲν παιδεύοντος, τοῦ δὲ παιδευομένου, ὁ μὲν ἄχθεται, ὁ δὲ παραμυθεῖται, ὁ μὲν ᾄδει, ὁ δὲ ἀκροᾶται. ἐρωτικὸν δὲ καὶ τὸ τυχεῖν ἐθέλοντα ἐξουσίας πρὸς μάχην, δακρῦσαι ὡς οὐκ ἀνεξομένου τοῦ ἐραστοῦ· ὁ δὲ ἐφίησι, καὶ τοῖς αὑτοῦ ὅπλοις κοσμεῖ, καὶ βραδύνοντος περιδεῶς ἔχει, καὶ ἀποθανόντος ἀποθανεῖν ἐρᾷ, καὶ τὴν ὀργὴν κατατίθεται. ἐρωτικὰ δὲ καὶ τὰ ἐνύπνια, καὶ τὰ ὀνείρατα, καὶ τὰ δάκρυα, καὶ τὸ τελευταῖον δῶρον ἤδη θαπτομένῳ ἡ κόμη.

It need hardly be pointed out that this central pair is not an isolated phenomenon. Ajax and Teucer (of whom we shall have occasion to speak again, p. 99), Idomeneus and Meriones, Diomed and Sthenelus, are obvious examples of similar relations among the subordinate characters.

of the Sacred Band of Thebans, who died to a man on the field of Chaeronea.

Those who have made any study of the social life of early Greece, will hardly need to be reminded how important a part this relationship between older and younger men played there. In some states, such as Megara, it was specially patronised by the government. Among the Cretans, and to a certain extent also among the Lacedæmonians,[1] it formed the basis of the military organisation.[2] At Thespiae, the festival of the Erotidia was consecrated to this form of love.[3] At Elis there was a periodical beauty-competition among the youths, the prizes consisting of arms and armour.[4] A somewhat similar contest took place every spring at the tomb of the hero Diocles at Megara.[5] Nor was this all. In many states this relationship came to be looked upon as well-nigh an emblem of constitutional liberty;[6] so much so, that

---

[1] Its prevalence among the Lacedæmonians, in spite of the influential position of women in the state, is vouched for by the usage of the word λακωνίζω. Vide M̄ Com. Fr. ii. pp. 200, 1088. (The derivation mentioned by ineke *l.c.*, seems due to Aristophanes, and need not)

[2] Athen. xiii. 561 E. O ciple, the Ἱερὸς Λόχος founded by Epaminondas was compo entirely of youths and their lovers, παιδικῶν γὰρ παρόντων ἐραστὴς πᾶν ὁτιοῦν ἕλοιτ᾽ ἂν παθεῖν ἢ δειλοῦ δόξαν ἀπενέγκασθαι. Athen. xiii. 602 A, cp. 561 F; Max. Tyr. xxiv. 2.

[3] Athen. xiii. 561 D. Cp. Paus. ix. 31, p. 771.

[4] Athen. xiii. 609 F. [5] Schol. *ad Theocr.* xii. 29.

[6] This view was, of course, especially prominent at Athens, where Harmodius and Aristogeiton had become well-nigh the 'patron saints' of the democracy. Very interesting in this connection is the remark in Ath. xiii. 562 A, that the Peisistratidae, after their expulsion, were the first persons who ventured to slander this form of intimacy. Cp. too Max. Tyr. xxiv. 2. The important part that it played in, at any rate, the old-fashioned Athenian education is shown by more than one passage in Aristophanes, of which the most striking is perhaps *Nubes*, 972 *seqq.*; cp. 1002 *seqq.*

the tyrants used to regard it as a standing menace to themselves, and actually took steps to suppress it.[1] Thus Polycrates destroyed the gymnasium[2] at Samos ὥσπερ ἀντιτείχισμα τῇ ἰδίᾳ ἀκροπόλει, and others are said to have behaved in a similar way.[3]

But while the social importance of this relationship cannot be questioned, its character is equally unmistakable. In principle, and also in practice, it was pure. Its first and most striking feature, a feature specially emphasised by almost every ancient writer who alludes at all to the subject, is its perfect purity. The very idea of sensuality in connection with it is almost invariably vigorously repudiated,[4] and the author of the "Erotic Oration" of Demosthenes is but expressing the universal convictions of his predecessors when he says, δίκαιος ἐραστὴς οὔτ' ἂν ποιήσειεν οὐδὲν αἰσχρὸν οὔτ' ἀξιώσειεν.[5]

How entirely this was the case will be still more apparent when we come to examine the writers who dealt with the subject. Here it may suffice to remark that, apart from that main sewer, the Old Attic Comedy, there are, in all the Greek poetry extant

---

[1] Athen. xiii. 602 D. διὰ τοὺς τοιούτους οὖν ἔρωτας οἱ τύραννοι (πολέμιοι γὰρ αὐτοῖς αὗται αἱ φιλίαι) τὸ παράπαν ἐκώλυον τοὺς παιδικοὺς ἔρωτας, πανταχόθεν αὐτοὺς ἐκκόπτοντες.

[2] The gymnasium is always a prominent feature in this connection. Cp. Catull. lxiii. 64; *Anth. Pal.* xii. 123; Ach. Tat. ii. 38, πάσης δὲ γυναικῶν μωραλοιφίας ἥδιον ὄδωδεν ὁ τῶν παίδων ἱδρώς.

[3] Athen. *loc. cit.*

[4] Athen. xiii. 561 D. σεμνόν τινα τὸν Ἔρωτα καὶ παντὸς αἰσχροῦ κεχωρισμένον. Very characteristic in this respect is the story of Agesilaus, related in Xen. *Ages.* v. 4, 5; cp. Max. Tyr. xxv. 5, xxvi. 8. Other noticeable instances will appear in the next few pages.

[5] Demosth. 1401.

down to the end of the fifth century, but a couple, or at most three, passages in which sensuality is so much as suggested in this connection.[1]

To trace the growth and development of this form of love—for love it was in the most modern sense of the word—would be extremely interesting; but it would be a long and difficult undertaking, which cannot be attempted here. The main outlines of its history are, however, sufficiently clear. Originating in the companionship of the battle-field, where the younger and weaker combatants would naturally look to their elders for help and support, it introduced itself also, as we have seen, into those peaceful exercises which serve to train the soldier; and hence, as soon as we find civilised communities, we find both the army and the gymnasium organised with reference to it. When a somewhat more settled condition of affairs had succeeded to the constant warfare of earlier times, we find it losing to some extent its distinctively military character, though this never entirely disappears, as is clear from the institution by Epaminondas of that "Sacred Band" of which we have had occasion to speak already. And so, in peace and war alike, it continues throughout classical times a dominating element in Greek society. Its highest development was due, of course, to Socrates and his followers; but from the end of the fifth century onwards it was beginning to lose its hold upon the Greek mind. The improved position of

---

[1] Hence it is not without significance that, according to a common story, the originator of this form of intimacy was said to be Orpheus See Ovid, *Met.* x. 83; Phanocles, *Fr.* 1.

women, and that improved way of regarding them which was gradually springing up about this time, could not fail to affect it prejudicially, while other equally potent causes were at work to bring about its overthrow; indeed, it is not long before we find writers speaking in open disparagement of it.[1] And in all probability this contempt for the "hypocrisy of the philosophers" was now, to a great extent, justified; for there is little reason to suppose that at this period that high standard of moral purity, with which this form of love had been originally associated, was any longer a prominent feature of it. The Macedonians, in destroying the old Greek states, were destroying at once the home of its birth and the cause of its existence. It is small wonder that it failed, like so many other of the old Greek institutions, to adapt itself to its new surroundings, and that it could not survive the downfall of those virtues of patriotism and independence of which it was at once the outcome and the emblem.

But the fragrance of its early purity and beauty was never quite lost, as long as the classical world remained. In well-nigh all the poetry dealing with it there is a tone of dignity and chivalry to which the

---

[1] Antimachus already seems to have been inclined to ridicule the story of Heracles and Hylas. (Vide *Fr.* 8.) Plato and "Platonic" love are, of course, stock subjects throughout the Middle Comedy. (Vide *e.g.* Amphis, *Dithyramb. Fr.* 2; Meineke, *Com. Fr.* iii. p. 307.) The nature of this general attack on the philosophers must not be misunderstood. It is an error to suppose that the more old-fashioned among the Athenians disapproved, in the first instance, of the philosophers because they were paederasts; it would be truer to say that they turned against paederasty because it was so intimately associated with philosophy.

poetry addressed to women never, perhaps, wholly attained. The charming grace of the 12th Idyll of Theocritus is unsurpassed in any of his other works; the passionate despair of the 23rd is unequalled. The contrast in tone between the 12th and the 5th books of the *Anthology* is one of the most remarkable features of that remarkable collection of poems.[1] Even Catullus, when striving to give expression to a love purer and more intense than any Roman had ever known, still feels the spell of early Greece upon him.

"tunc te dilexi, non tantum ut vulgus amicam,
sed pater ut natos diligit et generos,"

he exclaims. "I loved you, not as a man loves a woman, but as a man loves a youth!"[2]

We have hitherto been speaking chiefly of the social aspect of this form of love; we can now proceed to examine somewhat more in detail its influence upon literature. And here two striking facts will at once present themselves to us, the exact converse of those which met us when examining the early literary treatment of woman-love. From the earliest period onwards we shall find the love of man for man taking a prominent place in poetry, while at the same time this love as there depicted is remarkable for its chivalrous and unsensual character.

[1] The poems of Strato form, of course, an exception; but then the incidents on which they are based are professedly the product of his own, not always very charming, imagination. Cp. *Anth. Pal.* xii. 258. A further fact worth noticing is that abstract love-poems (*e g.* xii. 50) are regularly placed among the Παιδικά.

[2] The reader will perhaps be thinking of another love "passing the love of women." One might write many pages on the differences between these two similar emotions.

In other words, while the love of man to woman was among the early Greeks a love of the senses, the love of man to man was a love of the soul.

Of the *Iliad* we have spoken already, and we need not speak further, for though, as we have already pointed out, the relations between various of the Greek heroes there described are strong presumptive evidence of a state of affairs parallel to that which we know to have existed in historical times,[1] it is in the nature of an epic to be unable to supply proof of so positive a kind as is to be found in lyric poetry, which is generally, anyhow in early times, the expression of the writer's actual feelings with reference to actual surrounding circumstances.

In dealing with the lyric writers we shall therefore be on firmer ground.

Here, in the fragments of Archilochus already we find very strong evidence of the existence of love-poems addressed to men; indeed, it is impossible satisfactorily to explain *Fr.* 85—

ἀλλά μ' ὁ λυσιμελής, ὦ 'ταῖρε, δάμναται πόθος,

on any other supposition. This being so, and there being no evidence of any erotic poems addressed to women, it is justifiable to consider that *Fr.* 84 also belonged to this same class of poetry[2]; while there

[1] Whatever opinion one may have as to Homer's own intention, it cannot be denied that this was the Greek view of the relation between Achilles and Patroclus from a very early period. This is clearly shown by the fact that Aeschylus of all people treated it in this way in his *Myrmidones*. That the attachment was further regarded as a perfectly pure one might be equally proved from the fragments of that tragedy, if indeed proof were necessary. Insinuations like those elaborated at the end of Lucian's *Amores* are a much later aftergrowth.

[2] Vide *supra*, pp. 21, 22.

is further no reason to believe that these two passages were unique in the works of Archilochus. In other words, love-poems addressed to men are among the earliest known forms of subjective Greek poetry.

But while both Archilochus and Alcman[1] produced works of this kind, the fragments of these which remain are too scanty for it to be possible to feel any real certainty as to their exact nature; nor again was either of these two authors particularly celebrated in ancient times for this class of composition.

It is different with Alcaeus. Alcaeus was recognised throughout antiquity as the master *par excellence* of this form of poetry, and though the actual fragments of his works on this subject which remain are not much more satisfactory than is the case with his predecessors, we have most valuable evidence as to their nature in two poems of Theocritus, the one professedly and the other evidently imitated from them.[2] These poems contain certain evidently Alexandrian elements,[3] and, consequently, it would be unjustifiable to press any particular detail of them as illustrating Alcaeus, but, at the same time, there seems every reason to believe that in their general tone they reflect the spirit of their originals, and it is to their general tone that I wish to draw the reader's attention.

---

[1] Vide *supra*, p. 24.

[2] Theocr. xxix. and xxx.

[3] *E.g.* the image of Time with wings on his shoulders (xxix. 29). For this reason I have not cared to urge the expression Ἀχιλλέϊοι φίλοι in xxix. 34, as a proof that Alcaeus took this view of the relation between Achilles and Patroclus. (Vide *supra*, p. 82.)

To take the first of them (*Idyll* xxix.). The speaker is about to tell some unpleasant truths, but he feels constrained to apologise for so doing (1–4). After a passionate but dignified protestation of his love (5–8), he appeals to his friend's better feelings (9), and urges him to be constant in his affections (10–20).

ποίησαι καλιὰν μίαν εἰν ἑνὶ δενδρίῳ,
ὅπᾳ μηδὲν ἀπίξεται ἄγριον ὄρπετον.

"If you do so," he continues—

"ἀγαθὸς μὲν ἀκούσεαι
ἐξ ἀστῶν,

and Love will deal kindly with you, and save you from such pangs as I have suffered (21–24). For we grow older every day, and youth is the season for forming those friendships which last a lifetime (25–34). Now, I would readily do anything for your sake, but if you disregard my words, the time may come when even if you call me I will not answer" (35–40).

But anyone who has ever read this charming little poem will not need to have its character further forced upon him. The manliness, the dignity, the courtesy of it, are patent in every line; more striking still to those who know Greek literature is the spirit of self-negation which pervades the whole; and all this, combined with a passion which is none the less real because it is kept rigorously under control. Even in Alexandrian times it would be hard to find a poem addressed to a woman which can equal this in its chivalrous tone; to look for such a poem in early Greek literature would be vain indeed.

In the second of these two pieces (*Idyll* xxx.), also in all probability modelled on Alcaeus, the purely erotic side of the matter comes more to the front than in the one we have just been discussing, but here, too, one cannot fail to be struck by the quiet earnestness of the tone, which is as far removed from the good-humoured banter of Asclepiades as it is from the outspoken brutality of Archilochus.

But perhaps the most striking commentary on this state of feeling is that furnished by the other section of the Lesbian school of poets. It has troubled the minds of many modern commentators to think why Sappho should have addressed love-poems to Anactoria; for those who have formed a true idea of what "love" between a man and a woman meant in Greece of the seventh century, and compared this with the love then existing among men for one another, the question answers itself. Sappho, in addressing love-poems to Anactoria, was but adapting to her own circumstances and sex the universal contemporary principles of love-poetry. It seemed so unnatural then, and so impossible, to connect the sexual instinct with any pure or noble feeling, that Sappho, because her love was pure and its ideal a noble one, instinctively and inevitably chose as the object of this love her fellow-women, just as the men of her time chose their fellow-men.[1] To the Greek of the period the association of the

---

[1] Thus Maximus Tyrius (xxiv. 9) compares the love of Sappho to that of Socrates. ὁ δὲ τῆς Λεσβίας (ἔρως) . . τί ἂν εἴη ἄλλο, ἢ ἡ Σωκράτους τέχνη ἐρωτική; δοκοῦσι γάρ μοι τὴν κατὰ ταὐτὸ ἑκάτερος φιλίαν, ἡ μὲν γυναικῶν, ὁ δὲ ἀρρένων, ἐπιτηδεῦσαι.

sexes inevitably suggested sensuality; Sappho loved Anactoria, just as Alcaeus loved Lycus, in order that this suggestion might be as far as possible excluded. Sappho loved a woman because her love was too pure to allow her to love a man. All this sounds strange—monstrous almost—to modern ears; and yet, of all the scandal of the centuries which has heaped itself up around the name of Lesbos, what Sappho herself would have resented most would perhaps have been the story that she was in love with Phaon.

We have already had occasion to notice that Anacreon, while he was the originator of love-poetry addressed to women, at the same time addressed a large number of his poems, in fact, the majority, to boys. In his case, therefore, it is possible for the first time to compare the two forms of "love" in the same individual. The comparison is not much to the advantage of the newer feeling. While the outspoken sensuality of the poems devoted to women cannot be matter of dispute, even judging from such fragments of them as remain, the chaste and sober nature of Anacreon's relation to his boy-lovers is not only a feature of the extant fragments, but is also alluded to more than once by ancient writers, who had his complete works from which to draw their inferences. Thus Aelian (*Var. Hist.* ix. 4), speaking of the love of Anacreon for Smerdias (cp. Anacreon, *Fr.* 48) says—

εἶτα ἥσθη τὸ μειράκιον τῷ ἐπαίνῳ καὶ τὸν Ἀνακρέοντα ἠσπάζετο σεμνῶς εὖ μάλα, ἐρῶντα τῆς ψυχῆς, ἀλλ' οὐ τοῦ σώματος. μὴ γάρ τις ἡμῖν διαβαλλέτω, πρὸς θεῶν, τὸν ποιητὴν τὸν Τήϊον, μηδ' ἀκόλαστον εἶναι λεγέτω.

Maximus Tyrius again, who several times alludes to Anacreon (and always under the title of ὁ σοφός or ὁ σοφιστής), expressly compares his love to that of Socrates (xxiv. 9)—

ἡ δὲ τοῦ Τηίου σοφιστοῦ τέχνη τοῦ αὐτοῦ ἤθους καὶ τρόπου, καὶ γὰρ πάντων ἐρᾷ τῶν καλῶν καὶ ἐπαινεῖ πάντας. μεστὰ δὲ αὐτοῦ τὰ ᾄσματα τῆς Σμερδίου κόμης καὶ τῶν Κλεοβούλου ὀφθαλμῶν καὶ τῆς Βαθύλλου ὥρας· ἀλλὰ κἀν τούτοις τὴν σωφροσύνην ὅρα. ἔραμαι δέ τοι κ.τ.λ. (*Fr.* 44) καὶ αὖθις, καλὸν εἶναι τῷ ἐρῶντι τὰ δίκαια φησί.

A similar compliment to Anacreon seems to glimmer through Athenaeus' account of Polycrates. (xii. 540 E.)

How deep the difference really went, it is of course impossible, in the absence of the poet's complete works, to show, but, as already remarked, even in the few fragments we have, the distinction between the strong passion with which he speaks of his boy-loves and the frivolous tone of his addresses to women is very noticeable.

On the deep significance of the attempt of Ibycus to introduce personal erotic poetry into the choral hymns, we have also dwelt,[1] so that we can proceed without further delay to the works which bear the name of Theognis, a body of poems which, in the present connection, are perhaps the most interesting in all early Greek literature.

The great mass of these poems are in the form of short pieces addressed by the writer to his youthful friend Cyrnus, and, as such, are one long commentary on the subject we are discussing. Regarded from

[1] Vide *supra*, p. 35.

this point of view, several features at once force themselves upon the attention. Notwithstanding the fact that many of them are thorough love-poems, yet not only is the sensual side of the matter entirely ignored, but even the erotic, as far as that is subjective, is kept rigorously in the background. The counsel Theognis gives is such as a father might give to his son—[1]

σοὶ δέ τοι οἷά τε παιδὶ πατὴρ ὑποθήσομαι αὐτός
ἐσθλά. (l. 1049.)

Indeed, he is afraid lest Cyrnus' eagerness may lead him into temptation, and so even urges him not to be over-loving.

μή μ' ἀέκοντα βίῃ κεντῶν ὑπ' ἄμαξαν ἔλαυνε,
ἐς φιλότητα λίην, Κύρνε, προσελκόμενος.[2] (l. 371.)

He will not thrust himself upon his friend if the latter is unwilling; he will rather himself bear the pang of parting—

ἀργαλέως μοὶ θυμὸς ἔχει περὶ σῆς φιλότητος·
οὔτε γὰρ ἐχθαίρειν οὔτε φιλεῖν δύναμαι,
γινώσκων χαλεπὸν μέν, ὅταν φίλος ἀνδρὶ γένηται,
ἐχθαίρειν, χαλεπὸν δ' οὐκ ἐθέλοντα φιλεῖν.
(l. 1091.)

Yet he is always ready to sympathise with him when in trouble—

σὺν σοί, Κύρνε, παθόντι κακῶς ἀνιώμεθα πάντα.
(l. 655.)

Though Cyrnus does not heed him, he will yet make him immortal by his songs.[3]

---

[1] Cp. Theocr. xxix. 10,

ἀλλ' εἴ μοί τι πίθοιο νέος προγενεστέρῳ.

[2] A striking record of temptation resisted is to be found in l. 949 *seqq.*, but this is almost certainly by a later hand.

[3] l. 237 *seqq.*

Much more there is, similar in tone, chiefly advice as to the choice of friends and the like, but it would be an endless task to examine all this in detail. The reader may open the collection at random, and at once find further proof of what has been said here. Whatever the subject of the poems and whatever their occasion, they are all well-nigh equally remarkable for their dignity, their temperance, their manliness, and for their most un-Greek virtue of unselfishness, and remarkable, no less, for the absence from them of that meanness and spitefulness which even in modern times so often mark the unfortunate lover. It does one good to read these poems; they are keen and clear like a mouthful of mountain air; and it does one good, too, to think of the θοῖναι καὶ εἰλάπιναι where they were sung and where the spirit of them was understood. After all, modern writers may decry and defame these *amantes contra naturam* as much as they please, but they cannot deny that they were the first to teach that the mission of love was to make men better.[1]

The intimate connection between the poems that bear the name of Theognis and the *Scolia* has already been noticed; it will not therefore be surprising to find that the latter are almost as full as the former of references to our present subject, though, as it is in their nature to be commonplace, they need not detain us long.

Of the 25 *Scolia* preserved by Athenaeus,[2] 15 deal

[1] For an examination of the Second Book of Theognis, vide Excursus E.
[2] Athen. xv. p. 694 *seqq.* This number excludes the poems of Hybrias and Aristotle, which are different in character from the rest.

with friendships of this kind;[1] these may be roughly divided into two classes: those which sing the praises of famous pairs of friends, and those which contain general remarks on the subject. A striking instance of the first class is, of course, the well-known *Scolion* of Callistratus (9–12), in which it may be observed that in the second verse, where Harmodius is promised immortality among the celebrated heroes of antiquity, the two of these specially mentioned are Achilles, the lover of Patroclus, and Diomed, the lover of Sthenelus. Other examples are *Scol.* 21, referring to Admetus, and *Scol.* 17, 18 referring to Ajax, the latter of whom is a hero in the *Scolia* as early as the time of Alcaeus. In the second class, perhaps the most interesting are *Scol.* 23, with its very Theognis-like advice, and *Scol.* 19, of which we have already spoken.[2]

As is, of course, only to be expected, these poems do not add much to our knowledge of the subject or its treatment; but it was none the less worth while to call attention to them, owing to the fact that verse or doggerel of this kind, though it may not be of much importance itself, is yet able to furnish important evidence as to the nature of the popular feeling to which it owes its origin. The views expressed in these poems are not those of individual authors, they are the views of the whole community; and it is this fact which gives to the

---

[1] Of the remaining ten, the first four are religious, and only three contain any mention of women, two of these being coarse.

[2] [p. 31.]

Scolia a far deeper significance than would at first sight appear to belong to them.

So far, the examination of such fragments of the early Greek literature as have survived, has resulted in the discovery of a body of evidence which, if not very voluminous, is yet remarkably unanimous. It remains to be seen in how far it is possible to supplement this from the works of the Attic tragedians, which have been preserved in a more perfect condition. At the first glance the prospect is not very promising; love altogether, as we have seen, plays a very subordinate part in the Attic drama, while that form of love which we are immediately considering, seems at first sight to be especially neglected. And indeed, to a certain extent, this is really the case, for very obvious reasons. In the early days of tragedy, when the love-element was well-nigh entirely excluded, in obedience to the then artistic canons, it was not to be expected that exception would be made in favour of this particular form of it;[1] later, when the love-element was gradually forcing itself into the drama, the playwrights were all, whether they cared to confess it or not, under the influence of Euripides, who, as we know, was a special student of feminine nature, and as such, felt only a qualified interest in the mutual relations of

---

[1] For, as we have seen, one of the first of these canons was that the public expression of private emotions was an offence against art no less than against decency, and this would tend to exclude from the stage all forms of love equally. In the case of woman-love there were, of course, special objections; that was why the *Myrmidones* was the first erotic play of any kind produced; but this is beside the present issue.

men.[1] But at the same time, a closer examination of the Attic tragedians will perhaps reveal that this characteristically Greek emotion has had a greater influence on their work than one would, at the first moment, be disposed to believe.

Two plays, the *Myrmidones* of Aeschylus and the *Niobe* of Sophocles, are specially mentioned by Athenaeus[2] as introducing ἀρσενικοὶ ἔρωτες; unfortunately, however, in neither case are the fragments preserved of a kind to throw much light on the method of treatment adopted.

The *Myrmidones*, which seems to have been the first play of a trilogy, treated of the death of Patroclus and Achilles' lament for him,[3] which seems, to judge by such expressions as those preserved in *Fr.* 135,[4] 138, to have been of a passionate character; but whether the erotic element was the only interest in the play, and whether it was in any

---

[1] For the story in Aelian, *Var. Hist.* ii. 21, as to the relation between Euripides and Agathon, does not seem to be more than a vague piece of scandal.

To this must be added the fact that the earlier part of the century was the time when such a subject would most readily have appealed to the Athenian imagination. Later on, and especially from the fourth century onwards, the changed position of women was beginning to make itself felt in the way we have seen.

[2] Athen. xiii. 601 A, where it is further noted that these plays were received with applause.

[3] According to Schol. *Ar. Ran.* 911, first of all, μέχρι τριῶν ἡμερῶν οὐδὲν φθέγγεται.

[4] The reader must be careful here to give the proper sense to σέβας ἁγνόν, translating "ne sancta quidem reverentia qua casta atque intemerata tua femora servavi, te movit, ingrate, etc." *Fr.* 136, whether genuine or not—it reads very like a misquotation of its predecessor—must obviously mean the same, in spite of Theomnestus and Lucian.

way developed in the latter part of the trilogy, it is impossible now to say. The *Niobe* recounted the misfortunes of that heroine, with her subsequent grief and exile from Thebes, the scene of the tragedy, to Lydia. But a striking feature, the most striking, perhaps, if we may draw any inference from the statement in Athenaeus[1] that this play was commonly known as ἡ τραγῳδία ἡ παιδεράστρια, was the relation represented as existing among Niobe's sons.[2] This would appear to have been especially emphasised in the account of the death-scene[3]—a passage which we can gather indirectly to have been the most popular in the play;[4] whether it was at all prominent in the previous action we cannot tell; and, indeed, the fragments of the *Niobe* are of a quite particularly meagre description.

To these two plays mentioned by Athenaeus must be added a third, the *Chrysippus* of Euripides, a work which is peculiarly interesting for two reasons—its author and its subject. The *Myrmidones* and the *Niobe*, of which we have just spoken, seem, as far as can be judged by the little of them that remains, to have dealt with what may be called

---

[1] Athen. xiii. 601 B.

[2] Startling as it appears at first sight, this is probably the simplest way of understanding Athenaeus' τὸν τῶν παίδων (sc. ἔρωτα). Those who have properly appreciated what such ἔρως meant to the early Greeks, will not be surprised to find the term applied to the affection of an elder for a younger brother.

[3] Plut. *Amor.* 17, p. 760 D, τῶν μὲν γὰρ τοῦ Σοφοκλέους Νιοβιδῶν βαλλομένων καὶ θνησκόντων ἀνακαλεῖταί τις οὐδένα βοηθὸν ἄλλον οὐδὲ σύμμαχον ἢ τὸν ἐραστήν.

[4] Cp. Aristoph. *Vesp.* 579.

simple straightforward love-stories. Men are introduced as in love with other men, and this love is brought to a climax by the most usual of expedients —the death of the loved object. Euripides, on the other hand, was, as we have seen, above all things a student of the emotions in their more complex phases, and a *dénouement* of so ordinary a kind could not have failed to appear commonplace to a writer who took such an interest in the pathology of the senses, even when he for once abandoned his favourite field of the feminine passions, and undertook the examination of a form of love, the symptoms of which are notoriously more easily capable of diagnosis. And, as a matter of fact, the *Chrysippus* introduces us to a novel and most interesting side of the question. The story on which the play is founded is, to quote the words of the Argument to the *Phoenissae*, as follows:

οὗτος (ὁ Λάϊος) ἀφικόμενός ποτε εἰς Ἦλιν καὶ τὸν τοῦ Πέλοπος υἱὸν Χρύσιππον ἰδών, ὃς ἦν ἐξ ἄλλης αὐτῷ γυναικὸς καὶ οὐκ ἐκ τῆς θυγατρὸς Οἰνομάου Ἱπποδαμείας, καὶ ἁλοὺς τούτου κατάκρας τῷ ἔρωτι, ἁρπάσας εἰς Θήβας ἤνεγκεν. καὶ συνῆν αὐτῷ τὰ ἐρωτικὰ πρῶτος ἐν ἀνθρώποις τὴν ἀρρενοφθορίαν εὑρών, καθὼς δὴ καὶ ὁ Ζεὺς ἐν θεοῖς τὸν Γανυμήδην ἁρπάσας. ὁ δὲ Πέλοψ μαθὼν τοῦτο κατηράσατο Λάϊῳ μηδέποτε μὲν παῖδα τεκεῖν, εἰ δ᾿ ἄρα καὶ συμβαίη, ὑπ᾿ αὐτοῦ τούτου ἀναιρεθήσεσθαι.

Or, according to a slightly different version found in "Peisander":

ἱστορεῖ Πείσανδρος, ὅτι κατὰ χόλον τῆς Ἥρας ἐπέμφθη ἡ Σφὶγξ τοῖς Θηβαίοις ἀπὸ τῶν ἐσχάτων μερῶν τῆς Αἰθιοπίας, ὅτι τὸν Λάϊον ἀσεβήσαντα εἰς τὸν παράνομον ἔρωτα τοῦ

Χρυσίππου, ὃν ἥρπασεν ἀπὸ τῆς Πίσης, οὐκ ἐτιμωρήσαντο
. . . . πρῶτος δὲ ὁ Λάϊος τὸν ἀθέμιστον ἔρωτα τοῦτον ἔσχεν.
ὁ δὲ Χρύσιππος ὑπὸ αἰσχύνης ἑαυτὸν διεχρήσατο τῷ ξίφει.
(Schol. *ad Eur. Phoen.* 1760.)

The moral of both these stories is obvious. The behaviour of Laius towards Chrysippus was a crime deserving the most exemplary punishment.

Now this fact at once affords us a clue as to the real nature of Laius' conduct. It seems impossible that the statement that Laius πρῶτος τὸν ἀθέμιστον ἔρωτα τοῦτον ἔσχεν can be taken to mean that he was the founder of love as between man and man in the same way as this is related of, for instance, Orpheus. It seems impossible to believe that any legend should have described the originator of that form of love with which, as we know, the highest thoughts and ideals of the early Greeks were so intimately associated, as a criminal worthy of divine punishment. Euripides himself might not have shrunk from such a course, but it does not seem conceivable that he should have found any existing legend on which to begin to work;[1] and it seems, therefore, unquestionable that the meaning of the story cannot have been this. As a matter of fact, a careful examination of such evidence as we have,

[1] The marked differences in the versions of the legend, and the fact that it appeared in the *Theogamia* of the pseudo-Peisander—a writer who seems to have drawn his materials in most cases from early sources—seem to show that it must have been of a certain antiquity, and anyhow was not a pure invention on the part of Euripides. The evidence of Aelian (*N. H.* vi. 15), though of little value, is to the same effect: Λάϊος δὲ ἐπὶ Χρυσίππῳ, ὦ καλὲ Εὐριπίδη, τοῦτο οὐκ ἔδρασεν, καίτοι τοῦ τῶν ἀρρένων ἔρωτος, ὥς λέγεις αὐτός, καὶ ἡ φήμη διδάσκει, Ἑλλήνων πρώτιστος ἄρξας.

affords every reason for believing that its meaning was a very different one.

The true meaning of the legend is this. Laius was the first to violate the universal law that the love between man and man must be pure; and it was this transgression that involved himself, his family, and his country in such universal ruin.

That this meaning is in itself a more likely one than the other, will probably not be disputed by anyone who has formed a true conception of early Greek feeling on the subject; more than this one cannot expect. But while actual proof on the point is impossible, it may not be inapposite to draw attention to the way in which the sensuality and unreasoning animalism of Laius are emphasised at every turn, with the view doubtless, in the first case, of preventing any conceivable misunderstanding of the true purport of the tradition.

In the play itself, the nature of his passion is shown only too clearly by the famous distichs (*Fr.* 840, 841):

λέληθεν οὐδὲν τῶνδέ μ' ὧν σὺ νουθετεῖς,
γνώμην δ' ἔχοντά μ' ἡ φύσις βιάζεται.

αἰαῖ, τόδ' ἤδη δεινὸν ἀνθρώποις κακόν,
ὅταν τις εἰδῇ τἀγαθόν, χρῆται δὲ μή.

Cicero says as much (*Tusc.* iv. 33, 71): Quis ... non intellegit quid apud Euripidem et loquatur et cupiat Laius? Aelian, too (*N. H.* vi. 15), draws an unconscious comparison between this play and the pure old-Greek *Niobe* of Sophocles when, after describing how the dolphin that loved a boy ἐπιβιῶναι τοῖς παιδικοῖς οὐκ ἐτόλμησεν, he adds, Λάϊος δὲ ἐπὶ Χρυσίππῳ, ὦ καλὲ Εὐριπίδη, τοῦτο οὐκ ἔδρασεν.

The sensuality of the passion is clearly shown, too, by various features of the legend as recorded by various writers, above all by the fact that Hera is the goddess outraged, and by the peculiar nature of the curse of Pelops. The actual words, moreover, of the Scholiast of the *Phoenissae* (τὸν Λάϊον ἀσεβήσαντα ἐς τὸν παράνομον ἔρωτα τοῦ Χρυσίππου) and of the argument of that play (καὶ συνῆν αὐτῷ τὰ ἐρωτικὰ πρῶτος ἐν ἀνθρώποις τὴν ἀρρενοφθορίαν εὑρών), seem all to point the same way.[1]

In fact, the sensuality of Laius is made such a feature of the story in every case in which it is narrated, that it cannot well be doubted that this sensuality was a feature of the story in its earliest form; and if this be granted, there can be very little question as to the meaning of the story itself, as originally current.

We thus have three plays, one by each of the great dramatists, dealing with this subject, two of them dwelling upon the intense and unselfish nature of the passion in its true form, the third emphasising the disastrous consequences of any transgression of that purity which was so integral a part of it; but are these three the only ones of their kind? They

---

[1] The remark of the Scholiast that the behaviour of Laius to Chrysippus was parallel to that of Zeus to Ganymede, like the similar remark in Cicero (*loc. cit.*), belongs of course to an age when the primitive meanings of the legends had long been forgotten. The allusion to the legend in Aristoph. *Pelargi, Fr.* 1 is too general to give evidence either way. See Meineke, *Com. Fr.* ii. p. 1126 *seq.*

are the only three, perhaps, that dealt with the purely erotic side of the matter; but its general influence evidently extended over a far wider field. This influence makes itself felt in various ways and in varying degrees, and it would be a lengthy task, and one beside the present purpose, to endeavour to trace its workings wherever they are visible in Attic tragedy; but a few noticeable instances of it are well worthy of attention.

One of these is the *Ajax* of Sophocles. It is a common complaint against this play that the second half of it is inferior in interest to the first. The admirers of Sophocles, however, contend that, to an Athenian audience, the details of funeral arrangements were matters of such paramount importance that, in a play intended for the Athenian stage, a second act dealing entirely with this subject would not by any means be of the nature of an anticlimax. I am no great admirer of Sophocles, and still less am I an admirer of the mob that pelted Aeschylus and hooted Euripides, but yet I should be disposed to give the Athenians credit for rather higher tastes than this would seem to imply; while, even had the predilections of his audience been so strongly those of the undertaker, it might surely have been hoped that a poet of Sophocles' genius would have had the courage to ignore them. Indeed, as long as the interest of the second half of the *Ajax* is considered as centred on the dead body of the hero, it is impossible successfully to refute the charge of bathos; but a more careful consideration of this part of the play will, perhaps, show that the interest is by no means intended to be attached in this Mezentius-like manner to a corpse. The interest is meant to centre on Teucer, the *amasius* of the dead Ajax,[1] and on his efforts to prove himself worthy of his heroic lover; for his lover's sake, in spite of every obstacle, and in the face of what looks like certain death, he insists that due respect shall be paid to the dead; in fact, there are in this situation the germs of the situation which excites such general interest in the *Antigone*.[2] There the character whose weakness is made strength through love, is a woman, and so we moderns admire; here it is a man, and so we misunderstand; but it does not follow that the Greeks were equally narrow in their sympathies.

Another instance, less obvious at first sight, but equally convincing on nearer examination, is the *Alcestis*. The *Alcestis* is a very difficult play to understand, as far as the motives of its leading figures are concerned; nor is it enough to say that, because the play has been described as "something of a satyric drama," therefore all its characters are meant to be grotesque. The self-concentration of Admetus and the complete acquiescence therein of Alcestis, must surely be capable of some more

---

[1] That this is the relation between Ajax and Teucer in Homer already, is pretty clear. Vide *e.g. Il.* ix. 266 *seqq.*; cp. Schol. *Theocr.* xii. 29. This, no doubt, accounts for the frequent mention of Ajax in the *Scolia* (cp. p. 90).

[2] Supposing Tecmessa appeared as champion for the dead Ajax, everyone would acknowledge this, and no one would find the situation dull: only people will not understand that Teucer meant as much, and more, to the Greeks, than Tecmessa would to us.

satisfactory explanation.¹ This explanation is, perhaps, to be found in the relation existing between Admetus and Apollo. The story of the love of Apollo for Admetus is sufficiently familiar,² and has been alluded to on various occasions in the preceding pages. Both at Athens and Sparta the legend seems to have been well known,³ and there can be no doubt that an audience, when called upon to listen to a play dealing with Admetus, would instinctively call to mind this incident in his life.⁴ Granted this, it is not, perhaps, too bold to say that it is equally unquestionable that this recollection on their part must have influenced their view of the hero's character. He was unwilling to die; for any Greek to be unwilling to die was excusable in a way which we who live in English fogs can never understand; but for Admetus, the beloved of the Sun-god! If he, who for nine years had met Apollo face to face, shrank from the mould and the mud of Hades, what reason to wonder at it? To a Greek, to live was to see the sun; surely then, to one whom the Sun-god loved, life must be doubly precious, precious to a degree that less happy mortals could never

---

[1] The position of Alcestis has already been partly discussed on p. 57.

[2] Vide Call. *Hymn. in Apoll.* 49; Panyasis, *Fr.* 15 (Dübner); Schol. *ad Eur. Alc.* 2; Lact. i. 10, 3.

[3] Cp. *supra*, pp. 24, 31.

[4] When the Scholiast (*ad Eur. Alc.* 1) says that the version of the story of Apollo's servitude given in the Prologue is the usual one (ἡ διὰ στόματος καὶ δημώδης), he need mean no more by this than the fact that this was the case at the time of writing, when the influence of Euripides had naturally superseded all others. The Scholiast cannot be taken as throwing light on the state of feeling in Athens at the time when the *Alcestis* was produced.

comprehend.[1] Then, again, if one thought of who Admetus was. Surely the man whom the Sun-god loved was a man whom the world could not spare, a man for whom it was a privilege to be considered worthy to die. Patriotism, too, no less than personal affection, would seem to compel a sacrifice on behalf of the man in whose kingdom a god took such a special interest;[2] nor, again, was the gift of a divine lover a thing that it was safe lightly to put aside. All this, and much more of a kindred nature, must have been present in the minds of those who first saw this strange play, and must have served in part to mitigate its strangeness. It could not, perhaps, explain the central mystery; but then, the mystery of self-sacrifice has never been explained yet.

Another striking instance is the persistent way in which Orestes and Pylades figure in the Athenian drama. They play a prominent part in no fewer than five tragedies, in one of which, the *Iphigeneia in Tauris*, the scene between them became proverbial;[3] and thus we get repeated again and again the, to modern minds, almost grotesque situation of the intense affection between Orestes and Pylades, and the intense affection between Orestes and Electra,[4] and

[1] I am not concerned here to write an apology for Admetus, or I might add much that would militate against the ordinary, somewhat flippant, view taken of his character. One point, however: many readers do not seem to notice that the original question of dying or not is never in the play left to Admetus at all, but is settled by Apollo on his own responsibility. Cp. Eur. *Alc.* 11 *seqq.*, 32 *seqq.*

[2] Cp. Eur. *Alc.* 10, etc.

[3] Cp. the lengthy comments on the play in Lucian, *Amores* 47, vol. ii. p. 450.   [4] On this point cp. above, p. 48.

the supreme indifference between Pylades and Electra, the two lovers who are going to marry one another as soon as the curtain comes down. And yet, those who have read what has gone before will know that not only did this situation seem natural to the Athenian audience, but any other situation under the circumstances would have seemed to them monstrous or absurd.

It is hardly necessary to follow this subject further, for enough has been said already to make its main features perfectly clear. Still less is it necessary, for our present purpose, to study the history of this emotion during the succeeding centuries. As we have already pointed out, from the end of the fifth century onwards it begins to lose its hold on the popular imagination, and ceases to be a national institution; and when next we find traces of it in literature, we see at once that its nature has entirely altered. Paederastic poetry there is enough and to spare among the Alexandrians, but it is poetry which looks strange indeed by the side of Theognis.[1] What were the causes that led to this change, a change as great as that which about this time came over the relation between man and woman—how far it was due to Persian influence, how far to the employment of professional soldiers instead of the citizen-armies of an earlier period—all these are questions of the greatest interest in themselves, but they cannot be discussed here. The fact remains that that purity

[1] An exception to this general rule is, perhaps, Theocritus; whether, or how far, this was due to the influence of Aratus is an interesting question, but one for the discussion of which the evidence has yet to be collected.

and self-devotion which had been the rule in one generation became the exception in the next, and that the downward course was never again fully arrested throughout classical times.

And yet, even the most sensual of the later poets, somehow, sometimes, when speaking of this, rise to strange heights of beauty. Listen to Rhianus:

> ἰξῷ Δεξιόνικος ὑπὸ χλωρῇ πλατανίστῳ
> κόσσυφον ἀγρεύσας, εἷλε κατὰ πτερύγων·
> χὠ μὲν ἀναστενάχων ἀπεκώκυεν ἱερὸς ὄρνις.
> ἀλλ' ἐγώ, ὦ φίλ' Ἔρως, καὶ θαλεραὶ χάριτες,
> εἴην καὶ κίχλη καὶ κόσσυφος, ὡς ἂν ἐκείνου
> ἐν χερὶ καὶ φθογγὴν καὶ γλυκὺ δάκρυ βάλω.
> (*Anth. Pal.* xii. 142.)

Listen to Meleager, the last of the Greek poets:

> οὐκ ἐθέλω Χαρίδαμον· ὁ γὰρ καλὸς εἰς Δία λεύσσει,
> ὡς ἤδη νέκταρ τῷ θεῷ οἰνοχοῶν.
> οὐκ ἐθέλω· τί δὲ μοί τὸν ἐπουρανίων βασιλῆα
> ἄνταθλον νίκης τῆς ἐν ἔρωτι λαβεῖν;
> αἱροῦμαι δ', ἢν μοῦνον ὁ παῖς ἀνιὼν ἐς Ὄλυμπον
> ἐκ γῆς νίπτρα ποδῶν δάκρυα τἀμὰ λάβῃ,
> μναμόσυνον στοργῆς· γλυκὺ δ' ὄμμασι νεῦμα δίυγρον
> δοίη, καί τι φίλημ' ἁρπάσαι ἀκροθιγές.
> τἄλλα δὲ πάντ' ἐχέτω Ζεύς, ὡς θέμις. εἰ δ' ἐθελήσει,
> ἦ τάχα που κἀγὼ γεύσομαι ἀμβροσίας.
> (*Anth. Pal.* xii. 68.)

> δάκρυα σοὶ καὶ νέρθε διὰ χθονός, Ἡλιοδώρα, δωροῦμαι.

The foregoing discussion has covered a quantity of ground and dealt with a large variety of topics, some of which may have appeared but remotely connected with our immediate subject; but in the end it has succeeded in establishing certain facts very clearly. We have learnt from an examination of such parts of the early Greek literature as have survived, and from a consideration of the probable nature of the rest, that

(1) Love in the modern sense, as existing between men and women, was unknown in early Greece.

(2) Such love on the part of men for men was not only a fact, but was generally recognised as a social, and in some cases a national, institution.

From this it would seem inevitably to follow, that the change which we find at a later period to have come over the way of regarding women, was due to a transference to the sexual instinct, and an amalgamation with it, of that form of emotion which had previously been confined to the mutual relations of men. In other words, men first began to look upon women as fit objects of pure and chivalrous devotion, when they began (to quote the expression of Alcman)[1] to look upon them as "female boy-friends."

Now, my reason for calling attention to this point is the following: If one regards the origin of what, for briefness' sake, we have called the romantic feeling, as entirely a new growth of the fourth century, unconnected with anything that had gone before, it is obvious that such a growth, if indeed possible at all, can only have been made possible by a simultaneous movement on the part of a large number of persons; for it is inconceivable that any one man, however great his influence, could invent

[1] *Fr.* 125.

and popularise an entirely new emotion. But if, on the other hand, we regard the romantic feeling as simply due to the readjustment of an already existing emotion, it is no longer absurd to suppose that the original suggestion of this readjustment may have been due to some single individual. Indeed, the probabilities rather point in that direction, for it is a commonplace that revolutions of thought are generally due to the discovery, on the part of some individual, of the apparently obvious formula for which the rest of mankind have long been seeking in vain. This being so, it will be justifiable to apply the general principle to the case before us, and it will no longer seem a fruitless task to look about among the literary names of the close of the fifth century and the beginning of the fourth, for the man who gave the first impulse to that remarkable movement with which we are at present concerned.

The great obstacle which here confronts us at the outset, and, indeed, makes this whole investigation one of exceptional difficulty, is the fact that, of all the periods of Greek poetry, that which covers the first part of the fourth century—in other words, that which forms the transition from the classical to the so-called Alexandrian era—is just that of which the fewest monuments of importance have been preserved. From the death of Aristophanes to the time when Asclepiades began to write is pretty well 70 years,[1] but all the poetry which has come

[1] And the interval is in reality even longer, for but little of the later work of Aristophanes has survived.

down to us from this whole period consists of a few fragments of comedy,[1] most of which it is impossible even approximately to date, and a few epigrams, the history of which is often more obscure still. There is thus a great gap in our knowledge, and it is just during this interval of darkness that the romantic feeling must first have found expression, for while in Euripides, confessedly the most "modern" of the classical poets, no real trace of it is to be found,[2] in Asclepiades and his immediate contemporaries and followers we find it already so thoroughly established as a noteworthy factor in their work, that it is impossible to doubt that its origin must belong to a considerably earlier period. This being so, it is impossible to speak with any

---

[1] For an examination of the fragments of the Middle Comedy, *vide* Excursus F.

[2] It may not be out of place to emphasise here once more the difference that exists between regarding women as an object of interest or importance, and regarding them as an object of love; for the two have been confused by many, not only in estimating the influence of Euripides (cp. *supra*, pp. 40, 50), but also in considering the events of the earlier part of the fourth century. Thus many have pointed to the agitation in favour of "women's rights" satirised in the *Ecclesiazusae*, or to the great social importance of the Hetaerae (as illustrated in the Middle Comedy, &c.), or to the generally ameliorated condition of women of every class, as proofs of the existence at this period already of the romantic feeling. But to those who care to consider the matter clearly, it must be apparent that all these things are really beside the question. The improved state of women and their increasing power may have helped, and doubtless did help, to spread the romantic feeling when once it had originated; but they were in the first instance entirely independent of it. One does not *ipso facto* feel a romantic attachment for people because one is compelled to recognise them socially, while in these days of extended franchises it is surely not necessary to repeat that political recognition is not the same as love.

certainty. It seems, however, most probable that the initiation of the movement was due to Antimachus of Colophon.

Antimachus was a distinguished man in various ways. The author of an important critical edition of the text of the Homeric poems, he was himself an epic poet second only in the general estimation to Homer, and his *Thebaid* was still read and admired more than 500 years after his death.[1] But the work on which his present claim rests is his elegiac poem, *Lyde*. It may not be amiss briefly to recall the circumstances and nature of this poem.[2]

Antimachus, falling in love with some Lydian lady, married her, and went to live with her in her native country. Afterwards, on her death, he returned to Colophon, where he composed, in her memory, the elegy *Lyde*, a poem containing, in the form of digressions, accounts of most of the unhappy lovers of tradition or mythology.[3]

---

[1] Cp. Quint. x. 1, 53; *Anth. Pal.* vii. 409, &c.; vide Dübner, *Asii &c. Frag.* p. 28 *seqq.* (at the end of Didot's *Hesiod*).

If the epigram attributed to Antimachus in *Anth. Pal.* ix. 321, be really his, he must further be regarded as one of the originators of the Dedicatory Epigram. Cp. Reitzenstein, *Epig. u. Skol.* p. 131.

[2] For a full account of it, vide Bach, *Philetas, &c.*, Epimetrum iii. (p. 240); Dübner, *op. cit.* p. 40.

[3]
Λύδης δ' Ἀντίμαχος Λυσηΐδος ἐκ μὲν ἔρωτος
πληγεὶς Πακτωλοῦ ῥεῦμ' ἐπέβη ποταμοῦ.
Σαρδιανὴν δὲ θανοῦσαν ὑπὸ ξηρὴν θέτο γαῖαν,
Τμώλιον αἰξαον δ' ἦλθεν ἀποπρολιπὼν
ἄκρην ἐς Κολοφῶνα, γόων δ' ἐνεπλήσατο βίβλους
ἱράς, ἐκ παντὸς παυσάμενος καμάτου.

(Hermesianax, iii. 41.)

Ἀντίμαχος ὁ ποιητής, ἀποθανούσης τῆς γυναικὸς αὐτοῦ Λύδης, πρὸς ἣν φιλοστόργως εἶχε, παραμύθιον τῆς λύπης αὐτῷ ἐποίησε τὴν ἐλέγειαν

Now, in this there are two features which it is impossible to parallel in any previous Greek poem. The *Lyde* of Antimachus was a love-poem addressed to his wife, and written after her death. In these two facts we recognise, on the part of the writer, a view both of married life and of women in general, which is entirely new. Mimnermus had said that life without love was not worth living, but his was hardly the love to last after his lady's death. Simonides had sung the charms of the ideal housekeeper, but one would not expect to find emotional poetry addressed even to the most perfect housekeeper, as such. Euripides had expatiated on the powers and the capabilities of women; but there is a difference between regarding a woman as a particularly cunning and dangerous sort of beast, and regarding her as a fit object for a life's devotion. In Antimachus, for the first time, we meet with the new spirit which animates the new literature and forms the foundation of the Greek romantic conception; for it is respect for women and, above all, for marriage, that constitutes the fundamental principle of the romantic

---

τὴν καλουμένην Λύδην, ἐξαριθμησάμενος τὰς ἡρωϊκὰς συμφορὰς, τοῖς ἀλλοτρίοις κακοῖς ἐλάττω τὴν ἑαυτοῦ ποιῶν λύπην.

(Plut. *Cons. ad Apoll.* p. 106 B.)

The very important detail that he *married* her is confirmed by the passage in Athen. xiii. 597A, where the Lyde of Antimachus is expressly contrasted with τὴν ὁμώνυμον ταύτης ἑταίραν Λύδην.

Cp. too Ovid, *Trist.* i. 6, 1 :

    nec tantum Clario Lyde dilecta poetae,
      nec tantum Coo Battis amata suo est,
    pectoribus quantum tu nostris, uxor, inhaeres.

feeling throughout the later Greek poetry.[1] It was this spirit which rendered possible the artistic treatment of the story of Acontius and Cydippe, and the growth of the novel, with its one inviolable canon that, whatever trials or temptations might befall them, the two lovers must throughout remain pure and faithful to one another.[2] It was this that rendered possible the New Comedy, with its endless variations on the ever-fresh theme of the unhappy lover, made happy at the last by marriage with his lady.[3] It was this that rendered possible the Battis

---

[1] This respect for marriage (if one extends the idea of marriage sufficiently to cover every form of union which is faithfully observed—whether actually legalised by some particular ceremony or not, is, in this connection, not very material) will, I think, be found underlying the whole Greek conception of romance. This is, of course, diametrically opposed to the view of the mediæval barbarians, who held that the one woman in the world one could not love was one's wife. Whether Lyde or Isolde be the higher ideal is, perhaps, a matter of taste; *magno se iudice quaeque tuetur.* That I personally prefer the Greek to the barbarian is perhaps due to prejudice, but it is prejudice for which I am very grateful.

A further illustration may be found in the Latin elegiac poets. Propertius, the "Roman Callimachus," who is always calling attention to the Greek sources of his inspiration, addresses all his love-poems to the Hetaera Cynthia, to whom he remained faithful to the end. Ovid only invokes the Greeks (Antimachus in *Trist.* i. 6, 1; Philetas in *Trist.* i. 6, 2, *Pont.* iii. 1, 58) when addressing his wife. Tibullus and Catullus, the poets of adultery, never acknowledge in their love-poems their Greek predecessors, and Catullus even goes out of his way to abuse one of them.

[2] The *Cleitophon and Leucippe* of Achilles Tatius is, of course, an exception (the only extant one) to this rule, but then this late and curious work differs in other respects also from the typical Greek novel.

[3] It is most interesting to note how that, while in the earlier comedy marriage is the one great subject of ridicule, in the new comedy marriage is the hero's one great ambition.

of Philetas and the Leontium of Hermesianax, just as it rendered possible the Delia and the Lycoris of a later time. Under the old *régime* none of these things could have been. When Antimachus first sat down in his empty house at Colophon to write an elegy to his dead wife, consciously or unconsciously, he was initiating the greatest artistic revolution that the world has ever seen.

The circumstances under which the *Lyde* was produced were thus in themselves sufficiently unusual to have made a deep impression, and there is reason to believe further that the way in which Antimachus there treated his subject was also strikingly original. Not only was the actual literary form a novel one, and one that subsequently became very popular, but the general tone evidently differed in a marked manner from that of any love-poetry which had gone before. It was, above all things, noticeable for its seriousness, its gravity, and its self-restraint, characteristics entirely foreign to any previous love-poetry addressed to women. Thus Poseidippus expressly contrasts the temperate Antimachus with the licentious Mimnermus.[1] Something similar seems equally implied by the epithet σεμνοτέρη in the epigram of Asclepiades (*Anth. Pal.* ix. 63, 2). Indirect evidence of the same nature is to be found in the remark of Dionysius of Halicarnassus, who refers to Antimachus

---

[1] Ναννοῦς καὶ Λύδης ἐπίχει, δύο καὶ φιλεράστου
Μιμνέρμου καὶ τοῦ σώφρονος Ἀντιμάχου.
Anth. Pal. xii. 168.
For φιλεράστου Cod. Vat. gives φερεκάστου, which might also, perhaps, be retained in this sense.

as an instance τῆς αὐστηρᾶς ἁρμονίας.¹ Lastly, it is not, perhaps, too far-fetched to suppose that in Catullus xcv. the contrast between the *Smyrna* and the *Lyde* is not intended to be confined merely to the literary form, but is meant to further imply the poet's preference for the story of Myrrha over the less highly spiced anecdotes in Antimachus. Very interesting too, from this point of view, are the relations of mutual admiration which are known to have existed between Antimachus and his younger contemporary Plato, an admiration illustrated by several striking anecdotes.² That the philosopher's views on

---

[1] *De Compos. Verb.* p. 300. He is here, of course, speaking primarily of the literary style; but literary style is in most cases more or less a reflection of literary treatment.

The severe style of Antimachus' *Thebaid* is well known. (Vide Quint. x. 1, 53; *Anth. Pal.* vii. 409, 4.)

[2] Ἀντιμάχου τοῦ Κολοφωνίου καὶ Νικηράτου τινὸς Ἡρακλεώτου ποιήμασι Λυσάνδρια διαγωνισαμένων ἐπ' αὐτῷ (*sc.* Λυσάνδρῳ) τὸν Νικήρατον ἐστεφάνωσεν· ὁ δὲ Ἀντίμαχος ἀχθεσθεὶς ἠφάνισε τὸ ποίημα. Πλάτων δὲ νέος ὢν τότε καὶ θαυμάζων τὸν Ἀντίμαχον ἐπὶ τῇ ποιητικῇ, βαρέως φέροντα τὴν ἧτταν ἀνελάμβανεν καὶ παρεμυθεῖτο, τοῖς ἀγνοοῦσι κακὸν εἶναι φάμενος τὴν ἄγνοιαν, ὡς τὴν τυφλότητα τοῖς μὴ βλέπουσιν.—Plut. *Lysand.* 18.

Nec enim posset idem Demosthenes dicere, quod dixisse Antimachum, Clarium poetam, ferunt; qui cum, convocatis auditoribus, legeret eis magnum illud quod novistis volumen suum, et eum legentem omnes praeter Platonem reliquissent, Legam, inquit, nihilominus; Plato enim mihi unus instar est omnium milium.—Cic. *Brutus*, 51, 191.

Ἡρακλείδης γοῦν ὁ Ποντικὸς φησιν ὅτι τῶν Χοιρίλου τότε εὐδοκιμούντων Πλάτων τὰ Ἀντιμάχου προὔτιμησεν, καὶ αὐτὸν ἔπεισε τὸν Ἡρακλείδην ἐς Κολοφῶνα ἐλθόντα τὰ ποιήματα συλλέξαι τοῦ ἀνδρός.

Proclus, *Comm. in Plat. Tim.* i. p. 28.

Whether these anecdotes are actually true or not does not much matter. That the friendship between Antimachus and Plato was a well-known fact would be sufficiently proved by their invention; but there is nothing really contradictory or improbable in them, as some have asserted. In the story from Plutarch there is no need to suppose that

love were directly influenced by the poet cannot, of course, be absolutely proved. At the same time, the well-authenticated story of this intimacy, coupled with all that we know of the *Lyde*, is very suggestive of this, and might well furnish the subject for more elaborate research on the part of some Platonist. In spite therefore of the very scanty references to the *Lyde*, and the still scantier remains of the poem itself, it seems to be clear beyond doubt that, both in its circumstances of origin and its style, it was entirely different from any love-poem which had preceded it; and, further, that both circumstances and style may justly be described as romantic. In other words, the *Lyde* was a romantic love-poem.

But this is not in itself enough to show that the origin of the romantic feeling which appears in Alexandrian literature was due to its influence. It is further necessary to prove that those writers in

Plato was actually present at Samos; he may very well have met Antimachus afterwards elsewhere. The evidence of Proclus again merely says that Plato, in opposition to the prevailing opinion of his time, preferred Antimachus to Choerilus, and that he sent Heracleides to Colophon to make a collection of the works of the former, evidently after his death. It is consequently quite possible to reconcile all three narratives. Antimachus was defeated by Niceratus at the Lysandria, an event which, owing to his celebrity at the time (404 B.C.), naturally excited remark. Subsequently he met Plato, who, when the conversation turned on his defeat, complimented him in the way described—a compliment which Antimachus returned on another occasion (that alluded to by Cicero). Lastly, after Antimachus' death, Plato caused a collection of his works to be made. Where Plato met Antimachus is not quite clear, but the ascription to the former of the epigram in Athen. xiii. 589 C (*Anth. Pal.* vii. 217) would almost seem to imply that there was, at any rate, a tradition that Plato visited Colophon. If that was actually the case, he would naturally have come across Antimachus there.

whose works this feeling first appears — viz Asclepiades and Philetas — were actually readers and admirers of Antimachus.

This it is, perhaps, possible to do more conclusively than the general absence of evidence on the whole subject would have led one to expect. It is just Asclepiades and his particular followers who speak with the greatest enthusiasm of Antimachus. Very noteworthy are the words of Asclepiades himself—

Λύδη καὶ γένος εἰμὶ καὶ οὔνομα· τῶν δ' ἀπὸ Κόδρου
σεμνοτέρη πασῶν εἰμὶ δι' Ἀντίμαχον.
τίς γὰρ ἔμ' οὐκ ἤεισε; τίς οὐκ ἀνελέξατο Λύδην,
τὸ ξυνὸν Μουσῶν γράμμα καὶ Ἀντιμάχου;

Anth. Pal. ix. 63.

And the passage in Poseidippus, where Antimachus and Mimnermus, coupled but contrasted, are spoken of as the first two love-poets, is scarcely less emphatic.[1]

In the case of Philetas, the evidence is also strong. His elegies addressed to Battis are generally admitted to have been modelled, in form, at any rate, on the *Lyde* of Antimachus; and it does not seem unjustifiable to infer from this that their spirit and their general character were also, in the main, similar. The way in which the two poets are coupled by Ovid (*Trist.* i. 6, 1) seems to support this view, and, as we have already seen, there is no evidence to the contrary.[2] To sum up, then: the conclusions arrived at are briefly as follows:

[1] *Anth. Pal.* xii. 168.   [2] Cp. p. 70.

(1) In extant Greek poetry there is no trace of romantic love-poetry addressed to women, prior to the time of Asclepiades and Philetas.

(2) In the works of these writers this element suddenly appears, not in the nature of an experiment, but as a leading motive—an almost sure proof that they were not the originators of it.

(3) The *Lyde* of Antimachus was a work of such a kind, both in nature and in circumstances of production, that there is every reason to believe that it was a romantic love-poem.

(4) Philetas and Asclepiades were notoriously admirers of the *Lyde* of Antimachus.

(5) Therefore there is reason to believe that the romantic element appearing in their poems was due to the influence of Antimachus, who may thus be regarded as the originator of the romantic element in literature.

Vale, lector benevole, si quidem huc usque mecum perveneris.

WOMEN IN GREEK COMEDY

WOMEN IN GREEK COMEDY

I. THE CLASSIFICATION OF COMEDY

THE classification of Greek Comedy has been, from the earliest times, a subject of dispute. The ancient critics, for the most part, divided comedy into two classes only—the Old Comedy, which has a *parabasis*, and the New Comedy, which has none. According to these critics, the acme of the Old Comedy was reached during the Peloponnesian War, that of the New Comedy during the reign of Alexander. That this system of classification, though sound as far as it goes, is not an adequate one, will be admitted by every student of the subject, and need not be further discussed. The alternative division of comedy into three classes, corresponding roughly to the sixth, seventh, and eighth so-called periods of Greek literature [1]—a scheme of arrangement that has on the whole been most generally accepted in modern times—is also not a very satisfactory one; for, apart from the initial objection that it, like all similar chronological

---

[1] *I.e.* Peloponnesian War, 431–403; Lacedaemonian and Theban Supremacy, 405–336; Macedonian Age, 336 onwards.

arrangements, is far too rigid to be applied to anything so intangible as a literary tendency, there is the further and graver objection that there is really no essential difference whatever between the comedies performed at Athens during the reign of Philip and those performed there in the time of Alexander.

The *Orge* of Menander, produced in the year after the death of the latter monarch, might have been produced, as far as one can judge of its character by its remains, in any year of the previous fifty.

At the same time, however, it is certain that a division of comedy into three classes rather than two is necessary; for that the work of, say, Apollodorus Carystius, differs as much from that of Antiphanes as anything the latter ever wrote does from the work of Eupolis, is a fact that no one acquainted with the subject is likely to question.

The only satisfactory system of classification is that based, not on style or chronology, but on subject. Greek comedy falls naturally into three great divisions—the Political, the Social, and the Romantic,[1] and, to come at once to the point, these three divisions are characterised by three distinct ways of regarding women. The Political Comedy practically ignores women altogether; the Social Comedy admits the fascination of woman's society as an incident in a man's life; the Romantic Comedy claims woman's love as the one topic of absorbing interest for men.

[1] Of the sense in which the unfortunate word "romantic" has to be understood we have already spoken elsewhere. [p. 2.]

And here it may at once be observed that the relation between the first two forms of art is somewhat different from that which exists between them and the last. The Social Comedy was the natural and logical development of the original primitive comedy, and the Comedy of Cratinus, with its political motive, was but a temporary branch of the art, which, though growing at one time to such striking proportions as well nigh to conceal the parent stem, yet never actually prevented the growth and development of the latter. The Romantic Comedy, on the other hand, was the result, not of development, but of revolution. It was a deliberate attempt (undertaken in the first instance, it would seem, by a single man of genius) to inoculate the old Athenian drama with those romantic ideas which were by this time beginning to be freely expressed in various other parts of Greece, and to combine the teaching of the epic erotic legends, which were in essence ideal, with the realism of Social Comedy.[1]

This being the case, one would not unnaturally expect to find a more decided line of cleavage

[1] It may be remarked in passing that this ideal character of the "New" Comedy is not, as a rule, sufficiently recognised. People speak as if they thought that the stories in Menander, for instance, represented the ordinary events of life at Athens at the end of the fourth century. It need hardly, perhaps, be remarked that it would be about as reasonable to endeavour to get an idea of the ordinary life of English people at the present day by studying an Adelphi melodrama. As long as comedy at Athens confined itself to social satire, it is obvious that the social scenes it depicted must have been, even if somewhat burlesqued, yet, on the whole, true to life. When once it had abandoned this object, and began to aim at telling an exciting

between the writers of the two last phases of Comedy than is apparent in the previous case. And this is unquestionably so. Throughout the fifth century we find political and social comedy flourishing side by side, the great mass of the comedians being equally at home in either branch of the art, while, towards the close of that century and at the beginning of the next, the boundary line between the writers of "Old" and "Middle" Comedy is notoriously a very faint one. At the end of the fourth century, on the other hand, the victory of the Romantic Comedy was rapid and well-nigh complete, while there is generally no difficulty in saying without hesitation to which of the two classes, the modern or the old-fashioned, any given play of the transition belonged.[1]

But while the most satisfactory classification of Greek Comedy is unquestionably one on the lines

---

story, calculated to interest its audience in proportion to the strangeness and novelty of its *dénouement*, it is equally obvious that it must very soon have been compelled to abandon the ordinary affairs of everyday life. In taking over the business of the Epic, Comedy took with it the license of that form of composition and of its offspring, Tragedy. While no one will deny that incidents like those described by Menander may have occasionally taken place at Athens in the fourth century, just as some of them might conceivably take place in England at the present day, there can be hardly any real doubt that the stories of romantic comedy were as little true to the ordinary life of the time they professed to depict, as, say, the novel of Xenophon was to the ordinary life of the Roman provinces under the Antonines.

[1] It is true, of course, that the "New" Comedy took over from its predecessor certain characters (*e.g.* the parasite or the cook) and certain other features, practically unchanged; but all this was confined to minor points of detail, and any similarity between the two forms of art which such transference of ready-made *spécialités* may cause is a purely superficial one. The main subject of romantic comedy, and the treatment there of that main subject, are entirely distinct from everything that had gone before.

suggested above, the ordinary division into Old, Middle, and New Comedy, is so generally recognised that it has seemed to me inadvisable to ignore it altogether, and so these terms will be found occurring repeatedly in the following pages. To avoid the possibility of any misunderstanding, however, it may be remarked that the term, "New Comedy," will always be used in the sense of romantic comedy. The term, "Middle Comedy," will be used in its ordinary sense, except that it will be extended to cover all works, irrespective of author, which are akin to the school of Antiphanes and Eubulus. The unsatisfactory term, "Old Comedy," will only be used in those passages where the context renders its meaning unmistakable.

II. THE ORIGIN OF COMEDY.

Comedy was, in its origin, as seems indeed necessary from its nature, social rather than political. The scenes which the first comic actors aimed at depicting appear, beyond doubt, to have been representations of amusing incidents in the everyday life of ordinary people, and were in no way concerned with state policy; while the personalities with which this form of entertainment originally abounded, were aimed rather at rival actors than at well-known public characters, and had nothing at all in common with political lampoons. It is true that Comedy generally received its chief impulses at times of great popular license under democracies,[1] but this fact really means no more than that, at such periods, the amusements of the people received greater attention than would be the case under a tyranny or an oligarchy. No doubt these extempore slanging-matches became, at an early time already, very general in character, and contained, among other promiscuous allusions, occasional references, probably none too complimentary, to important contemporary events or personages; but that this was not their main feature, nor that which supplied their chief interest, seems shown, *inter alia*, by the fact that the first artistic development they received at the hands of Epicharmus was by no means in this direction. Nor, indeed, do the earliest Attic comedies appear to have been political in character, the few fragments of them which survive seeming, in every case, to deal with social subjects.[2]

The first writer to make Comedy political—that is, the first writer to give to the "Old" Comedy of

---

[1] Thus the Megarian Comedy dates from the expulsion of Theagenes (Arist. *Poet.* iii. 5), while the Athenian reappears, after a silence of some 70 years, on the expulsion of Hippias.

[2] The titles of the plays attributed to Chionides do not in themselves contradict this view. The *Heroes* describes life as it would be in a state engaged in war, but there is no reason to believe that the play discussed any real phase of any contemporary war. The *Persae*, too, to judge by its second title of *Assyrii*, was devoted rather to ridiculing Persian customs than to dealing with the Persian War. In like manner the *Lydi* of Magnes introduced the Lydian dances to Athens (cp. Hesych. λυδίζων, χορεύων, διὰ τοὺς Λυδούς sc. Μάγνητος), while the *Barbatistae* appears to have been equally aimed at the æsthetic tastes of some part of the community. Titles again, like *Ornithes*, *Batrachi*, and *Psenes*, give no suggestion of political motives, any more than does the *Satyri* of Ecphantides.

Athens that which is, by modern readers, generally regarded as its most essential characteristic—was Cratinus. He, abandoning in great part that endeavour to amuse which had been the primary object of his predecessors, deliberately made use of Comedy as a political party engine, or, as he would perhaps have preferred to call it, as a means of attacking those who did harm to the state.[1] The success of the new element thus imported seems to have been very great; but, at the same time, it must not be supposed that the work of Cratinus was all of this nature. In the first place, some of his plays were of a distinctly general character. Thus the *Odysses* was a simple parody of the *Odyssey* of Homer, and, as such, was the distinct forerunner of a class of piece very common in the Social Comedy of the fourth century.[2] The *Cleobulinae*, with its enigmas, is equally suggestive of another feature of the same period of art. In like manner, the *Panoptae*, with its attacks on the philosopher Hippo, the *Seriphii*, with its mythological allusions, and the *Horae*, with its apparent discussions of tragedy, all point to the

---

[1] τῷ χαρίεντι τῆς κωμῳδίας τὸ ὠφέλιμον προσέθηκε τοὺς κακῶς πράττοντας διαβάλλων καὶ ὥσπερ δημοσίᾳ μάστιγι τῇ κωμῳδίᾳ μαστίζων (Anon. *de Com*. p. 32). οὐ γὰρ ὥσπερ ὁ Ἀριστοφάνης ἐπιτρέχειν τὴν χάριν τοῖς σκώμμασι ποιεῖ . . . ἀλλ' ἁπλῶς καὶ κατὰ τὴν παροιμίαν γυμνῇ κεφαλῇ τίθησι τὰς βλασφημίας κατὰ τῶν ἁμαρτανόντων (Platon. *de Com*. p. 27).

[2] τοιοῦτος οὖν ἐστὶν ὁ τῆς μέσης κωμῳδίας τύπος, οἷός ἐστιν . . . οἱ Ὀδυσσεῖς Κρατίνου (Platon. *de Com*. p. 34). οἱ γοῦν Ὀδυσσεῖς Κρατίνου οὐδενὸς ἐπιτίμησιν ἔχουσι, διασυρμὸν δὲ τῆς Ὀδυσσείας Ὁμήρου (*ibid.* p. 35).

The elaborate details as to cookery in the fragments of this play are also very suggestive of one of the features of "Middle" Comedy.

direction in which lay the true development of the art of Comedy.[1]

But, popular as the indiscriminate mud-throwing of Cratinus undoubtedly was with a large section of that cultured Athenian audience which one is taught to admire, a certain reaction was, in course of time, almost inevitable; and such a reaction was actually furnished by the comedies of Crates. Crates is described as the first Attic comedian to develop Comedy on the lines of Epicharmus, and to introduce a plot with apparently fictitious or allegorical characters, instead of merely bringing public characters on the stage and making them ridiculous.[2]

From a very early period, therefore, Comedy at Athens falls into two classes, the personal, which is usually also political, and the general or social, though the line of demarcation is not, of course, a very rigid one, since writers of the latter class would seldom feel much hesitation in attacking anyone who had made himself particularly obnoxious to them, even if he were a political character, while those of the former were also frequently compelled, for equally

---

[1] It is further to be observed that, though Cratinus nearly always indulges in personal abuse, this abuse is by no means necessarily directed against *political* characters. Any person, whatever his capacity, who was sufficiently well known to be recognised by the Athenian audience, was liable to be the butt of his scurrility.

[2] Arist. *Poet.* v. 5. As Meineke (*Com. Fr.* i. 59) well expresses it: "Cratetem primum apud Athenienses exstitisse qui Epicharmi exemplo comicae poeseos materiam a singulorum hominum i·risione ad generales morum notationes rerumque descriptiones traduceret." Crates thus differs from Cratinus in that his plays were not political, while he differs from the earlier comedians in that he avoided personalities and treated of general subjects, and this is the meaning of the word πρῶτος in Aristotle, *l.c.*

personal reasons, to set a limit to their righteous indignation. Thus Pherecrates, the most important of the actual imitators of Crates,[1] is by no means averse to an occasional personality, while a writer of the very opposite school, Hermippus, was yet the author of the *Athenas Gonae*.[2] Plato and Aristophanes are, of course, equally striking instances of the same fact occurring at a later date.

From the preceding paragraphs, which might have been considerably extended, had it not lain somewhat outside the present subject to extend them, one fact at least will be abundantly clear. That system of treating subjects rather than persons as material for comedy which is sometimes spoken of as a distinctive feature of "Middle" Comedy (using that term in its chronological sense), had already been in vogue at Athens from the very earliest times; in fact, what are commonly called "Old" and "Middle" Comedy are, in spirit, intimately associated with one another, and the most important differences between them are in purely external matters, brought about by external causes.[3]

[1] ἐξήλωκε Κράτητα. Anon. *de Com.* p. 29.

[2] The law of Morychis, during the operation of which this play, like the *Odysses* of Cratinus and various others, seems to have been brought out, is interesting as an early instance of the influence of political events upon the development of early Athenian comedy, an influence entirely absent in the case of the romantic comedy.

[3] Thus the final disappearance of the *parabasis*, though an important enough event for the history of the form of Comedy, is but an incident in the real development of the art. This is shown by the fact that, when, under the law of Morychis, the *parabasis* was temporarily suspended, the result was the immediate appearance, at this date already, of plays which belong, in spirit, entirely to "Middle" Comedy.

This fact will not be without its importance in considering our immediate subject. In the first place, it will cause us to find in the early Athenian comedy two distinct ways of regarding women, which, while contemporaneous, have very little else in common with one another. The comedy of the school of Cratinus,[1] being concerned with public characters and with them alone, naturally ignores women almost entirely.[2] The comedy of the school of Crates, on the other hand, is very similar in its treatment of women to the comedy of the beginning of the fourth century, except that, in so far as the position of women in Athenian society was a less important one in the middle of the fifth century than it was some seventy years later, the female element is not such a pronounced feature of these early works as it is of the later.

A detailed examination of the treatment of women in early comedy, as far as such is possible by means of the fragments, will serve to illustrate the foregoing somewhat general remarks.

---

[1] This means the school of Cratinus, when unrestricted by legislation, and allowed to take its own course. Prohibitive legislation naturally tended to put the two schools of comedy on much the same footing.

[2] The few exceptions will be considered presently. [p. 127.]

III. EARLY COMEDY.

Cratinus, in that work at any rate which is truly characteristic of his genius, is entirely engrossed in public affairs, and in attacking the characters of public men. It is not, therefore, surprising to find that in his plays women are almost entirely ignored. The one notable exception is Aspasia, who is, it is true, alluded to more than once, and that in no very complimentary terms; but this is, of course, only what one would expect of an opponent of Pericles.[1] The poet's views of married life are sufficiently illustrated by his *Pytine*. It is, however, to be observed that, in those of his plays which, from legislative causes, approximated more closely to the contemporary social comedy, the female element is more apparent, though even here it is never really prominent. Thus the *Cleobulinae* appears to have introduced a chorus of women propounding enigmas, while both the *Nemesis* and the *Seriphii* contained at least allusions to erotic mythological incidents.[2]

The other early poets of the political school are

[1] [The author contemplated, but does not seem to have written, an Excursus on "Pericles and Aspasia."]

[2] In neither of these must it, of course, be supposed that the erotic element was at all the leading motive. Most of the fragments of the *Nemesis* seem to refer to events which must be supposed to have taken place some time after the erotic incident had been closed, while in the *Seriphii* the description of Andromeda as δελέαστρα (*Fr.* 12) is the only allusion to her preserved. Indeed, it is vain in Cratinus to look for any leading motive at all, for, as Platonius says of him (*de Com.* p. 27), εὔστοχος ὢν ἐν ταῖς ἐπιβολαῖς τῶν δραμάτων καὶ διασκευαῖς, εἶτα προϊὼν καὶ διασπῶν τὰς ὑποθέσεις οὐκ ἀκολούθως πληροῖ τὰ δράματα.

still more barren of references to women; indeed the fragments of Teleclides, Hermippus, and Eupolis,[1] put together, do not furnish a single noticeable instance.

It is otherwise, as already remarked, with the school of Crates. The fragments of Crates himself do not indeed furnish much of interest in this connection, except, perhaps, the rather *risqué* remarks in *Fr. Incert.* 3 and 4, but from Pherecrates there is more to be learnt. In the first place, three of his plays, the *Corianno*, *Thalatta*, and *Petale*, are named after Hetaerae, a common enough feature in later times, but rare at this early period; while the first two of these, at any rate, were evidently devoted to a study of the life of this class of person. Thus the *Corianno* describes (*Fr.* 1, 2, 3, 4) the drinking propensities of its heroine;[2] while the *Thalatta* gives one even further particulars, *Fr.* 7 describing the arrival at Thalatta's house of her lover[3] (perhaps the Epilesmon, the "Absent-minded Man," from whom the piece had its second title), and *Fr.* 2, 3, and 5 their supper together, while *Fr.* 4 shows clearly that a lover's quarrel of some sort duly found its place in

---

[1] The apparent allusion to the Hetaera Myrrhina in Eupolis, *Autolycus*, *Fr.* 10, is too uncertain to be of any value.

[2] The *Tyrannis* (another suggestive title) also satirised the drunkenness of women (cp. the fragment *ap.* Athen. xi. 481 B). It may be remembered in this connection, that the introduction of drunken persons on the stage was an invention of his master Crates.

[3] τὸν ἱδρῶτα καὶ τὴν ἄρδαν ἀπ' ἐμοῦ σπόγγισον.

The tone of address will surprise no one who remembers the scene between Diphilus and Gnathaena (*ap.* Athen. xiii. 583 F), and others like it. [This subject was to have been dealt with further in an Excursus.]

the piece.[1] Of the *Petale* no important fragment remains. Whether the *Pannychis* dealt with one of those incidents which are so common in New Comedy, it is impossible to say.

IV. ARISTOPHANES.

The remains of Pherecrates, therefore, notwithstanding their very meagre character, supply ample evidence that, at this period already, some of the most popular characters and scenes of early fourth-century comedy had found a place on the Athenian stage[2]; but a still more interesting field of study is furnished by those poets who belong to the period of transition which commences with the decline of the Athenian power, and more especially by those who began life as adherents of the personal and political school of Cratinus, and were afterwards compelled, by force of circumstances, to identify themselves with a different style of art. Foremost among these is, of course, the name of Aristophanes. The earlier plays of Aristophanes contain few allusions to women, and throughout his works it may be doubted whether he ever introduced a female character on the stage except with the ultimate intention of leading up to some form of indecency. At the same time, since the fact that his plays have been preserved affords a better opportunity

---

[1]   κἂν μὲν σιωπῶ, δυσφορεῖ καὶ πνίγεται,
    καί φησι, τί σιωπᾷς; ἐὰν δ' ἀποκριθῶ,
    οἴμοι τάλας, φησίν, χαράδρα κατελήλυθεν.

[2] The precise nature of the differences between these early "Hetaera-plays" and those generally in vogue at a later date, will be examined when we come to consider the latter class of composition. [p. 153.]

of judging of his views than is to be had in the case of any other writer of the period, it will perhaps be well to examine some of his characteristics in greater detail.

The first and, perhaps, the most striking feature in the Aristophanic treatment of women—a feature which is very prominent indeed in certain plays—is the respect which the poet professes to feel for women's judgment and powers of organisation. Thus, in the *Lysistrata*, the treaty between Athens and Sparta, which is admitted on all sides to be desirable, can only be brought about through the intervention of a woman. Similarly, in the *Ecclesiazusae*, when the government of the city has fallen into a deplorable state, it is reorganised by the women, and their scheme of reorganisation is, we are given to understand, a complete success, for the time being at any rate. Again, in the lost play of the *Scenas Catalambanusae*, there seems little doubt that the motive of the action was an appeal on the part of the poet from the male audience who had not appreciated him, to a female audience which he expected to find endowed with better taste.

All this is very pleasing as far as it goes. The question is:—How far is this respect professed for women, genuine? Enquiry would seem to show that very little of it, if any, is genuine at all. Of the *Scenas Catalambanusae* it is impossible to speak with certainty,[1] but, as for the other two plays mentioned

[1] One can at least gather from *Fr.* 1, 2, 3, that the coming together of the women was made the occasion of a series of jokes at their expense, something after the manner of Mnesilochus and the baby in *Thesmoph.* 689 *sqq.*

above, it is hard to believe that the women are introduced for any other purpose than that of leading up to the various scenes of indecency which afford the main interest of both pieces. The climax of the *Lysistrata* is the pathetic speech of Cinesias (865 *seqq.*), that of the *Ecclesiazusae* the struggle between the γραῦς and the νεανίς (877 *seqq.*), and neither of these scenes can be said to show much respect for female nature. As for the success of the women's efforts in both these plays, it is perhaps sufficient to observe that in each case the poet's main object was to point out the advantages of a particular course of action, not to suggest any novel method of procedure by means of which this course was to be adopted. The political object of both comedies is merely to attack the government of the day. No one who has ever read these plays would be likely to argue that they advocated the extension of the franchise to women, or indeed concerned themselves in any way with any subject of the kind. To put it shortly, the women are introduced for indecency's sake, and their revolutions succeed simply because they are revolutions against the existing order of things, an order of which Aristophanes did not approve. It would be as reasonable to suppose that the *Aves* was a serious piece of advice to the Athenians to consult with birds about the management of the State, as to assume that the *Ecclesiazusae* meant to imply that the views of women were really worthy of consideration or adoption.

The incessant allusions in these plays, no less than

in others, to the incontinence,[1] the drunkenness, and the various other faults with which it was usual at the time to tax women—allusions which frequently take the form of frank confessions on the part of the women themselves—are so numerous that there is no need to quote any of them.

Another rather striking feature is the way in which several of the plays of Aristophanes conclude with the wedding of one of the characters—a feature at first sight very suggestive of the comedy typical of a much later period. The best known instance of this is perhaps in the *Eirene*, but the same seems to have been the case in the *Polyidus* (where the successful soothsayer is rewarded with the hand of the king's daughter, Phaedra), and in the *Geras*, where the hero, having been miraculously restored to youth, repudiates his former wife, and marries one more suited to his recently acquired—or lost—years. It must, however, be observed that in none of these plays, as far as one can see, is the wedding of the hero by any means the logical result of the action of the piece; it is merely an incidental episode introduced, in the *Eirene* at any rate, and very possibly also in the others, simply with the view of providing the chorus with an effective exit. In the *Polyidus*, moreover, it is clear that though Minos gives his daughter as a reward, he has his own

---

[1] This seems to have been one of the main motives of the *Lemniae*; at any rate, the nature of Aeschylus' play on the same subject would have afforded an excellent opportunity of the kind—Αἰσχύλος δ' ἐν Ὑψιπύλῃ ἐν ὅπλοις φησὶν αὐτὰς [τὰς Λημνίας] ἐπελθούσας χειμαζομένοις [τοῖς Ἀργοναύταις] ἀπείργειν, μέχρι λαβεῖν ὅρκον παρ' αὐτῶν ἀποβάντας μιγήσεσθαι αὐταῖς. Schol. *ad Apoll. Rhod.* I. 773.

opinion as to the value of the gift, an opinion which is hardly complimentary to Phaedra[1]; while in the *Geras* there can be little reasonable doubt that the connubial arrangements were made the occasion for a plentiful supply of obscenities, *quae nunc desiderantur*, if one can use the words in such a connection.[2] One must be careful, therefore, not to exaggerate the importance of this feature in the Aristophanic treatment of women, though it cannot, of course, be denied that to introduce a wedding at all on the stage was a distinct advance on strict Athenian views with reference to such events.[3]

Aristophanes was above all things, by profession at least, a conservative and a *laudator temporis acti;* but, strangely enough, this characteristic of his is but little noticeable in his treatment of women. Nothing would have been more natural, one would have thought, than that he should, in the course of some of his highly-coloured pictures of primeval felicity before the days of Euripides and the philosophers, have dwelt upon the purity of ancient family life and the chastity of a previous generation of women, in contrast to that present depravity to which he makes such frequent allusion. But, true to his Athenian temperament, he never follows any such line, nor indeed does he ever take up high ground on this subject. Ready as he is to moralise seriously on

---

[1] ἰδού, δίδωμι τήνδ' ἐγὼ γυναῖκά σοι
  Φαίδραν· ἐπὶ πῦρ δὲ πῦρ ἔοιχ' ἥξειν ἄγων.
  (*Polyid. Fr.* 2.)

[2] Cp. *Geras, Fr.* 5, 6, 7.

[3] Cp. *e.g.* the remarks of Phocion to his son: ἐμοῦ μέν, ὦ παῖ, τὴν σὴν μητέρα γαμοῦντος οὐδ' ὁ γείτων ᾔσθετο. Plutarch. *Phoc.* 30.

other matters, even on matters so distinctly erotic as the relations of man to man,[1] his tone with regard to women is invariably flippant.

Women are, above all things, conservative:

μοιχοὺς ἔχουσιν ἔνδον ὥσπερ καὶ πρὸ τοῦ.
(*Eccles.* 225.)

Euripides may have made rude remarks about women, but his suggestions are politeness itself compared with what might have been said.[2] Indeed, the main charge of the women against Euripides in the *Thesmophoriazusae* is not that he has maligned them, but that he has opened the eyes of their husbands to what they actually do.[3] It is needless to multiply instances; the general tendency is plain. Woman in Aristophanes is invariably an object of ridicule. So incapable was he of treating her otherwise, that his one ideal woman, Eirene, for whom the knight-errant Trygaeus flies up to heaven on the dung-beetle, was a colossal failure, a κολοσσικὸν ἄγαλμα that was the general laughing-stock of his contemporaries.[4]

This being so, there is but little need to dwell on such "erotic" passages as do occur, here and there in his works, between men and women. Such scenes, of which the best instance is perhaps that in the *Ecclesiazusae* (877 *seqq.*), are never the main motive

---

[1] *Vide e.g. Nubes,* 973 *seqq.*, 1002 *seqq.*

[2] Cp. the speech of Mnesilochus, *Thesmoph.* 466 *seqq.*, the spirit of which, all allowance for comic exaggeration being made, cannot be mistaken.

[3] *Vide Thesmoph.* 383 *seqq.* The subject and style of the *Daedalus* were equally uncomplimentary. Cp. *Fr.* 3.

[4] κωμῳδεῖται δὲ (ὁ Ἀριστοφάνης) ὅτι καὶ τὸ τῆς Εἰρήνης κολοσσικὸν ἐξῆρεν ἄγαλμα, Εὔπολις Αὐτολύκῳ, Πλάτων Νίκαις. Schol. *Plat. Apol.* p. 331.

of the plot; they are merely more or less irrelevant incidents, developed or not according to the chances they afford for the introduction of amusing indecencies. In these scenes Aristophanes is often to be seen at his very best, but they cannot of course be drawn upon with the object of supplying evidence as to his real views of women, except in so far as they serve still further to emphasise what has already been said as to the poet's disinclination to deal seriously with the subject of women at all. Indeed, his view of the proper relation between love and art is sufficiently illustrated by the famous argument in the *Ranae* (1043 *seqq.*) between Aeschylus and Euripides, where, after the former has stated with pride:

οὐδ' οἶδ' οὐδεὶς ἥντιν' ἐρῶσαν πώποτ' ἐποίησα γυναῖκα,

and the latter has defended his own erotic treatment on the ground that it is realistic:

πότερον δ' οὐκ ὄντα λόγον τοῦτον περὶ τῆς Φαίδρας ξυνέθηκα;

the answer comes back:

μὰ Δί', ἀλλ' ὄντ'· ἀλλ' ἀποκρύπτειν χρὴ τὸ πονηρὸν τόν γε ποιητήν.

The treatment of erotic subjects in a realistic manner is not the business of a true poet!

V. THE COCALUS.

With this before one, it would seem hardly necessary to say anything further about the erotic element in Aristophanes. There is, however, one play of his

—the last, or last but one, that he wrote—which seems at first sight to differ so entirely in spirit from the rest, that it is well worthy of separate notice.

This play is the *Cocalus*, a work of which it is distinctly stated by ancient authorities that it anticipated one of the most characteristic features of romantic comedy—nay more, that it actually served as the model for Menander and Philemon. Thus, in the *Vita Aristophanis*, p. xxxviii., it is said: ἐγένετο δὲ καὶ αἴτιος ζήλου τοῖς νέοις κωμικοῖς, λέγω δὴ Φιλήμονι καὶ Μενάνδρῳ ... ἔγραψε Κώκαλον, ἐν ᾧ εἰσάγει φθορὰν καὶ ἀναγνωρισμὸν καὶ τἄλλα πάντα ἃ ἐζήλωσε Μένανδρος, and again, p. xxxv.: πρῶτος δὲ καὶ τῆς νέας κωμῳδίας τὸν τρόπον ἐπέδειξεν ἐν τῷ Κωκάλῳ, ἐξ οὗ τὴν ἀρχὴν λαβόμενοι Μένανδρός τε καὶ Φιλήμων ἐδραματούργησαν.

Of these statements, the one part, startling as it is, must presumably be accepted without question. In the face of such definite evidence, it would be rash to attempt to deny that one of the features of Aristophanes' play was φθορὰ καὶ ἀναγνωρισμός—a feature which is, as is well known, not only one of the commonest in romantic comedy, but also peculiarly characteristic of the love-element as there treated. The sort of story of which we are speaking is sufficiently familiar to every reader of Terence. A man seduces a girl, either without knowing at all who she is, or else under the impression that she is a foreigner or a slave. Afterwards she is proved to be an Athenian citizen, and he, being still in love, marries her, with the double object of atoning for his fault and of continuing his amour on a legitimate basis.[1]

But here a question arises. Granted that Aristophanes anticipated one of the most characteristic situations of the romantic comedy, in how far, if at all, did he anticipate the romantic treatment of that situation, such as we subsequently find it? Aristophanes, as we have seen, has the first part of the romantic love-story in his *Cocalus;* is it probable that he also had the second? He has the seduction and the recognition; is it probable that he had also the *amende honorable* prompted by feelings of respect and devotion? And, as a natural pendant to this, is it probable that the *Cocalus* was really, as asserted, the model after which the later romantic comedy was formed?

It is not probable. No one who knows the works of Aristophanes, and considers the character of the Athenians of his day, would expect such a thing; and, apart from this inherent improbability, there are various reasons which seem to suggest that the second part of the anonymous grammarian's statement was based upon a misconception. But, before discussing any of these points, it will be necessary to investigate, as far as possible, the exact nature of this play of Aristophanes, for which so much is claimed.

[1] It is worth noticing that, while a man who seduced an Athenian citizen seems to have been legally bound to marry her, and therefore, to a certain extent, there was no great virtue in his action if he did so, at the same time this legal necessity was never, so far as we know, in any way urged in any play of the New Comedy. The point will be more fully discussed when we come to this part of our subject. [See p. 169.]

An examination of the actual remains of the *Cocalus* will not afford very much information, for the fragments preserved are few and unimportant, while the mercurial nature of Aristophanes' plots, as we know them from existing plays, makes it obviously hazardous to venture conjectures as to what they may or may not have included. Certain facts, however, seem sufficiently clear. For one thing, the play was based, at any rate originally and ostensibly, on the legendary history of Cocalus, Daedalus, and Minos. This history was, briefly, as follows :—

Daedalus, after his flight from Crete, took refuge with Cocalus, king of Sicily, and rose to high favour at his court. When Minos, having learnt his whereabouts, demanded his surrender, Cocalus at first seemed willing to comply, and invited Minos to his palace. The latter, suspecting nothing, accepted the invitation, and was at once murdered in his bath, either by Cocalus himself or by his daughters.[1]

---

[1] Minos, quod Daedali opera multa sibi incommoda acciderunt, in Siciliam est eum persecutus petiitque a rege Cocalo ut sibi redderetur. cui cum Cocalus promisisset et Daedalus rescisset, ab regis filiabus auxilium petiit. illae Minoem occiderunt. Hygin. *Fab.* 44.

Μίνως δέ, ὁ τῶν Κρητῶν βασιλεύς, θαλαττοκρατῶν κατ' ἐκείνους τοὺς χρόνους καὶ πυθόμενος τὴν Δαιδάλου φυγὴν εἰς Σικελίαν, ἔγνω στρατεύειν ἐπ' αὐτήν . . . ὁ δὲ Κώκαλος, εἰς σύλλογον προσκαλεσάμενος καὶ πάντα ποιήσειν ἐπαγγειλάμενος, ἐπὶ τὰ ξένια παρέλαβε τὸν Μίνω. λουομένου δ' αὐτοῦ, Κώκαλος μὲν παρακατασχὼν πλείονα χρόνον ἐν τῷ θερμῷ τὸν Μίνωα διέφθειρε, καὶ τὸ σῶμα ἀπέδωκε τοῖς Κρησί, πρόφασιν ἐνεγκὼν τοῦ θανάτου διότι κατὰ τὸν λουτρῶνα ὠλίσθηκε καὶ πεσὼν εἰς τὸ θερμὸν ὕδωρ ἐτελεύτησε. (Diodorus, iv. 79.)

The story is told somewhat differently in Zenobius iv. 92. There Minos, in order to discover Daedalus, goes about the world offering large rewards to anyone who can run a linen thread through a spiral

That the latter version of the final incident was accepted by Aristophanes seems probable, but even so it is hard to see how the φθορὰ καὶ ἀναγνωρισμός can be brought into the story. It is, perhaps, justifiable to assume that the hero of the amour was Daedalus, and that the lady was subsequently recognised as a daughter of Cocalus; but how this all came about, it is well-nigh impossible to say. In some of the fragments we are apparently introduced to a regular Hetaera (*e.g.* 2, 10; and, perhaps, 6, 7); in another, however (*Fr.* 3), a woman seems vigorously repudiating some slur cast on her character. It cannot, of course, be proved that the plot[1] was not

---

shell, being convinced that no one but Daedalus would be able to do such a thing. When he comes to Sicily, Cocalus, in order to gain the reward, gives the shell to Daedalus, who bores a hole at the end, ties the linen thread to an ant, and so does what is required. λαβὼν δὲ ὁ Μίνως τὸν λίνον διειρμένον ᾔσθετο εἶναι παρ' ἐκείνῳ τὸν Δαίδαλον καὶ εὐθέως ἀπῄτει. Κώκαλος δέ, ὑποσχόμενος δώσειν, ἐξένισεν αὐτόν. ὁ δὲ λουόμενος ὑπὸ τῶν Κωκάλου θυγατέρων ἀνῃρέθη ζέουσαν πίσσαν ἐπιχεαμένων αὐτῷ.—This is the version of the story followed by Sophocles in the *Camici*. (Cp. *Fr.* 301, 302.)

It is worth noticing that Daedalus, according to Diodorus, iv. 78, made a cave at Selinus, in which patients were treated by being subjected to a gradually-increasing temperature. (τρίτον δὲ σπήλαιον κατὰ τὴν Σελινουντίαν χώραν κατεσκεύασεν, ἐν ᾧ τὴν ἀτμίδα τοῦ κατ' αὐτὴν πυρὸς οὕτως εὐστόχως ἐξέλαβεν ὥστε διὰ τὴν μαλακότητα τῆς θερμασίας ἐξιδροῦν λεληθότως, καὶ κατὰ μικρὸν τοὺς ἐνδιατρίβοντας μετὰ τέρψεως θεραπεύειν τὰ σώματα, μηδὲν παρενοχλουμένους ὑπὸ τῆς θερμότητος.) It is, perhaps, not impossible that Aristophanes may have described Minos' death as occurring in this cave.

[1] By the word "plot" as here used, must of course be understood merely the erotic incident. That the action was not confined to one subject of this kind is obvious to every reader of Aristophanes. Whatever may have been the treatment of the erotic element, there can be practically no doubt that this element was only one, perhaps not the most important one, among the many that went to make up the play.

one of the regular New Comedy kind: The daughter of Cocalus, being stolen as a child, became the property of a *leno*, and was thus brought in contact with Daedalus, &c. But it seems to me much more probable that the structure of the story was somewhat of the following kind. The daughter of Cocalus is violated by Daedalus on the occasion of a nocturnal orgy, without being recognised by her lover. She, however, is aware of his identity, and consequently, when the time comes, murders Minos, an event which necessitates explanations (the ἀναγνωρισμός of the grammarian).[1] One thing there is to be said in favour of this scheme of reconstruction, though, of course, when the evidence is so slight, it is impossible to feel anything like confidence with regard to this or any other suggestion. If this view be adopted, Aristophanes may be assumed to have chosen his story with the object of satirising the *Pannychides* and other similar orgies, which were always a favourite subject of attack with him, and which he had already abused in the *Horae*,[2] the *Lemniae*, and, perhaps, elsewhere.

But, be this as it may, one thing is plain. There is nothing, either in the story of the *Cocalus* or in its treatment, as far as the fragments allow one to

---

[1] *Fr.* 4 seems to suggest that there may have been a regular trial instituted, as in the *Vespae* (cp. *Vesp.* 807 *seqq.* with *Cocal. Fr.* 12), at which Daedalus was accused of complicity in the murder, and his services to Cocalus as a builder (*Fr.* 5; cp. Diodorus, iv. 78) urged on his behalf. This trial may well have had features in common with the last scene in Euripides' *Andromeda*.

[2] The fact that this play led to the abandonment of certain nocturnal orgies is, of course, no proof that such habits altogether ceased, even for a time; indeed, it is notorious that they did not.

judge of this, which has any real sympathy with that later feeling which inspires the romantic comedy. For one thing, the erotic incident, such as it is, belongs entirely to that primitive class in which the action is all on the side of the woman. The daughter of Cocalus saving her lover is but a reflection of Medea or Ariadne. In the later romantic comedy, on the other hand, the action is regularly on the side of the man; for, as is well known, the attempts of the lover to outwit his father or the *leno* supply pretty well the whole stock of the incidents of New Comedy. Again, there is no suggestion whatever, as far as one can judge, of any marriage by way of reparation, or, indeed, of any marriage at all;[1] and marriage, as we shall see very clearly later on, is the fundamental principle of Greek romance. Again, there is no suggestion—and this is still more important—that the love of Daedalus was described as more than a mere temporary emotion; and here is another

[1] Even if it could be proved that the play ended with a wedding—such endings are, as we have seen, not uncommon in Aristophanes—and that this is what the grammarian means by his τἆλλα πάντα ἃ ἐζήλωσε Μένανδρος, this would not, in itself, be enough to make the play a romantic one after the manner of the later works. The marriage would have to be *an act of reparation inspired by love*, and it need hardly be remarked how utterly foreign any such feeling would be to the work of Aristophanes. Such a difference in spirit and motive, however, important and obvious as it seems to us, may very well have escaped the ancient critics, whose criticism of art was well-nigh exclusively concerned with its external and superficial qualities. Hence, if by any chance Aristophanes' characters were despatched off the stage to the sounds of a wedding march, it is easy to see how clear a proof this would have seemed to them that the *Cocalus* belonged to the same phase of art as the plays of Menander, when, in reality, it did nothing of the kind.

point of difference between this play and the romantic New Comedy. In fact, if one comes to examine the story of the *Cocalus* carefully, it becomes apparent that the essential features of Greek romance are entirely wanting. Indeed, the only real affinity of this play to the New Comedy seems to be that it anticipated, or possibly suggested, some of the rather cumbrous conventional machinery of the latter form of art.

A further fact, which well-nigh precludes the possibility of regarding the *Cocalus* as the real model of New Comedy, is furnished by the dates. The date of the *Cocalus* cannot be fixed later than the year 380 or thereabouts. The first play of Philemon, admittedly the most ancient poet who wrote romantic comedies, appeared in 330. Thus, even if it were granted that such romantic comedies were among the earliest of Philemon's works, which was almost certainly not the case,[1] there would still be an interval of at least fifty years during which the "romantic" *Cocalus* of Aristophanes did not find a single imitator. The works of Antiphanes, Eubulus, and, indeed, all the typical writers of "Middle" Comedy, do not contain so much as a suggestion of a romantic element, and yet, before the time of all of them, there was in existence a perfect romantic comedy, which only needed to be revived by Philemon to bring about a complete revolution of the canons of dramatic art. In fact, the introduction of the romantic element into comedy—that is, the birth of the modern drama

[1] Cp. *infra*, p. 189 *seqq*.

—was due to a chance resuscitation by Philemon of an obscure piece that had been lying unnoticed for more than fifty years. *Credat Apella.*

Moreover, if one comes to consider the matter, there were powerful causes at work in the minds of the early critics, which may very well have led them to assign an undue degree of importance to the *Cocalus*. Such causes would be mainly of two distinct kinds.

In the first place, there was the tendency, with which every student of ancient and mediæval criticism is familiar, to exaggerate the merits of certain individuals, and to ascribe to certain admittedly great names an even more extended influence than they actually possessed.[1] It seemed only natural, therefore, to the ancient critic to expect that Aristophanes, being admittedly the greatest of the comedians, should not only have profoundly influenced his own immediate field of art, but should also have laid the foundations of every subsequent form of comedy. The grammarian, therefore, who found in the story of the *Cocalus* a certain resemblance to stories with which he was familiar in the plays of the New Comedy, felt no hesitation in affirming that the *Cocalus* was actually the model on which these plays of the New Comedy were based, just as Platonius (p. xxxiv.) speaks of the *Aeolosicon* as ὁ τῆς μέσης κωμῳδίας τύπος.

In the second place, the story of the *Cocalus* had

[1] Thus, to quote one instance among many, the habit, common among the writers of the Empire, of describing Vergil as not only a supreme, but also a universal, genius, is sufficiently familiar. (Cp. Mart. viii. 18, &c.)

actually been converted into a "New" Comedy play—the *Hypobolimaeus* of Philemon[1]—and the existence of this neo-comic version of the story may very possibly have influenced the recollections of the original; for it is more than probable that the play of Philemon, while adopting the main features of the story as it appeared in Aristophanes, yet differed considerably in its general treatment of the erotic incidents. In other words, there is little reason to doubt that Philemon, actuated by the changed spirit of his time, developed the romantic capabilities of the story to the utmost, and gave a romantic interpretation to various situations, where nothing of the kind had been done or intended by Aristophanes. And hence the fact that a romantic version of the *Cocalus* was familiar, served to spread the idea that the original *Cocalus* was romantic also, and, as such, a forerunner of the romantic element in New Comedy, whereas, as a matter of fact, it was nothing of the kind, owing its romantic colouring entirely to the influence of the ideas disseminated by that New Comedy which it was erroneously supposed to inspire.

To sum up, then: There seems little reason to believe that the *Cocalus* is really as important for the history of the romantic element as would at first sight appear. Apart from the strong *prima facie* improbability of finding a romantic love-story in a play by Aristophanes, there is the further

---

[1] τὸν μέντοι Κώκαλον, τὸν ποιηθέντα Ἀραρότι τῷ Ἀριστοφάνους υἱῷ, Φιλήμων ὁ κωμικὸς ὑπαλλάξας ἐν Ὑποβολιμαίῳ ἐκωμῴδησεν. (Clem. Alex. *Strom.* vi. p. 267 [628].)

remarkable fact that the Aristophanic suggestion, if really given, found no one to take it up for more than fifty years. Again, while the legendary history of Cocalus and the fragments of the play, as far as such have been preserved, do not actually preclude the possibility that the erotic incident may have been treated in a romantic manner, they certainly furnish no evidence whatever in favour of such a view. There are, besides, various reasons which may have induced the ancient critics to see a greater resemblance between the *Cocalus* and the plays of the New Comedy than was actually present. On the whole, therefore, it would appear that the similarity between this work of Aristophanes and the romantic comedies of Menander and his followers, is merely an accidental and superficial one, and that it is incorrect to say, as some have done, that the latter class of composition was derived from or inspired by the former.

VI. THE POETS OF THE TRANSITION.

To return after this somewhat lengthy digression to our examination of the poets of the transition.

Plato, even more than his model Aristophanes, was a follower of the political school of Cratinus, revelling in personal attacks of the most violent kind, and hence there seems little reason to doubt that such of his plays as bear the stamp of Middle Comedy belong to his later period, and were only produced, decidedly *invita Minerva*, when the free license of abuse had been artificially checked. Hence the allusions in his works to women or erotic subjects seem to have been unusually scarce. In the *Adonis*, mention is made of the rival lovers of the hero, Aphrodite and Dionysus; but there is nothing to indicate that this play contained anything of the nature of a serious exposition of the respective claims of male and female love. The *Zeus Cacumenus* very probably introduced Zeus in his usual comic character of the adulterer, as did the *Nyx Macra*,[1] and the *Europe* may very possibly have treated of a similar subject. More original, however, and interesting than these is the *Phaon*, which seems to have been one of the poet's latest works, and which furnishes a good specimen of his manner of treating women. Phaon, having been presented by Aphrodite with the cosmetics which were to inspire universal passion, appears surrounded by a crowd of admiring women, who are, however, refused access to his presence, unless they perform certain propitiatory rites (*Fr.* 2), and otherwise prove themselves worthy of the honour. The means by which one lady eventually qualifies (*Fr.* 4) can only be guessed, but the language of *Fr.* 3 seems to suggest that the contest was somewhat after the manner of those described in *Anth. Pal.* v. 35 or Alciphron i. 39, 4 *seqq.*[2] The

---

[1] ἐπεπόλαζε γὰρ τότε ταῦτα, Ἡρακλῆς πεινῶν, καὶ Διόνυσος δειλός, καὶ μοιχὸς Ζεύς. Schol. *ad Aristoph. Pac.* 740. The *Zeus Cac.* of Plato is said to have borne a close resemblance to the *Daedalus* of Aristophanes, which certainly contained matter of this kind. Cp. Aristoph. *Daed. Fr.* 3.

[2] It is interesting to observe the absence, as far as one can judge, of any reference to Sappho, the favourite butt of a somewhat later school of comedians. Could the fact of this absence be conclusively proved, it would afford valuable evidence for determining the date of the origin of the Phaon and Sappho legend. The earliest reference to it at present known is, perhaps, that in the *Leucadia* of Menander.

interest of this piece lies in the fact that the plot is, despite its ribald handling, unequivocally a love-story, and, as such, perhaps distinct from any piece that we have hitherto had occasion to examine. That the love-story is, however, of the kind which belongs essentially to Middle Comedy, and has nothing whatever in common with those of the later romantic comedy, will become abundantly clear when we come to deal with the points of difference between these two schools of art.[1]

The information to be gained from the remains of the other poets of the transitional period is sadly scanty. The *Moechi* of Ameipsias, a play which, to judge by the title, might have thrown much light on the present subject, is hopelessly lost. Of the *Sappho* even the title is doubtful. The celebrated *Ichthys* of Archippus seems to have contained punning allusions to the Hetaerae Sepia and Aphye, a sign of the growing inclination to discuss this class of persons on the stage. The latter lady, or a namesake of hers, is mentioned by Callias in his *Cyclopes*. Of the *Atalanta* of the same writer, one line is preserved:

κέρδος αἰσχύνης ἄμεινον· ἕλκε μοιχὸν ἐς μυχόν,

which seems in some sort to suggest that episode in the life of the mythical Atalanta, daughter of Schoeneus, which led to her metamorphosis[2]; but, seeing that even the title *Atalanta* is doubtful, this conjecture cannot be considered as very certain. Strattis appears to have introduced Lais on the stage

---

[1] We may further observe the mention of Lais in *Fr.* 10 of this play.
[2] Cp. Ovid, *Met.* x. 686 *seqq*. The incident might be utilised in various ways.

in his *Macedones* (*Fr.* 5), and in his parodies of the *Medea*, the *Phoenissae*, &c., the female characters of Euripides doubtless came in for their full share of ridicule, though no definite evidence to this effect has been preserved.

A little more information is to be gained from the works of those poets who belonged to the very end of the period of transition. Thus, the plays of Theopompus, which deal almost exclusively with Middle Comedy subjects, furnish several instances of that treatment of female characters with which one is familiar in the plays of the Middle Comedy proper. The *Aphrodisia* introduces us to the Hetaerae celebrating their customary festival. *Fr.* 1 affords a specimen of the remarks passed on absent friends on such occasions,[1] while *Fr.* 2 gives further details of the festivities. The solitary but considerable fragment of the *Nemea* (called after the Hetaera of that name) gives a lively description of a scene in which an intending lover is doing his best to gain the approval of the lady's *lena*, a class which was, doubtless, as devoted then to the *curto vetus amphora collo* as it was 400 years later.[2] In the *Capelides* it is equally possible to get a glimpse of the action of the piece. A man dropping in at the bar of a house he has been in the habit of frequenting, and finding himself less effusively welcomed than he had had reason to hope

---

[1] Cp. Alciphron i. 39, 7. καταπαννυχίσασαι δ'οὖν καὶ τοὺς ἐραστὰς κακῶς εἰποῦσαι ... ᾠχόμεθα ἔξοινοι.

[2] *Vide* Athen. xi. 470 F. σπινθήρ in l. 8 seems not to be the proper-name of a slave, but may simply be translated "spark." The expression is as natural in Greek as in English, even if no other instance of this exact usage occurs.

(*Fr.* 3, 4), threatens to attack the proprietress and the rival of whom he is jealous (*Fr.* 5). Of the rest, the *Hedychares* described a wedding ceremony (*Fr.* 3),[1] the *Callaeschrus* contained an allusion to the expensiveness of certain Hetaerae, and general erotic allusions are not uncommon (*e.g. Odysseus* 1, *Medus* 2). The *Stratiotides* seems to have had some points in common with the *Ecclesiazusae* of Aristophanes. Alcaeus, who is one of the very latest in date of the writers usually ranked as belonging to the "Old" Comedy, deals in nearly all his plays with erotic subjects, mostly in the shape of mythological stories burlesqued. To this class belong the *Pasiphae*, the *Hierus Gamus*, the *Endymion*, the *Ganymedes*, and perhaps the *Callisto*, unless this be, like the *Palaestra*, named after an Hetaera. From this list of titles it may be seen that every style of love came in for treatment, but in no case are the fragments sufficiently numerous, for it to be possible even to hazard a guess as to what the nature of that treatment may have been. As to the plot of the *Adelphae Moecheuomenae*, we are equally in the dark, though the title seems to suggest the *Aeolosicon* of Aristophanes and the *Canace* of Euripides. Lastly, in the *Antea* of Eunicus and the *Thalatta* of Diocles, both named

---

[1] The "Hedychares" of the title seems to be Plato, so that it is rather tempting to imagine a scene something like the following. The hero, after dilating sufficiently on the virtues of "Platonic" love, is eventually discovered by one of the other characters, in company with a woman under circumstances which suggest the propriety of their getting married immediately—a fact which induces the intruder to exclaim :

φέρε σὺ τὰ καταχύσματα κ.τ.λ. (*Fr.* 3.)

The late date of this play (cp. *Fr.* 4) makes a plot of this kind by no means impossible, but, of course, *hariolandi est infinita libertas.*

after Hetaerae, we have two further instances of a class of piece with which we have been steadily growing more familiar, the nearer we have approached the confines of the typical "Middle" Comedy.

VII. THE MIDDLE COMEDY.

The poets of the transition, of whom we have just been speaking, have introduced us, more or less, to most, if not all, of the features which belong to the Middle Comedy proper; at the same time, it may not be amiss, for clearness' sake, to recapitulate briefly those features, in so far as they affect our immediate subject.

The points on which it is essential to concentrate the attention are three in number:—

(1) In Middle Comedy, the preponderance of politics as the main dramatic interest—a preponderance which, naturally, tended to exclude women from the stage—disappears, and, consequently, female characters step inevitably into a more prominent position.

(2) The restriction of the original license of Comedy, had led the comedians to devote their talents to parodying mythological subjects; the parodists of mythology would naturally find their readiest materials in the stories of the amours of the various gods, and hence erotic stories of a sort at once come to the fore.

(3) Middle Comedy being in great part, if not entirely, devoted to the realistic treatment of contemporary social life, the Hetaerae, who formed an

important feature in that life, were necessarily brought into prominence.[1]

Of these three main features,[2] the first two will not require special illustration,[3] but the last is one on which it will be necessary to dwell for some time.

---

[1] Great care must be taken not to misunderstand the causes of this prominence of the Hetaera in Middle Comedy. The fall of Athens, and the events immediately preceding it, resulted in a revolution of the Athenian social system, which was even more momentous than the political overthrow. From this time onwards, the individual appears at Athens as opposed to the state, in a manner that would not have been possible under the earlier *régime*. Hence in the Middle Comedy, which is perhaps the earliest individualistic poetry which Athens produced, ordinary habits and private life come to be treated with an interest and a realism which had never previously been attempted, and, as a consequence of this, the Hetaerae come to the fore in literature. This fact does not, therefore, imply that the position of these women in the thoughts of men was any higher than had previously been the case, or that there was a growing idea among the people that love for women was a worthy subject for artistic study and representation. It simply means, as will be abundantly clear later on, that the Hetaera was an important feature in private life, and that, therefore, when private life came to be represented on the stage, she was bound to appear there also, just in the same way and for the same reasons as the cook and the fishmonger, who are also such features of this literature.

[2] With the other distinctive features of Middle Comedy, though occasional reference may be made to them, we have less to do. It may not however be amiss, in passing, just to notice the spirit of the age, which, while it required personal attacks on men to be more or less veiled, allowed personal attacks of the fiercest description to be made on women openly by name. A remarkable instance of this is the *Antilais* of Epicrates, but it is far from being the only one. As for those Middle Comedies which are called after public men (*e.g.* the *Theramenes* of Cratinus junior), it would be easy to believe that these were all, as some of them certainly were, composed after the deaths of the persons whose names they bear, and that these names were simply used as types, in the way that Juvenal speaks of Tigellinus, &c.

[3] With regard to what we have described as the second feature of Middle Comedy, it may perhaps just be remarked that this constant habit of parodying and ridiculing love-stories would inevitably tend, in

The Hetaera-plays[1] are one of the most characteristic features of the fourth century; indeed, it may almost be said that admiration for the Hetaera, and ridicule of the wife, were the two main social canons of the period. These plays seem to have been realistic representations of contemporary life, and their general character is sufficiently demonstrated by the well-known retort of Antiphanes to Alexander;[2] but while they all thus have, as it were, a certain family likeness, it would appear, beyond doubt, that they may be also divided into two distinct classes, viz., those that have a distinct erotic plot, and those that have none, the latter naturally belonging to an earlier period of development than the former.

Plays dealing with Hetaerae were not, as we have already seen, exclusively a feature of the fourth-century Comedy, though the majority of such plays

some sort, to bring the whole matter of love into contempt. And that the feelings of contempt so produced, and the similar feelings which originated them, would act and react on one another till both became even more accentuated, was equally inevitable. Nor must it be forgotten that the influence of tragedy, which might otherwise have served to counteract this tendency, was much less than it had been at an earlier period, for the revivals and imitations of Euripides, which held the tragic stage throughout the century, popular though some of them may have been, belonged in spirit to the previous generation, and were thus to a certain extent out of touch with contemporary feeling.

[1] Many plays of this class are called after real or imaginary Hetaerae, such as the *Chrysis* of Antiphanes, &c., &c., but these are, of course, not the only ones that deal with the subject.

[2] Ἀντιφάνης ὁ κωμῳδοποιὸς ὡς ἀνεγίνωσκέ τινα τῷ βασιλεῖ Ἀλεξάνδρῳ τῶν ἑαυτοῦ κωμῳδιῶν, ὁ δὲ δῆλος ἦν οὐ πάνυ τι ἀποδεχόμενος· δεῖ γάρ, ἔφησεν, ὦ βασιλεῦ, τὸν ταῦτα ἀποδεχόμενον ἀπὸ συμβόλων τε πολλάκις δεδειπνηκέναι καὶ περὶ ἑταίρας πλεονάκις καὶ εἰληφέναι καὶ δεδωκέναι πληγάς. (Athen. xiii. 555A.)

does, of course, belong to this period. In the very beginnings of Comedy at Athens, we have at least three plays of this class from the pen of Pherecrates,[1] while, at a later period of the fifth century, other works of a similar character seem certainly to have appeared.

The general character of these plays, however, seems, in spite of the modernity of their subject, to have been essentially that prevailing during the early period to which they belong. Pherecrates and his imitators seem to have been merely concerned in drawing a picture—perhaps a somewhat burlesque one—of the general life of an Hetaera and her followers, and in dwelling upon the various comic incidents which might occur in her environment, without troubling to connect these incidents by means of any very definite story. In other words, the Hetaera-play of Pherecrates was still, in the main, that mixture of pantomime and variety-show with which one is familiar in Aristophanes, and with which one's ideas of the early Athenian Comedy are usually associated. And that plays of this class continued to be produced with success till well into the fourth century, there seems no reason to doubt.

The typical Hetaera-play of the Middle Comedy, however, is of an entirely different character. In this there is a definite plot, of which the Hetaera is the heroine, while the action of the piece is supplied by the struggles *de nocte locanda* of her various rival lovers. In fact, the Hetaera-play of Antiphanes or Alexis is a comedy in the modern sense of the word,

---

[1] [*Supra*, p. 128.]

while the Hetaera-play of an earlier period is still nothing but an extravaganza. The author of this great change is not known; perhaps it was Anaxandrides.

It is stated of Anaxandrides that he was the first to introduce ἔρωτας καὶ παρθένων φθοράς[1] into Comedy. This statement is, at first sight, rather difficult to understand, when one considers plays like the *Nemesis* of Cratinus, or the *Cocalus* of Aristophanes, not to speak of erotic episodes like the one which terminates the *Ecclesiazusae* of the latter writer; and it must be apparent that the mere introduction on the stage of such subjects cannot be the merit claimed by Suidas for Anaxandrides. The most simple explanation of the apparent anomaly would therefore seem to be, that what Suidas means to imply, is that Anaxandrides was the first to make erotic subjects the main interest of his plot, and to introduce his principal characters as taking part in them; for this, as we have already seen, was not the case with the earlier plays which dealt with erotic matters.

Whether this great advance was really due to Anaxandrides cannot, unfortunately, be proved with anything like certainty, for such fragments of his works as have survived are remarkably reticent on

---

[1] No one who is familiar with the Middle Comedy is likely to wish to maintain that the words παρθένων φθοράς imply that the plays of Anaxandrides were similar in character to such plays as the *Andria* or the *Adelphi* of Menander. The exact nature of the παρθένων ἔρωτες of the Middle Comedy, which form, in fact, an infinitesimal part of the erotic element in that literature, will be fully discussed lower down. [pp. 159, 213.]

this particular subject;[1] but there can be no doubt that it took place about his time, so that there is at least a strong probability, under the circumstances, that it was the result of his influence.

On the first and older class of Hetaera-play, it is useless to dwell further; a certain vague idea of their general nature is all that can be gained by the study of their fragments, and the external evidence as to their character is equally meagre, while the intentional want of coherence which marked their action makes it obviously absurd to endeavour in any way to reconstruct them. The character of the second and, for our purposes, more important class, will be best explained by a brief examination of one or two striking specimens, the remains of which are sufficiently important to render it possible to follow their story, at any rate for a certain distance.

Thus, in the *Campylion* of Eubulus, we are introduced to two men, one of whom sighs with quite modern plaintiveness over the heavy burden of his love for a certain κοσμία ἑταίρα:

> τίς ἦν ὁ γράψας πρῶτος ἀνθρώπων ἄρα
> ἢ κηροπλαστήσας Ἔρωθ᾽ ὑπόπτερον;
> ὡς οὐδὲν ᾔδει πλὴν χελιδόνας γράφειν,
> ἀλλ᾽ ἦν ἄπειρος τῶν τρόπων τῶν τοῦ θεοῦ.
> ἔστιν γὰρ οὔτε κοῦφος οὔτε ῥᾴδιος
> ἀπαλλαγῆναι τῷ φέροντι τὴν νόσον,
> βαρὺς δὲ κομιδῇ· πῶς ἂν οὖν ἔχοι πτερά
> τοιοῦτο πρᾶγμα; λῆρος, εἰ καὶ φησί τις.
> (*Fr.* 3 *ap.* Athen. xiii. 562C.)

---

[1] Curious in this connection is the fact that, while the *Captivi* of Plautus is the only extant play derived from Anaxandrides, it is, at the same time, the only extant play of Latin Comedy which is not concerned with erotic subjects.

Through the agency of the friend, who is evidently more of a man of the world, the lovers meet at a supper party, which was probably at least a *partie carrée*. Here the friend gives vent to various cynical remarks on women:—

> ὦ γαῖα κεραμί, τίς σε Θηρικλῆς ποτὲ
> ἔτευξε κοίλης λαγόνος εὐρύνας βάθος;
> ἦ που κατειδὼς τὴν γυναικείαν φύσιν
> ὡς οὐχὶ μικροῖς ἥδεται ποτηρίοις.
>
> (*Fr.* 2 *ap.* Athen. xi. 471 E.)

and, evidently a little sceptical as to the inviolable κοσμιότης of the lady, makes various efforts to induce her to commit herself, either by eating or drinking to excess[1] (*Fr.* 1, 5), or by displaying her talents in a questionable "song and dance." (*Fr.* 6.) His efforts seem, however, to be unsuccessful, and at the end of the evening the hero is as hopelessly in love as ever:—

> ὡς δ' ἐδείπνει κοσμίως, he exclaims,
> οὐκ ὥσπερ ἄλλαι, τῶν πράσων ποιούμεναι
> τολύπας, ἔσαττον τὰς γνάθους καὶ τῶν κρεῶν
> ἀπέβρυκον αἰσχρῶς, ἀλλ' ἑκάστου μικρὸν ἂν
> ἀπεγένεθ' ὥσπερ παρθένος Μιλησία.
>
> (*Fr.* 4 *ap.* Athen. xiii. 571 F.)

The *dénouement* of this interesting little story we do not know; let us hope it was a satisfactory one.

In the *Agonis* of Alexis again, we find a girl

---

[1] That τραγήματα was merely a polite word for drinking, seems clear from Alexis, *Polycleia*:—

> ὁ πρῶτος εὑρὼν κομψὸς ἦν τραγήματα·
> τοῦ συμποσίου γὰρ διατριβὴν ἐξευρέ πως
> κἀργοὺς ἔχειν μηδέποτε τὰς σιαγόνας.

remonstrating with her mother, who wishes her to accept a rich but dissolute lover in preference to the νεανίσκος of her choice.

> ὦ μῆτερ, ἱκετεύω σε, μὴ 'πίσειέ μοι
> τὸν Μισγόλαν· οὐ γὰρ κιθαρῳδός εἰμ' ἐγώ.

The mother, however, insists, in spite of the young man's professions of (imaginary?) wealth (*Fr.* 2), in carrying off her daughter to the rich lover's house, where, however, the hero also manages to turn up and make some cutting remarks on the family portraits (*Fr.* 3).[1] He then succeeds in making the mother drunk (*Fr.* 4), and so, we are led to believe—for the end is again veiled in obscurity—is enabled to elude her vigilance.[2]

Further evidence as to the character of this style of art may be obtained by studying several of the plays of Plautus, such as the *Truculentus*, the *Mercator*, or the *Mostellaria*, which seem to have been adapted directly from Greek works of this class, without being in any way influenced by the later romantic ideas.

But while the incidents which occur in the individual plays are naturally of an endless variety, certain broad features are recognisable throughout this literature.

Firstly, not only is love for an Hetaera enthusiastically praised, but it is specially described as the one

---

[1] σῦκα are doubtless used here in the same sense as "mariscae" in Iuv. ii. 13, or "ficus" in Mart. vii. 71.

[2] Or, perhaps, the νεανίσκος tries the effect of the θηρίκλεια on the girl herself (cp. the epigram of Hedylus, *Anth. Pal.* v. 199); *sed haec omnia incerta.* In any case, the scene seems somewhat to suggest that in Petr. 85 *seqq.*

love in life worth loving. The advantage of the Hetaera over the wife is such a stock subject, that it will be unnecessary to do more than mention one or two of the most striking passages in which the feeling finds expression, such as that cited in Athenaeus, xiii. 559 A, from the *Athamas* of Amphis:

> εἶτ' οὐ γυναικός ἐστιν εὐνοϊκώτερον
> γαμετῆς ἑταίρα; πολύ γε καὶ μάλ' εἰκότως.
> ἡ μὲν νόμῳ γὰρ καταφρονοῦσ' ἔνδον μένει,
> ἡ δ' οἶδεν ὅτι ἢ τοῖς τρόποις ὠνητέος
> ἄνθρωπός ἐστιν ἢ πρὸς ἄλλον ἀπιτέον.

or that quoted in the same place from the *Corinthiastes* of Philetaerus:

> ὡς τακερόν, ὦ Ζεῦ, καὶ μαλακὸν τὸ βλέμμ' ἔχει.
> οὐκ ἐτὸς ἑταίρας ἱερόν ἐστι πανταχοῦ,
> ἀλλ' οὐχὶ γαμετῆς οὐδαμοῦ τῆς Ἑλλάδος.

But this is not all. The advantages of Hetaera-love over adultery are expounded after a fashion that cannot fail to be startling to anyone who has not formed a clear conception of what "love" meant in the Athens of Demosthenes. A striking instance of this occurs in the *Nannion* of Eubulus,[1] and the same idea is still further developed in the *Pentathlus* of Xenarchus.

---

[1] ὅστις λέχη γὰρ σκότια νυμφεύει λάθρᾳ,
πῶς οὐχὶ πάντων ἐστὶν ἀθλιώτατος;
ἐξὸν θεωρήσαντι πρὸς τὸν ἥλιον,
γυμνὰς ἐφεξῆς ἐπὶ κέρως τεταγμένας,
ἐν λεπτοπήνοις ὕφεσιν ἑστώσας, οἵας
Ἠριδανὸς ἁγνοῖς ὕδασι κηπεύει κόρας,
μικροῦ πρίασθαι κέρματος τὴν ἡδονήν,
καὶ μὴ λαθραίαν κύπριν, αἰσχίστην νόσων
πασῶν, διώκειν, ὕβρεος οὐ πόθου χάριν.

As for that "love of a man for a maid," which is, so to speak, the very essence of the love-element in later Greek literature, it is simply ignored in Middle Comedy. A girl that one is going to marry has all the disadvantages of a wife, but for one thing. While the wife *in esse* is, as a later writer feelingly expresses it, "an immortal necessary evil," and, therefore, cannot be altogether escaped from, there is no need to meet troubles halfway by drawing attention to the wife *in posse*. Let us eat and drink, for to-morrow we marry; and while we do so, let us have no Alexandrian skeleton at the feast to remind us of the fatal hour. And so, if the question be asked, "What did the Middle Comedy writers think of such love?" the answer is, "They did not think of it at all."[1]

And this will serve to introduce us to a further question, in the answer to which lies the key to the whole of this part of our subject. What is actually meant by the "love" which we hear so often ex-

---

[1] The one or two apparent exceptions to this rule, such as those in the *Marathonii* of Timocles or the *Philaulus* of Theophilus, are in reality no exceptions at all. This will be clear enough if we consider what is meant in these passages by a κόρη, and do not confuse the sentiment there expressed with a sentiment which does not occur till a later period. The κόρη in question (a κιθαρίστρια in the *Philaulus*) is merely an Hetaera *in posse* instead of *in esse*, an Hetaera who has not yet entered into regular business, and herein consists her superiority from the point of view of those who do not share Diogenes' view as to the parallel between women and houses. That her attractions do not differ in kind from those of the regular Hetaera will be plain enough to anyone who takes the trouble to turn to the passage in the *Marathonii*, and that the character of the "love" she inspires is also similar will be equally apparent from the same lines. That this was the character of the παρθένων ἔρωτες with which, according to Suidas, Anaxandrides dealt, seems beyond question.

pressed for these Hetaerae? The answer may be simple and brief: *ornari res ipsa vetat, contenta doceri*: the love of the Middle Comedy is animal passion, pure and simple; the Hetaera caters for the appetites of the time in exactly the same way, even if in a different sphere, as the cook and the fishmonger, of whom we also hear so much, both to praise and blame, in this literature.[1] Of love in the modern sense of the word, of love as distinct from lust, there is nowhere any suggestion in the writers of the Middle Comedy. This fact is so patent to anyone who is familiar with the plays of this period, that one may, perhaps, be spared the trouble of its illustration. If anyone is inclined to doubt it, let him open the third volume of Meineke's *Comic Fragments* at random, and read; he will soon be satisfied.

When this is the case, it is not surprising that we find "Platonic" love held up to consistent ridicule during the time of the Middle Comedy. A sufficiently striking example of this method is the passage quoted in Athenaeus, xiii. 563 C, from the *Dithyrambus* of Amphis:

> τί φῄς; σὺ ταυτὶ προσδοκᾷς πείθειν ἐμέ,
> ὡς ἔστ' ἐραστὴς ὅστις, ὡραῖον φιλῶν,
> τρόπων ἐραστής ἐστι, τὴν ὄψιν παρείς;
> ἄφρων γ' ἀληθῶς. κ.τ.λ.   [*Fr.* 2.]

But the clearest proof of all is that furnished by the fact that Plato himself, and Sappho, whose style of love was, as we have already had occasion to observe,[2] recognised as similar in spirit to that

---

[1] Alexis himself says this, in almost as many words, in the passage quoted below, p. 163.   [2] *Supra*, p. 85.

advocated by the philosopher, are, perhaps, the two favourite butts for the wit of the Middle Comedy. That the *Plato* of Aristophon, like the *Hedychares* of Theopompus, of which we have already spoken, and the *Sappho* of Antiphanes, Amphis, Ephippus, and Timocles, were, at least some of them, in part devoted to this subject, it seems only reasonable to believe, while sporadic allusions to the matter are, of course, sufficiently common. The one possible exception to this general rule appears in the *Helene* of Alexis, where a character is introduced upholding the Platonic view of love; but it would be bold, in the face of so much evidence on the other side, to assert that this isolated statement in any way indicates the general tone of the comedy in question. It is far more likely that the champion of these views (perhaps Theseus[1]) was made to see the error of his ways and repent his lost opportunities before the play was out.

And akin in spirit to the above is the tendency, so common that it hardly needs special illustration, to throw ridicule on the married state and on family life in general.[2] When the man, who is called the

[1] The "Platonic" nature of Theseus' admiration for the undeveloped charms of Helen is a well-known feature of the legend. A comparison with Aristoph. *Thesmoph. B, Fr.* 26, seems to suggest a further reason why Theseus should have been introduced as a mock "Platonic" lover. Cp. Phot. s.v. κυσολάκων. τὸ δὲ τοῖς παιδικοῖς χρῆσθαι λακωνίζειν ἔλεγον. Ἑλένῃ (so Ruhnken for Μελαίνῃ) γὰρ Θησεὺς οὕτως ἐχρήσατο.

[2] In this connection we may remark that the tendency of the mythological stories commonly parodied by Middle Comedy was also almost entirely in this direction. The Ζεὺς μοιχός with whom the Athenian audience of the day was so familiar, was hardly the type of character to inspire respect for married life. How different was the New Comedy treatment of the adulterer, we shall see further on.

M

originator of the erotic element in Middle Comedy, can write words like these:

> ὅστις γαμεῖν βουλεύετ', οὐ βουλεύεται
> ὀρθῶς, διότι βουλεύεται χοὔτω γαμεῖ,
>
> (Anaxandrides, *Incert.* 1.)

and mean them, there can be little doubt as to the tendency of that erotic element which he was the first to introduce. In fact, not only is marriage a favourite subject of ridicule, but it is one on which the writers of this period make some of their happiest remarks. There are few things in Antiphanes as good as the passage in the *Philopator*, where one man, meeting another, enquires after a friend, and hears that he has got married.

> τί σὺ λέγεις; he exclaims in horror. ἀληθινῶς
> γεγάμηκεν, ὃν ἐγὼ ζῶντα περιπατοῦντά τε
> κατέλιπον;

Alexis is seldom as amusing as when he proclaims (*Incert.* 34) marriage worse than disfranchisement.

> εἶτ' οὐχὶ κρεῖττόν ἐστι τῷ γ' ἔχοντι νοῦν
> ἄτιμον εἶναι μᾶλλον ἢ γυναῖκ' ἔχειν;
> πολλῷ γε· τοὺς μὲν γοῦν ἀτίμους οὐκ ἐᾷ
> ἀρχὴν λαχόντας ὁ νόμος ἄρχειν τῶν πέλας·
> ἐπὰν δὲ γήμῃς, οὐδὲ σαυτοῦ κύριον
> ἔξεστιν εἶναι.

Such, then, is the erotic element of the Middle Comedy—the praise of sensuality and the ridicule of all that is ennobling or virtuous. Alexis tells us all when he says:

τὰς ἡδονὰς δεῖ συλλέγειν τὸν σώφρονα.
τρεῖς δ' εἰσὶν αἵ γε τὴν δύναμιν κεκτημέναι
τὴν ὡς ἀληθῶς συντελοῦσαν τῷ βίῳ,
τὸ πιεῖν, τὸ φαγεῖν, τὸ τῆς Ἀφροδίτης τυγχάνειν.
τὰ δ' ἄλλα προσθήκας ἅπαντα χρὴ καλεῖν.
(*Incert.* 31.)

Processit Vesper Olympo. It was time the Macedonian barbarians swept all this away and made place for cleaner things.[1]

VIII. THE NEW COMEDY.

The feeling on passing from the Middle to the New Comedy is like the fresh air on coming out of the bar of a public-house. The Middle Comedy is the last decaying branch of the old literature; the romantic New Comedy is one of the earliest and most vigorous offshoots of that new literature which sprang from the genius of Antimachus, and has continued to the present day. In the Middle Comedy, we are still face to face with the women of typical Athens, with the women of Aristophanes, at best with the women of Euripides,—and with the way in which typical Athens treated these women; in the New Comedy this is changed, and woman—the woman that can be loved as wife and mother—steps into her true place as object of, and partner in, the intensest and the purest passions of which humanity is capable.

It will be remembered that the Middle Comedy treatment, of women and love for women, had four main characteristics.

---

[1] Another phase of the Middle Comedy treatment of women, the discussion of which here would lead us too far away from our immediate subject, will be considered in Excursus I.

(1) The glorification of the Hetaera and of love for the Hetaera.

(2) The purely sensual nature of the love thus extolled.

(3) The ridicule of all love that was not sensual.

(4) The ridicule of family-life.

The New Comedy flatly contradicts every one of these principles. The love of which it treats is love for a *virgin*,[1] and the consummation of this love is *marriage*. Such love is by no means purely sensual; indeed, at times it is almost of a "Platonic" character. And lastly, not only is the sanctity of marriage strictly insisted upon, and the advantages of marriage as a system strongly maintained, but the family relations, anyhow among the younger generation, are often of a very pleasant character.

In fact, while the action of the Middle Comedy is concerned with a love, the consummation of which is a temporary sensual gratification, the action of the New Comedy is supplied by the efforts of its heroes and their adherents, to secure that the love which occupies so much of their thoughts may be made at once legitimate and permanent. It was New Comedy that first introduced on the stage the love of a life, as opposed to the love of an hour. If anyone were to ask what was the chief merit of Menander, the answer would be that he was the first to show the Athenians that "love for ever,"

---

[1] That the ψευδοκόρη, as the Athenian stage-managers rather quaintly called her—a class of character sufficiently common, it must be admitted—differs *toto caelo* from the regular Hetaera, is almost too obvious to need mention.

with which every poetaster and novel-reader has now been familiar for so many centuries.

But the differences between the treatment of women in the new literature, and that to which they were exposed in the literature we have just been studying, will be most readily made clear if we proceed at once to the detailed examination of the former.

The first and most prominent feature of the New Comedy treatment of the love of men for women is its insistence on marriage—that is to say, on a definite guarantee of permanence and constancy—as the one proper consummation of such love. In fact, as we have already had occasion to observe in another place, the idealisation of marriage is the basis of Greek romance.[1]

This insistence on marriage is, of course, most strikingly exemplified in the typical New Comedy plot, which is sufficiently familiar to every student of the Latin comedians. Thus, in five of these Latin plays, the *Heauton Timorumenos* (of Menander), the *Phormio* (of Apollodorus), the *Rudens* (of Diphilus), the *Curculio*, and the *Poenulus*,[2] the story is of exactly the kind that subsequently appears in the Greek novel—a young man falls in love with a virgin, and, after various misfortunes which threaten to separate the pair, they are eventually married, and live happily ever afterwards.

---

[1] *Supra*, p. 109.
[2] Of the *Casina*, which would appear at first sight to belong to this class, we shall speak in another place. [The Excursus, dealing with this subject, seems not to have been written; comp. Excursus K.]

On this class of plot it is unnecessary to dwell, except that it may be worth while just to draw attention to the extremely passionate nature of the love which makes these young men so anxious to marry. The modern reader would instinctively expect that the confinement of love to these legitimate and, as one would now consider them, commonplace channels, would inevitably lead to a lessening of its charm, and a diminution of its force. As a matter of fact, the result was the very reverse. Not only has the character of man's love for woman changed, but this love has developed an intensity of poetry and passion which has never belonged to it before.[1] Instances are easy to find; the most striking one is perhaps shown us at the meeting of Phaedromus and Planesium, in the *Curculio* (i. 3):

> PL. tene me, amplectere ergo! PH. hoc etiam est quamobrem cupiam vivere.
> quia te prohibet herus, clam hero potior. PL. prohibet, nec prohibere quit,
> nec prohibebit, nisi mors meum animum abs te abalienaverit.
> PH. sibi sua habeant regna reges, sibi divitias divites,
> sibi honores sibi virtutes sibi pugnas sibi proelia!
> dum mi abstineant invidere, sibi quisque habeant quod suum est![2]

---

[1] It is hard for us, in our generation, to realise what the first dawn of pure love for women must have meant to the men who saw it. It needs a conscious effort of will to clean away from one's eyes and one's heart the dust of the centuries, and to look back clearly; but if once the effort be successfully made, it is no longer hard to understand why, at the end of the fourth century, the pure girl was a more inspiring ideal than "the woman with a past," and why the παρθένος could stir depths of passion that the ἑταίρα had left untouched.

[2] These last lines are very suggestive of Theocr. viii. 53. It is worth noticing that in this play (v. 2, 72) the girl is specially asked whether she is willing to marry.

But there are others, almost equally forcible, in the *Rudens* (iv. 8)—where particular enthusiasm is expressed at the prospect of marriage, as opposed to the relation which had previously been the lover's highest possible ideal,—the *Poenulus* (v. 4, 49)[1], and elsewhere.

But another and equally important type of story is that in which the man first seduces the woman, and then subsequently marries her. Plays of this description are the *Andria*, the *Eunuchus*, the *Adelphi* (all by Menander), the *Aulularia*, and the *Cistellaria*.[2]

Of these, the *Cistellaria* is different from the rest. Here, the girl Silenium, who, though supposed to be the daughter of a *lena*, has been brought up as a virgin (i. 3, 24), is induced by a promise of marriage to live with the man Alcesimarchus, a promise which is afterwards fulfilled only after a considerable delay. (i. 1, 90-100.) In the other four cases, however— and this is very important—the promise of marriage is subsequent to the seduction, and takes the form, not of an inducement to, but of a reparation for the latter. The lover regards the seduction as a crime, for which he is willing to make amends to the utmost of his power, while at the same time he is anxious to perpetuate and legalise his amour. He therefore adopts what we are accustomed in modern times to call an "honourable course," and

---

[1] "patrue mi, ita me di amabunt ut, ego si sim Iuppiter,
    iam hercle ego illanc uxorem ducam, et Iunonem extrudam foras!"
    etc.
[2] Probably by Menander. At any rate, *Cistell.* i. 1, 90 *seqq.* is a translation of Menand. *Incert.* 32.

offers marriage to the woman whom he has loved and still loves. The importance of this feature is twofold—firstly, the close association thus brought about between marriage and love of the most "romantic" and unconventional description; and secondly, the perpetuation and legalisation of a form of love which is obviously by nature temporary and illegitimate. And thus the love-stories of the New Comedy may be said to begin where those of the Middle Comedy end; while the heroes of the latter are concerned with achieving the temporary satisfaction of their sensual desires, the heroes of the former are occupied in striving to make permanent atonement for the indiscretions which such desires have led them to commit.

To quote instances of what has been said: in the *Andria* the promise of marriage is distinctly an act of reparation, which the lover feels himself in duty bound to make. This is evident from the argument of Sulpicius Apollinaris,[1] and from various passages in the play.[2] The same is the case in the *Adelphi*.[3] Here Aeschinus, as soon as he considers what he has done, comes to the mother of Pamphila, and begs with tears to be allowed to marry her by way of reparation.[4] In the *Aulularia*, the petition of Lyconides to the miser Euclio is animated by a very

---

[1] "Glycerium vitiat Pamphilus,
gravidaque facta dat fidem, uxorem sibi
fore hanc," etc.

[2] *e.g.* Ter. *And.* i. 5, 36 *seqq.*, iv. 2, 11 *seqq.*

[3] In the *Adelphi* of Menander, this feature was, in all probability, even more prominent than it is in Terence's contaminated version.

[4] Ter. *Adelph.* iii. 2, 34 *seqq.*; cp. iii. 4, 23 *seqq.*

similar spirit.[1] In the *Eunuchus* (which is, it must be remembered, the love-story of a boy of sixteen)[2], there is no opportunity for any such behaviour on the part of Chaerea, though his sincere regret (ii. 3, 33 *seqq.*), and his enthusiasm when the possibility of marriage becomes apparent (v. 8, 1 *seqq.*), show clearly enough that he is not intended to be an exception to the general rule.

It must not, however, be supposed that the feeling, which prompts the various characters of whom we have spoken to make reparation for their wrong-doing, is merely a feeling of repentance, or a regard for public opinion. It is love, and love of a most passionate kind, that makes them so anxious to marry the women they have wronged. Of the enthusiasm of the hero of the *Eunuchus* at the prospect of marriage we have already spoken; in the *Adelphi*, Aeschinus is equally elated under similar circumstances;[3] in the *Aulularia*, the anxiety and persistency of Lyconides are evidently inspired by the same feeling;[4] in the *Andria*, Pamphilus protests that nothing short of death will divide him from Glycerium.[5] That love which the Middle Comedy could not conceive of as outliving its sensual gratification, appears in the New Comedy, not weakened, but strengthened by time, and obstacles only serve to make the lover more determined to perpetuate and to legalise those emotions

---

[1] Plaut. *Aulul.* iv. 10.
[2] Cp. Ter. *Eun.* iv. 4, 26.   [3] Ter. *Adelph.* iv. 5, 62 *seqq.*
[4] Cp. Plaut. *Aulul.* iv. 7 and 10; the conclusion of the play, in which the marriage of the hero was finally settled, is lost.
[5] Ter. *And.* iv. 2, 14.

which had, to a previous generation, owed their chief charm to their freedom from the restraints of constancy and propriety.

In the *Hecyra* again, it is by marriage that, through a strange coincidence, the hero is eventually able to repair the wrong done to the heroine. In the *Stichus*, too, the plot turns on the constancy of two wives to their absent husbands,[1] while, in the *Trinummus*, there seems strong reason to believe that it is not all love for Lesbonicus which makes Lysiteles so anxious to marry the former's sister.[2]

To this evidence from the plays themselves may be added some further evidence of a more general kind. Marriage is mentioned by the anonymous author of the epigram in the *C. I. G.* 6083, as the most characteristic feature of Menander's plays—

φαιδρὸν ἑταῖρον Ἔρωτος ὁρᾷς, σειρῆνα θεάτρων,
τόνδε Μένανδρον, ἀεὶ κρᾶτα πυκαζόμενον,
οὕνεκ' ἄρ' ἀνθρώπους ἱλαρὸν βίον ἐξεδίδαξεν,
ἡδύνας σκηνὴν δράμασι πᾶσι γάμῳ.

Still more emphatic is the testimony of Plutarch, who asserts (*Sympos.* vii. 712 C) that Menander is peculiarly suited for married men to hear and read—

ἔχει δὲ καὶ τὰ ἐρωτικὰ παρ' αὐτῷ καιρὸν πεπωκόσιν ἀνθρώποις καὶ ἀναπαυσαμένοις μετὰ μικρὸν ἀπιοῦσι παρὰ τὰς ἑαυτῶν γυναῖκας ... αἵ τε φθοραὶ τῶν παρθένων εἰς γάμον ἐπιεικῶς καταστρέφουσι. κ.τ.λ.

Indeed, the essentially "proper" character of the Menandrean drama is emphasised by more than one

---

[1] Here, too, there can be little doubt that in the original (the *Philadelphi* of Menander), this erotic element was more prominent than it is in the Latin. [2] Cp. Plaut. *Trin.* v. 1, 1 *seqq.*; 2, 64.

ancient writer. That Comedy could be anything but indecent was a revelation to Athens of the fourth century, and it was a revelation for which she does not seem to have been particularly grateful; but the fact that it was a writer whose works were fit "pueris virginibusque legi," who revolutionized the dramatic art, is one that a modern student of that revolution cannot afford to forget.[1]

Two of the plays mentioned above, the *Hecyra* and the *Stichus*, lead naturally to the consideration of another feature of the New Comedy treatment of marriage—a feature which, though less strongly marked than that of which we have just been speaking, is yet, if one considers what Greek feeling had previously been on this matter, perhaps even more remarkable. Not only is marriage held up as the lover's ideal, but the actual married state is described as a state of happiness, and married people, even those who have been married for some time, are introduced to us as strongly attached to one another. How complete a revolution in Greek feeling such a state as this implies, need hardly be emphasised.[2] Yet, in the *Stichus*, we have a plot based on the determination of two women to remain faithful to their husbands (who have been absent for

---

[1] Some further interesting evidence on this subject will be discussed later. [Cp. p. 189; but the reference seems to be to a part of the work which was not written.]

[2] In Tragedy, of course, the faithful and loving wife was not so entirely unknown. The Athenian might accept an Alcestis, who lived in pre-historic and heroic times, though even here his natural tendency was to jeer (cp. Aristoph. *Equit.* 1251); but, imagine such a character in Comedy, which was taken from real contemporary life? The idea was preposterous.

three years) in spite of the efforts of their father to induce them to do otherwise; they insist on remaining faithful, though their husbands are poor (Plaut. *Stich.* i. 2, 75 *seqq.*), and though they are uncertain whether their devotion is returned (i. 1, 36 *seqq.*). In the *Hecyra* again, it is the behaviour of Philumena after marriage which wins her husband's heart (Ter. *Hec.* i. 2, 85 *seqq.*)—a remarkably modern form of love-story.

Various fragments, too, of Menander have a similar import, such as the famous passage from the *Misogynes* on the advantages of marriage—

ἐλθόντ' εἰς νόσον
τὸν ἔχοντα ταύτην ἐθεράπευσεν ἐπιμελῶς,
ἀτυχοῦντι συμπαρέμεινεν, ἀποθανόντα τε
ἔθαψε, περιέστειλεν οἰκείως. (*Fr.* 1, 9.)

or Menand. *Incert.* 73, where the husband takes up the cudgels in his wife's behalf. *Incert.* 101, again, dwells on the close relationship existing between man and wife—

οἰκεῖον οὕτως οὐδέν ἐστιν, ὦ Λάχης,
ἐὰν σκοπῇ τις, ὡς ἀνήρ τε καὶ γυνή,

Incert. 100 points out that a wife must rule her husband by love—

ἕν ἐστ' ἀληθὲς φίλτρον, εὐγνώμων τρόπος.
τούτῳ κατακρατεῖν ἀνδρὸς εἴωθεν γυνή,

and a careful reader will have no difficulty in finding other more or less important examples of the same spirit, both in Menander and in the Latin Comedians.

One important exception there is, of course, to

this state of affairs, and that is the relation between the old men and their wives. The types of the henpecked husband and the Xanthippe-like wife are too familiar to need illustration. But here it is to be observed, that the husbands who appear in this position, are always old or elderly men, and this fact is probably not without its significance. In describing his elderly married men as unhappy, Menander was ridiculing, not marriage, but the *mariages de convenance* which had, before his time, been the regular thing at Athens. "These men are unhappy," says Menander, "not because they are married, but because they have married wives whom they never loved, and whom they chose merely because of their money, or to please their relations. If they had married for love, the case might well have been different." And thus the hen-pecked husband, who belongs to the old *régime*, is only a further argument in favour of the romantic love-matches of which Menander approved.

Of course the matter did not stop here. It was so easy to raise a laugh with a row between husband and wife, that Comedy was sure not to abandon the subject, even after its *raison d'être* had disappeared; and a modern audience, we know, is just as ready to laugh at the husband who has lost his latch-key as were the Athenians of the fourth century. But the point to be remembered is, that a pair of characters like Chremes and Sostrata in the *Heauton Timorumenus*, or Laches and Sostrata in the *Hecyra*, furnishes no real argument against the view that Menander and his followers of the New Comedy regarded marriage, if properly entered upon, as a state of happiness.

Another exception, and one that is perhaps in reality a more important one, is furnished by Menander's *Misogynes*, a work which gained very great popularity, doubtless owing to the way in which it appealed to the lower instincts of the audience whom its author was trying to educate up; but here it has to be observed that, in the first place, as the play is lost, it is impossible to say what the actual *dénouement* was; while, secondly, there was no reason why a man of Menander's versatile genius should not for once treat the subject of married life in an unusual manner, without in any way abandoning his general views on the subject.[1]

A further feature of the New Comedy treatment of marriage is the universal respect for its sanctity.[2] The adulterer, who is the favourite hero of mediaeval romance, is here invariably held up to contempt and hatred. The most familiar instance of this is, of course, the story in the *Miles Gloriosus* of Plautus, but it is far from being an isolated one. The *Halieis* of Menander evidently treated of a somewhat similar subject,[3] which appears once more in the *Eunuchus*.[4] In the *Andria* again, Charinus is horror-stricken at

[1] It is of course obvious that characters such as Clitipho in the *Heauton Timorumenus*, or Lesbonicus in the *Trinummus*, do not regard matrimony with much enthusiasm, but, in all these cases, the reasons for their objection are so apparent that no one would consider them as real exceptions to the general rule that the *young man* of the New Comedy looks on marriage with favour.

[2] And here one may remark at once that the incontinence of women, which is one of the favourite subjects both of Aristophanes and of Euripides, is nowhere emphasised in New Comedy.

[3] Cp. *Fr.* 10.   [4] Cp. Ter. *Eun.* v. 4, 21 *seqq.*

the idea of committing adultery with the woman he loves, though, when accused of seducing the same woman, his only regret is that he cannot plead guilty to the charge.[1] An even more remarkable instance, and one perhaps without parallel, is furnished by the *Hecyra*, where the Hetaera Bacchis asserts that she had refused to admit her lover, Pamphilus, as soon as she learned that he was married.[2] It may be argued, of course, that she did this out of pique, but the very cordial nature of the meeting between the two (Ter. *Hec.* v. 4, 16, *seqq.*), and the fact that Bacchis knew that her lover had abandoned her sorely against his will (i. 2, 45 *seqq.*), and was still devoted to her (i. 2, 82), seem to suggest that this is not the most natural explanation of her conduct.[3]

---

[1] Ter. *And.* ii. 1, 15 and 25. [The author is assuming that the words "quam vellem!" in the latter passage, are spoken by Charinus, not by Pamphilus: the editors differ on this point.] This curious passage furnishes a further instance, if further instances be needed, of the fact that what the Greek required of a woman for a love-match was not so much physical purity as constancy to a particular lover. Hence we find that by far the greater mass of Greek romantic love-poetry is addressed, not to virgins, but to women to whom the writer is, in one way or another, married. Thus, too, in the romance of Xenophon Ephesius, the adventures of the lovers all take place after marriage (the wedding occurs already in chapter viii of book I.), and in this the *Ephesiaca* are at least as Greek as, if not more so than the *Pastoralia* of Longus, or the novel of Eumathius, where the most ridiculous and desperate expedients have to be resorted to in order that the heroine may preserve her virginity till the end of the last chapter. But this whole matter will be more fully discussed when we come to consider the Callimachean ideal of woman. [The reference is to a part of the work which was not completed.]

[2] Ter. *Hec.* v. 1, 24 *seqq.*; cp. i. 2, 82.

[3] The *Casina* (of Diphilus) and the *Orge* of Menander seem equally emphatic on the point, but as both these plays belong, strictly speaking, to Middle Comedy, which had other and less romantic reasons for decrying adultery, they need not be further noticed here.

The passages just described may serve to introduce us to a further feature of our subject—a feature in which the New Comedy is, if possible, even more remarkably unlike the Middle Comedy than in those which have already been discussed. In the Middle Comedy, as we have already had frequent occasion to observe, the wife and the husband are invariably held up to ridicule when compared with the Hetaera and her lover; in the New Comedy we may find this position exactly reversed. Instances are rare, (as is indeed to be expected, when we consider, in the first place, the strong current of popular feeling on the subject, and, secondly, the personal relations between the leading writers of the New Comedy and the prominent Hetaerae of the time,) but they do unquestionably occur. The most striking example is perhaps that in the *Heauton Timorumenus*, where not only is the Hetaera contrasted unfavourably with the virgin, (as she herself admits,)[1] but her lover is made consistently ridiculous as compared with the lover who contemplates marriage, and in the end comes off badly in the extreme. Very similar evidence is furnished by the *Hecyra*. In the struggle for the love of Pamphilus, which takes place in that play between the wife and the Hetaera, the former is completely successful, and her victory is gained by sheer amiability of temper (Ter. *Hec.* i. 2, 85 *seqq.*); indeed, so charming is she, that the Hetaera is

---

[1] Cp. Ter. *Heaut. Tim.* ii. 4, 1 *seqq.*
edepol te, mea Antiphila, laudo et fortunatam iudico,
id cum studuisti, isti formae ut mores consimiles forent, etc.
words which raise strange memories of a well-known passage in the *Dame aux Camélias.*

driven in the end to congratulate her husband on his good fortune in having married her. (v. 4, 22.) And this victory of the wife becomes the more remarkable, when we observe that the Hetaera is evidently intended to be a very favourable specimen of her class, in every way deserving of the lover she is compelled to lose.[1]

While on this point, it may not be amiss to remark that it is by no means impossible that the famous *Thais* of Menander really belonged to this class of plays, and that the Hetaera, who gives her name to the piece, is intended as a *parody* on the typical Hetaera of Middle Comedy. This view, which is not improbable in itself, receives some support from the mock-heroic tone of *Fr.* 1 of the *Thais*,[2] and still more from Mart. xiv. 187;[3] but cannot, of course, be regarded as more than a possible suggestion.[4]

Of mere vulgar ridicule or abuse of the ordinary Hetaera, as heartless,[5] mercenary,[6] and the like,

---

[1] Cp. *inter alia*, v. 1, 30; 3, 35.

[2] ἐμοὶ μὲν οὖν ἄειδε τοιαύτην, θεά, κ.τ.λ.

[3] "haec. (*sc.* Thais Menandri) primum iuvenum lascivos lusit amores;" where *lusit* must almost certainly mean "parodied" or "ridiculed," and *lascivos amores* "Hetaera-loves" as opposed to the more orthodox amours of which the New Comedy proper treats.

[4] In any case, however, it is tempting to read in Prop. ii. 6, 3:
      turba Menandreae fuerit nec Thaidos olim
      tanta in qua *populum* lusit *Erichthonium.*

[5] *E.g.* Plaut. *Cist.* i. 1, 66.
    SL. at mihi cordolium est.
    GY. quid id? unde est tibi cordolium, commemora, obsecro, quod neque ego habeo neque quisquam alia mulier, ut perhibent viri?

[6] *E.g.* Plaut. *Trin.* ii. 1, 15 *seqq.* etc., etc.

there is, of course, enough and to spare; but it would be unjustifiable to claim expressions such as these as distinctive of New Comedy, in the face of passages like Epicrates, *Antilais*, 2, or Anaxilas, *Neottis*, 1. Menander indeed makes a more serious charge, perhaps, when one of his characters asserts that an Hetaera cannot be good, for she makes a trade of sin:

οὐδέποθ' ἑταίρα τοῦ καλῶς πεφρόντικεν,
ἣ τὸ κακόηθες πρόσοδον εἴωθεν ποιεῖν.
(*Incert.* 107.)

This is, however, an isolated expression, for Menand. *Incert.* 36, at first sight similar, is really different.

But, though the writers of the New Comedy are careful, as a general rule, to avoid anything that might have seemed too severe a stricture on that system of Hetaera-worship which was so distinctive a feature of the age, they are unmistakably emphatic in their assertion that such sensual love is not the only kind of love of which a man is capable. The chivalrous manner in which the lover of New Comedy often behaves to his lady, is one of the clearest features of the change which the authors of the romantic school had succeeded in bringing about on the Athenian stage.

At once the most striking and the most perplexing illustration of this is furnished by the character of Thrasonides in Menander's celebrated play, the *Misumenus*. This Thrasonides, who belongs to the regular type of the *Miles Gloriosus*, is in love with a slave-girl, whom he has obtained in the course of his wars;[1] but he has so disgusted her with his boasting (like Leontichus in Lucian) that she has conceived a most violent hatred for him. He then, though she is his slave, and though his passion is so great that he cannot sleep for thinking of her,[2] instead of using his undoubted power to accomplish what he wishes,[3] tries every means that he can imagine in order to conciliate her, "sending her gifts, and weeping, and praying,"[4] that she may look more favourably upon him.

The *dénouement* of the play is lost. It is not impossible that in the end the slave-girl was identified as an Athenian, and carried off by some more acceptable lover, who thus profited by the chivalrous conduct of his rival, or she may even have turned out to be the soldier's sister, as in the *Curculio* or the *Epidicus*, in either of which cases the scruples of Thrasonides would be necessary to the working of the plot. But all this is, for our present purpose, of no importance. What is of importance, and of the utmost importance, is the fact that Thrasonides, though he is so violently in love with the girl, will not make use of his unquestioned power to gratify this passion, because of the dislike which she feels for him. In fact, his love is of such a kind that he

---

[1] παιδισκάριόν με καταδεδούλωκ' εὐτελές,
ὃν οὐδὲ εἷς τῶν πολεμίων οὐπώποτε. (*Fr.* 3.)
Cp. Arrian, *Dissert. Epictet.* iv. 1.

[2] Cp. *Fr.* 10, 11.

[3] παρ' ἐμοὶ γάρ ἐστιν ἔνδον, ἔξεστιν δέ μοι
καὶ βούλομαι τοῦτ', οὐ ποιῶ δέ. (*Fr.* 5.)

[4] *Vide* Arrian, *loc. cit.* where the whole subject of Thrasonides is discussed.

does not merely want to satisfy a sensual appetite—he wants to be loved. Unless he can feel that she loves him, none of those privileges, which, to the ordinary Hetaera-lover of the day, would have been of themselves the complete consummation of love, are of any value to him. ἔξεστί μοι τοῦτο καὶ βούλομαι, οὐ ποιῶ δέ.

The aim of the lover is not to gratify himself, but to inspire love.[1] That we are here face to face with a form of love which is not only actually absent from Middle Comedy, but is by nature absolutely foreign to that literature and could not possibly appear in it, is too obvious to need further emphasis.[2]

This much, then, is clear; but there remains a most perplexing question, which, though it is a little aside of our immediate subject, is yet too interesting to be passed by altogether. Why is it Thrasonides, the *Miles Gloriosus* whom all the Comedians are banded together to ridicule, who appears as the most chivalrous lover of the whole of New Comedy?[3] Why is a man who is universally regarded as a fool, made to give expression to such elevated sentiments, and to follow such a noble line of conduct?

---

[1] This is the view taken of the case by Diogenes Laertius (vii. 130), when he is discussing the Stoic doctrine of love.

εἶναι δὲ τὸν ἔρωτα ἐπιβολὴν φιλοποιίας διὰ κάλλος ἐμφαινόμενον· καὶ μὴ εἶναι συνουσίας, ἀλλὰ φιλίας. τὸν γοῦν Θρασωνίδην, καίπερ ἐν ἐξουσίᾳ ἔχοντα τὴν ἐρωμένην, διὰ τὸ μισεῖσθαι ἀπέχειν αὐτῆς. εἶναι οὖν τὸν ἔρωτα φιλίας. κ.τ.λ.

[2] One need merely think of Thais, the ideal Hetaera, μηδενὸς ἐρῶσαν.

[3] That this is no mere coincidence is shown by the characters, of Stratophanes in Menander's *Sicyonius*, and others, of whom we shall speak presently. [p. 182.]

The first explanation that suggests itself is, of course, "Because he is a fool." This view is certainly advanced in a passage of Plutarch, where Thrasonides is compared to the miser who starves rather than make use of the food he has in the house,[1] and seems to find favour too with Thrasonides' own slave.[2] But this explanation is not a very satisfactory one, somehow. However great a fool Menander might wish to make of the mercenary soldier of the time, this does not seem the natural line for his folly to take, nor was it the line, as we know from historical evidence, that the folly of these people actually did as a rule take. A Pyrgopolinices must, one would have thought, have been a far more familiar figure to citizens who had enjoyed a Macedonian occupation, than a Thrasonides. One might, perhaps, imagine that the behaviour of Alexander to the wife and daughters of Darius—behaviour which was regarded in Greece as somewhat remarkable[3]—had suggested the character of Thrasonides, for, after all, the ideal soldier of the age, whether for good or evil, is always Alexander; only it seems doubtful whether a single action of an unusual kind could

---

[1] Plut. *de Cupid. Div.* 524 F.
[καίτοι πῶς οὐ μανικὸν οὐδὲ οἰκτρὸν τὸ πάθος, εἴ τις ἱματίῳ μὴ χρῆται διὰ τὸ ῥιγοῦν, μηδὲ ἄρτῳ διὰ τὸ πεινῆν, μηδὲ πλούτῳ διὰ τὸ φιλοπλουτεῖν; ἀλλ' ἐν τοῖς Θρασωνίδου κακοῖς ἐστίν·

παρ' ἐμοὶ γάρ ἐστιν ἔνδον, ἔξεστιν δέ μοι,
καὶ βούλομαι τοῦτ' . . . .

ὡς οἱ ἐμμανέστατα ἐρῶντες,

. . . . οὐ ποιῶ δε. . . . . κ.τ.λ.]

[2] *Misumenus, Fr.* 6.

[3] Cp. Athen. xiii. 603 C, where not only is his continence emphasised, but also his treatment of his captives as if they were free. Cp. Menand. *Sicyon. Fr.* 3.

serve to form so constant a type as the chivalrous soldier-lover. At one time I thought that, as the soldier of New Comedy has generally served in Asia, perhaps he might be supposed to have imported his advanced romantic ideas from one of those Greek Asiatic cities which were, as we know, the original home of Greek romance, and indeed of all important developments of Greek erotic literature.[1] But there is to modern notions so great an incongruity in the idea of, say, the Colonel of a West India regiment so influenced by the latest school of literature as to model his life on it, that, though such a character would not, perhaps, have seemed so absurd to the Greeks as it does to us, still, in the absence of all definite evidence, I have preferred not to lay undue stress upon what is, after all, entirely a matter of conjecture. Indeed, the question remains to me a very obscure one, and I cannot at present see any satisfactory solution of it.

But, whatever may have been the causes which led to the creation of this particular character, the soldier-lover of a more or less Thrasonides type is an unquestionable feature of New Comedy. Besides the hero of the *Misumenus*, of whom we have spoken, in the *Sicyonius* (also by Menander) we find another soldier, Stratophanes, who buys a slave-girl, and then treats her as if she were a free woman.[2] To the same class of feeling, though expressed in a some-

---

[1] Mimnermus, Anacreon, and Antimachus were all, of course, natives of Greek Asia, where the cult of women seems always, from the earliest times onwards, to have been more developed than in Greece itself. There is a certain grim irony in the tradition that would make Anaxandrides, too, a native of Colophon. [2] *Vide Fr.* 3.

what different way, belongs the remorse which the soldier Polemon (in the *Periceiromene* of Menander) feels for the wrong he has done to his αἰχμαλώτῳ ἐρωμένῃ.

A case in some respects similar, though in others different, is that of the soldier Stratippocles, in the *Epidicus*, who falls in love with his captive, but does not touch her.[1] The differences, of course, here are that, firstly, the play belongs to Middle Comedy, its moral being that Stratippocles will be happier with his *fidicina* than with the girl of high birth, for whom he has formed the chivalrous attachment;[2] while, secondly, the continence of the hero is not so much a feature of his character as a necessity for the development of the plot; and, thirdly, the soldier is here not a mercenary, but an Athenian citizen, who has been fighting against the Thebans. But though, therefore, the case of the *Epidicus* does not belong to the same category as those previously discussed, the association in it of the soldier with chivalrous behaviour towards women is yet worthy of notice, and, even if only a coincidence, is still an interesting one.[3]

Apart, too, from these very remarkable instances, there are not a few passages scattered about in the

---

[1] Plaut. *Epid.* i. 2, 7.

[2] Cp. v. 1, 45, where the lover's regrets are promptly answered by the assertion that there is another woman ready who will do just as well or better:
    stultus, tace!
    tibi quidem quod ames domi praesto.

[3] That the character of the soldier belonged essentially to *erotic* comedy is further shown by Plaut. *Capt.* prolog. 57:
    hic neque periurus leno nec meretrix mala
    neque miles gloriosus.

remains of the New Comedy which serve to show that the "love," of which there is so much talk in that literature, is not the merely animal passion of an earlier period. Of these, a striking one is that preserved in Plutarch, *ap.* Stob. *Flor.* lxiii. 34:

τῶν Μενάνδρου δραμάτων, says Plutarch there, οὐκ ἴσως ἁπάντων ἓν συνεκτικόν ἐστιν ὁ ἔρως, οἷον πνεῦμα κοινὸν διακεχυκώς· ὃν οὖν μάλιστα θιασώτην τοῦ θεοῦ καὶ ὀργιαστὴν ἴσμεν, τὸν ἄνδρα συνεπιλαμβάνωμεν εἰς τὴν ζήτησιν, ἐπεὶ καὶ λελάκηκε περὶ τοῦ πάθους φιλοσοφώτερον. ἄξιον γὰρ εἶναι θαύματος φήσας τὸ περὶ τοὺς ἐρῶντας, ὥσπερ ἐστὶν ἅμα λαλεῖ. εἶτα ἀπορεῖ καὶ ζητεῖ πρὸς ἑαυτόν·

τίνι δεδούλωταί (*sc.* ὁ ἐραστής) ποτε;
ὄψει; φλύαρος. κ.τ.λ. . . . . .
. . . . . καιρός ἐστιν ἡ νόσος
ψυχῆς.   (Menand. *Incert.* 14.)

That is: Menander, a writer familiar with love in its most passionate forms (θιασώτην καὶ ὀργιαστήν), gives us a sober and serious view of the matter. After expressing his astonishment at the ways of lovers, he furnishes us with a realistic account of love as it actually is (ὥσπερ ἐστὶν ἅμα λαλεῖ),[1] and then proceeds to investigate its causes. For a moment he is puzzled, and questions with himself, but soon he finds the true answer. καιρός ἐστιν ἡ νόσος ψυχῆς. Love is an affection of the soul as distinct from the body, and has only an accidental connection with the latter.[2]

Equally forcible, though in another way, is a

---

[1] This doubtless refers to some lines, now lost, which preceded the passage subsequently quoted.

[2] This is, of course, nothing but a versified version of the doctrine of the Stoic, Euclides. Cp. Diog. Laert. ii. 108.

passage from the *Poenulus*. The lover and his slave are watching the two girls, and the slave expresses his utter contempt for his master's "Platonic" affection, to which the latter answers that he loves Adelphasium as he loves the gods.[1] Another case is in the *Curculio*, where the love of Phaedromus for Planesium is fed on nothing more substantial than kisses;[2] another in the *Hecyra*, where it is distinctly pointed out that the love of Pamphilus for his wife is induced by other than sensual considerations.[3] Other instances, of more or less significance, every reader of the Latin comedians will be able to supply for himself; and it is further worth observing that when a New Comedy character, as occasionally does happen, is made to speak slightingly of "Platonic" love, such a character is always a slave, never a person of refinement.[4]

To proceed to the final point of essential difference between Middle and New Comedy, it will be remembered that, in the former class of literature, family life and the mutual relations of members of a family were among the stock subjects of ridicule, and that no remarks expressive of any other views on this matter are to be found there,

---

[1] MI. etiamne (a me didicisti) ut ames eam, quam nusquam tetigeris? nihil illuc quidem est.
AG. deos quoque edepol et amo et metuo, quibus tamen abstineo manus. (i. 2, 69.) A remark in v. 4, 49, is similar in spirit.

[2] Plaut. *Curc.* i. 1, 50 *seqq*. Further moralisings on the power of a kiss (which almost suggest Daphnis in Longus' *Pastoralia*, i. 18) occur in Menand. *Incert.* 7.

[3] Ter. *Hec.* i. 2, 60 *seqq*.; 85 *seqq*.

[4] *e.g.* the "Geta" in Menander's *Misumenus*, Milphio in the *Poenulus* of Plautus, &c.

at any rate before a very late period.[1] Family life, as depicted in the New Comedy, is by no means ideal; indeed, as we have already had occasion to remark, the unhappy relations between husband and elderly wife are, under certain circumstances, a favourite subject of ridicule, even with Menander.[2] But yet instances to the contrary are to be found, and are, in fact, by no means very uncommon. Not to speak of the cases of devotion of wife to husband and husband to wife—such as those in the *Stichus*, &c., already sufficiently discussed[3]—the relations between father and children, and, still more, mother and children,[4] are often described as of the most delightful character.

Of the former, there are interesting examples in Menand. *Incert.* 59:

>αἰσχύνομαι τὸν πατέρα, Κλειτοφῶν, μόνον.
>ἀντιβλέπειν ἐκεῖνον οὐ δυνήσομαι
>ἀδικῶν· τὰ δ' ἄλλα ῥᾳδίως χειρώσομαι.

Incert. 108:

>ὁ σκληρότατος πρὸς υἱὸν ἐν τῷ νουθετεῖν
>τοῖς μὲν λόγοις πικρός ἐστι, τοῖς δ' ἔργοις πατήρ.

Incert. 113:

>μηδὲν ὀδύνα τὸν πατέρα, γιγνώσκων ὅτι
>ὁ μέγιστον ἀγαπῶν δι' ἐλάχιστ' ὀργίζεται.

Incert. 117:

>οὐδέποτ' ἀληθὲς οὐδὲν οὔθ' υἱῷ πατὴρ
>εἴωθ' ἀπειλεῖν, οὔτ' ἐρῶν ἐρωμένῃ.[5]

---

[1] Such a passage as Alexis, *Incert.* 35, would belong to this date. It is very different to the ribald remarks in the *Philometor* of Antiphanes.

[2] Cp. *supra*, p. 173.   [3] *Ibid.* p. 171.

[4] The "mater indulgens" is mentioned in Apuleius, *Florid.* 16, as one of the stock characters in Philemon.

[5] Menand. *Incert.* 109, 114, 115, are all equally to the point.

The charming interview between the father and his two daughters in the *Stichus* (i. 2, 32 *seqq.*), is a further, equally striking instance.

Of the latter relation, that between mother and children, there is a good instance in this same play (i. 2, 51), where, after the father has propounded his intention of marrying again, his daughter reminds him that it will be hard for him to find a second wife like his first.

AN. pol ego uxorem quaero, postquam vostra mater
    mortua est.
PA. facile invenies et peiorem et peius moratam, pater,
    quam illa fuit; meliorem neque tu reperies neque
    sol videt.

A still more striking case is that in the *Hecyra*, where the mother of Pamphilus, thinking that it is her presence which renders it impossible for her son's wife to live with him, resolves to sacrifice herself, and go into voluntary exile into the country.[1] The same idea, though less pleasantly expressed, is apparent in Syrus' remark in the *Heauton Timorumenus* (v. 2, 38):   matres omnes filiis in peccato adiutrices, auxilio in paterna iniuria.

But it is needless to multiply instances of a state of affairs with which every attentive reader of Plautus and Terence must be sufficiently familiar.[2]

[1] *Vide* Ter. *Hec.* iv. 2, 1 *seqq.*, a passage of great interest.
[2] Some further remarks on the family relations in New Comedy will be found in Excursus K.

[Frequent reference is made in these pages to Plautus and Terence, as illustrating the New Comedy. The justification of such reference was to have been dealt with in an Excursus. The author was of opinion that the Latin comedians might be cited to illustrate plot and subject, though we could not be certain that the actual words or expressions in any given passage were due to Greek originals.]

IX. THE ORIGINS OF THE ROMANTIC COMEDY.

The above investigation into the nature of New Comedy, and into the points of difference between it and the earlier literature, leads naturally to the consideration of a further and final question—that of the origin of these differences which are so strikingly apparent. We have seen that the romantic New Comedy differs entirely in its treatment of women from every form of dramatic art which had preceded it.[1] In fact, we have seen that, while the Middle Comedy belongs still entirely to the first or classical period of Greek literature, the New Comedy, with its striking romantic features, belongs essentially to that second period, which it is usual to call the Alexandrian, and forms, indeed, one of the departments of literature in which the romantic tendencies of that period can be studied to the best advantage. What we have to consider is therefore this: How did Athenian Comedy acquire these romantic features which are so conspicuously absent from its earlier phases? when did it acquire them? and to whom was the acquisition due?

The last of these three questions may be best considered first. There seems every reason to believe that this introduction of the romantic element was due to Menander rather than to Philemon.[2] There

---

[1] That there was no romantic element in Greek tragedy has already been shown at length. [See above, pp. 37-67.]

[2] The claims of Diphilus need not be considered. His leanings towards Middle Comedy are generally admitted; in his fragments

can be no question that of the two writers, Philemon is the less distinctively romantic. Of the typical New Comedy love-stories preserved in Plautus and Terence, not one professes to be derived from him. The allusions to women altogether are proportionately much fewer in his fragments than in those of Menander; while a large proportion, again, of such allusions as there are, are either references to Hetaerae, or else belong to the old-fashioned misogyny of Middle Comedy. The detailed examination of his style of art, which occurs in the *Florida* of Apuleius, is altogether strongly suggestive of Middle Comedy;[1] indeed, Apuleius actually describes him as "mediae comoediae scriptor." It is further to be remarked that the number of coarse allusions to women is proportionately far greater in Philemon than in Menander. Indeed, the whole study of Philemon's treatment of women leaves one with the impression, not only that he was at heart a follower of the old school, but that even when he did for

there is no suggestion of any romantic treatment of women. In fact, the only real reason for assigning him to New Comedy at all is, perhaps, the story of the *Rudens*, which, Arcturus states in the Prologue, is derived from this writer. Of the *Casina* we shall speak elsewhere. [See page 165, note 2.]

[1] Poeta fuit hic Philemon, *mediae comoediae scriptor*; fabulas cum Menandro in scenam dictavit, certavitque cum eo, fortasse impar, certe aemulus. namque eum etiam vicisse saepenumero, pudet dicere. reperias tamen apud ipsum multos sales, argumenta lepide inflexa, agnatos lucide explicatos, personas rebus competentes, sententias vitae congruentes, ioca non infra soccum, seria non usque ad cothurnum. *rarae apud illum corruptelae*, et, uti errores, concessi amores. nec eo minus et leno periurus et amator fervidus et servulus callidus et amica illudens et uxor inhibens et mater indulgens et patruus obiurgator et sodalis opitulator et miles proeliator; sed et parasiti edaces et parentes tenaces et meretrices procaces. Apul. *Flor.* 16.

any reason adopt the romantic principle, he developed this principle from a more sensual point of view than Menander. That this tendency to coarseness is in sympathy with the earlier spirit of Athenian comedy, but is entirely foreign to its romantic development, need hardly be emphasised, after all that has already been said on the subject. And it may not be altogether beside the question here, to call attention to Philemon's invariable pessimism—pessimism most characteristic of a conservative mind in an age of progress, but hardly consistent with such qualities as would be required of the originator of a great artistic and social revolution.[1] Furthermore, Philemon is regularly spoken of as the rival of Menander;[2] the reverse is never the case, notwithstanding the fact that the relative ages of the two playwrights would have made the latter the more natural way of putting the case. Again, the much greater success of Philemon at the time, notwithstanding the well-nigh unanimous contrary verdict of subsequent ages,[3] seems to show clearly that he was the more old-fashioned of the two; for, as is well known, originality is seldom very welcome on the stage. And lastly, the very large proportion of Philemon's works which appear to have belonged to Middle Comedy pure and simple—a point which will be further discussed directly—seems to be further evidence that this was

[1] A curious instance of this feeling is his often-expressed opinion that animals are happier than men. Cp. *Incert.* 3, 4, 8, etc.

[2] Cp. *inter alia* Apul. *Flor.* 16.

[3] Among many expressions to this effect, we need only mention that of Quintilian: atque ille quidem (*sc.* Menander) omnibus eiusdem operis auctoribus abstulit nomen et fulgore quodam suae claritatis tenebras obduxit. *Inst.* x. 1, 72.

his natural *métier*, and that it was only a spirit of rivalry with Menander which made him turn his attention to a style of art with which he had no real sympathy.[1] As for the *Hypobolimaeus*, that proves nothing, for there is no evidence whatever by which to fix the date of this resuscitation of the *Cocalus* of Aristophanes; indeed, if anything, it rather suggests that Philemon found such subjects so little congenial, that he had to borrow his materials, instead of being able to produce them himself.

All this, it may be argued, proves little as to the claims of Menander over Philemon. Indeed, it may even be urged that the very fact that Philemon is the less distinctively romantic of the two, renders it probable that the first introduction of the romantic element was due to him. But such an argument, though at first sight plausible enough, rests on an imperfect comprehension of the real nature of the romantic principle in Greek comedy. Were this principle a direct development of tendencies characteristic of the earlier phases of the literature, it would doubtless be right to assume that its first appearance in any tangible shape would be of an unemphatic and tentative kind; but the romantic principle is no

---

[1] To take an instance from modern times. M. Daudet is said to have written his *Sappho* with the expressed object of showing that he, too, could produce a work which could not be left lying about. Similarly, M. Zola may be imagined to have produced *La Rêve*, in order to prove that even he could be decent if he tried. But any attempt to judge of the general character of these authors by the two books mentioned would be obviously futile. In like manner, in the case of Philemon, one has to consider how much of the romantic element in his comedies is due to conviction, and how much to a desire to show that romantic love-stories were a game two could play at.

such development of previous tendencies It is not a development, but a regeneration; it is not a growth from within, but an annex from without. Whatever anyone may suppose to be the origin of the romantic element, no one with any acquaintance with the subject is likely to wish to maintain that the virgin-love of New Comedy is developed out of the Hetaera-worship of its predecessor on the stage. Indeed, there can be little doubt that, so far from New Comedy appealing to those tastes which Middle Comedy had fostered, its remarkable success was in great part due to a strong reaction against the latter. And thus there is every reason to believe that, when once the new emotion found expression on the stage, such expression was immediately clear and unmistakable; and that therefore, in looking for the originator of the movement, one must look for that writer of the period whose works exhibit the romantic features most strongly and consistently, and must regard those other writers, in whom such features are less prominent, as more or less unwilling imitators. And if this be so, there can be little real doubt as to the validity of Menander's claim.

The next question to be considered is—When was this introduction of the romantic element into Greek comedy first brought about? We know that Philemon began to exhibit in 330, and that the date of Menander's first play is 322; but these facts do not of themselves furnish any information as to the origin of New Comedy proper. For it is an unquestionable fact, and one of the greatest importance in this connection, that both Philemon and Menander wrote plays which are not romantic, and which belong, therefore, to Middle, rather than to New Comedy. And on this fact hinges the whole question of the date of the introduction of the romantic element into Athenian Comedy.

Of the ninety-seven plays of Philemon, which Platonius states were in his time extant,[1] hardly fifty titles are preserved, and of these, well-nigh a third obviously belong to what were evidently Middle Comedies.[2] When we consider how extremely probable it is that the majority of the plays now entirely lost belonged also to this class (for it is obvious that a later age would tend to preserve such plays as were in harmony with the romantic tastes then prevailing, rather than those that were not), it becomes clear that a very large proportion of the plays of Philemon were not New Comedies at all. With Menander the same is to a certain extent, though not in an equal degree, also true. Of about a hundred plays that he produced during the thirty-two years of his literary activity, while

[1] Platon. *de Com.* p. 30. *ad fin.* The passage distinctly suggests that these ninety-seven plays were not all that Philemon actually wrote. σώζεται δὲ αὐτοῦ (Φιλήμονος) δράματα ἑπτὰ πρὸς ἐνενήκοντα. Μένανδρος . . . . γέγραφε δὲ πάντα δράματα ρη'.

The view that the total number of his plays was greater than ninety-seven seems to acquire further probability from the fact that he lived well-nigh twice as long as Menander, and continued to write up to the day of his death. Cp. Apul. *Flor.* 16.—It need hardly be remarked that if plays of Philemon were already lost in the time of Platonius, such plays were, in all probability, Middle rather than New Comedies.

[2] I have reserved the detailed proof of this fact, and the similar one concerning Menander, for another place, in order that the sequence of the argument may not be disturbed. *Vide* Excursus. [This Excursus does not appear to have been written.]

a dozen or so, presumably unsuccessful efforts of his earlier years, are entirely lost, some twenty besides, of those whose titles we know, must be ranked with the old, rather than with the new form of dramatic art.

Now when we further reflect that it is not probable that, after a writer has once taken to a new and successful development of art, he will then fall back again to any considerable extent upon the old, and that therefore the Middle Comedies of Menander, and also of Philemon,[1] belong, in all probability, to their earlier period and are anterior to the introduction of the romantic element, it becomes obvious that the date of the introduction of this element into Comedy, (that is to say, the date of the birth of New Comedy,) must be put considerably later than is usually done, and that, instead of fixing this date at 330, or even at 322, we must rather fix it somewhere between the years 315 and 310. For assuming, as we seem in every way justified in doing, that about a quarter of the plays of Menander belonged in spirit still to Middle Comedy, and that his rate of production increased rather than diminished with advancing years, a simple calculation will enable us to put the date within these limits.

Granted then that the introduction of the romantic element into Comedy was due to Menander, and

---

[1] It is hard to speak so positively of Philemon if, as is probable, he was merely the imitator and rival of Menander in this respect; but, of course, if it be granted that his romantic plays are subsequent to Menander's introduction of the subject, it is a matter of indifference for the present argument whether he afterwards reverted to the older style or not.

took place about the year 312, there remains the final question, Where did Menander get the idea from? It has, I trust, been made sufficiently clear by this time that he did not derive it from his predecessors in Comedy, nor yet from his favourite model Euripides. He may, of course, have evolved it independently for himself, but this, seeing that a similar conclusion had been arrived at some hundred years before, is not very probable. It has already been demonstrated that the romantic idea, (that is to say, the idea that a woman is a worthy object for a man's love, and that such love may well be the chief, if not the only, aim of a man's life,) had originally been propounded by Antimachus of Colophon at the end of the fifth century[1]; it seems, therefore, well-nigh certain that this idea must have been communicated in some way to Menander from Antimachus, and the only point that remains to be considered is the probable method of this communication.

It is possible that the influence may have been direct. It is possible that the accident of a copy of the *Lyde* coming into Menander's hands may have suggested to him the idea which he subsequently developed with such success. It is possible, and, in the absence of evidence, one way or the other, it would be bold to assert that it was not the case; but, at the same time, it seems on the whole more probable that the influence was of a different kind, and that Menander's attention was first called to the views propounded by Antimachus through the medium of some third person. While it is, of

---

[1] [*Supra*, p. 107 *seqq.*]

course, futile to expect proof in such a case as this, there is, perhaps, one personality among those we know belonging to the period, in favour of which, rather than of any other, the evidence seems to tend. This is Asclepiades, the originator of the erotic epigram, and a poet of great influence upon various contemporary writers. It is true that it is usual to place the date of Asclepiades somewhat later than that which we have decided must be fixed for the appearance of the New Comedy, but this later date does not rest on any very strong evidence. Asclepiades is mentioned along with Philetas in Theocritus vii. 40, in a way which, at any rate, does not exclude the possibility that he was a contemporary;[1] Philetas, as we know, was born in the reign of Philip,[2] say, 338; Asclepiades may have been born several years later, even in 330, and yet have had an influence on Menander, for, as we know, he began his career as an erotic poet at a very early age.[3] It is by no means improbable that he may have visited Athens to complete his education; his epigrams show an acquaintance with Athenian comedy and life as there described which could hardly have been acquired elsewhere; such visits were paid to Athens by Callimachus, Aratus, and others. It will, of course, be urged that the influence may have been just the

---

[1] The Scholiast here, and others, go so far as to assert that Theocritus was a pupil of Asclepiades as well as of Philetas.

[2] Φιλητᾶς . . . ὢν ἐπί τε Φιλίππου καὶ Ἀλεξάνδρου. Suidas *s.v.*

[3] Cp. *Anth. Pal.* xii. 46.—The fact that Asclepiades was tired of life at twenty-one is, of course, no proof that he died early. Many people, especially poets, who were very anxious for death in their youth, have developed a wonderfully tenacious hold upon life as they grew older.

reverse, and that Menander suggested the romantic idea to Asclepiades; but this is improbable for two reasons. In the first place, Asclepiades is known to have been a student of Antimachus,[1] while Menander, as far as we know, was not; in the second, though Asclepiades shows, as has been said, evident traces of the influence of comedy, such comedy is not New, but distinctly Middle Comedy, as is sufficiently plain from the drinking-scenes described in *Anth. Pal.* v. 181, 185, from the frequent, or rather, constant allusions to Hetaerae in his epigrams, and from the complete absence from them of those particular features of the romantic idea which Menander himself developed. It is therefore well-nigh certain that, if there was influence from either side,—and, when one considers the close sympathy between the ideals of the two writers, the conclusion that there was some more than merely fortuitous affinity between them is almost irresistible—such influence came from the side of the brilliant young Samian, who would thus deserve the credit of having originally inspired not merely the romantic epigram, but also the romantic drama.[2] That this was actually so, no one can of course affirm; but that it may have been, no one who is familiar with the "wild-flowers of Asclepiades" will be likely to deny.

[1] Cp. *Anth. Pal.* ix. 63; *supra*, p. 113.
[2] The fact that Menander called one of his plays *Samia*, a title which had not been used since the time of Anaxandrides, is one of those interesting coincidences that prove nothing at all.

EXCURSUS A.

[P. 31.]

THEOGNIS (261 *seqq*).

THE great difficulty in the way of a satisfactory reconstruction of this passage lies in the fact that it is not certain whether it is to be regarded as simply a description of an erotic incident, or whether it is a γρῖφος; in the latter and, perhaps, more probable case, it is impossible to emend without first finding the solution, and to guess a riddle without knowing what that riddle is, rather requires a Daniel or some similar commentator. It is not quite so impossible, however, to improve the passage if it is looked upon as merely descriptive of an actual event, in which case the account of apparently similar scenes in the Romance of Eumathius may, perhaps, throw some light on the subject.

In the scene depicted in Theognis, the παῖς τέρεινα is fenced off from her lover, not only by an objectionable suitor, but also by the presence of her severe "water-drinking" parents. Under these circumstances, it does not seem very probable that the lover would (as the ordinary reading makes him do) throw his arms round her waist and kiss her on the neck; such behaviour on his part (and its natural consequences) might, it is true, account for the abrupt termination of the poem, but still would not be, as I have said, exactly probable, especially after he had been drinking only water. The scene actually described was, perhaps, rather somewhat of the following kind. When the time for drinking was come, the girl in question got up and went round, like the Hysmine of Eumathius, to hand the cup to the guests,[1] going, however, first to her parents;[2] as these were only drinking ψυχρόν, her office is contemptuously described as being that of a water-carrier. The last two lines I would then read:

ἔνθα μέσην περὶ παῖδα λαβὼν ἀγκῶν' ἐφίλησα,
δειλήν, ἡ δὲ τέρεν φθέγγετ' ἄνις στόματος.

i.e., as she came on her round to her lover, he put his arm on her waist and kissed her on the elbow; and she, though she said nothing with her lips, "her eyes were speaking."[3]

Whether the actual words ought not to be still further emended, is questionable; but, anyhow, the general sense thus given is a little more complimentary to Greek "company" manners.

The chief objection to this interpretation is, of course, that it bestows on the epigram a decidedly erotic character, which is not elsewhere to be found in this book, and would certainly be an anachronism if the lines belong to the fifth century.

---

[1] Ὑσμίνῃ παρθένῳ τῇ θυγατρὶ Σωσθένης οἰνοχοεῖν ἐγκελεύεται· ἡ δὲ ἀνεζώσατο τὸν χιτῶνα, ἐγύμνωσε τὼ χεῖρε μέχρις ἀγκῶνος κ.τ.λ. Eumath. i. 8.

[2] ἔπιε μὲν οὖν ὁ Σωσθένης· οὐκ ἔπειθε γάρ με αὐτοῦ προπιεῖν. εἶτα καὶ ἡ Πανθία (ἡ τῆς Ὑσμίνης μήτηρ) συνέπιεν· ἐμὲ δὲ τρίτον εἶχεν ἡ πόσις. id. *ibid.*

[3] καὶ πίνων τὸν πόδα θλίβω τῆς κόρης, πόδα κατεπιθεὶς τὸν ἐμόν· ἡ δὲ σιγῶσα τῇ γλώττῃ, τῷ σχήματι λαλεῖ, καὶ λαλοῦσα σιγᾷ κ.τ.λ. id. iv. 1.

EXCURSUS B.

[P. 48.]

THE fragments of the *Phaedra* of Sophocles (among which may be included Soph. *Fr.* 855, and Eur. *Fr.* 431, which both very possibly belong to this play) are interesting for the many parallels they show to the Homeric Hymn to Aphrodite (*Hom. Hymn.* iv).

There, too, special emphasis is laid on the universal sway of Aphrodite, not only over men (l. 3), but also over animals (l. 4–6), and over Zeus and the gods (l. 34 *seqq.*). The animals fawn on her as she comes (l. 69, 70, cp. Soph. *Fr.* 625). From l. 7 one might guess that Soph. *Fr.* 855, 13 was originally

τίν' οὐ παλαίουσ' ἔς τε τρεῖς σφάλλει θεῶν,

or something similar. Both l. 45 and Soph. *Fr.* 619 give Zeus as well as Aphrodite the power of inspiring love; and other less important parallels could be pointed out.

These parallels are very striking; and though one must, of course, beware of drawing conclusions from what may be merely accidental or external, it cannot be denied that, if it could be proved that Sophocles was working with this hymn in his mind and with its conception of Aphrodite before him, this fact alone would render it very unlikely that he would treat his love-element in that "modern" way in which it has hitherto been the fashion to assume that he did.

Anyhow, it may not be inapposite to glance at the love-incident which occurs in this Hymn, for, if nothing else, it is interesting as a very typical Greek "love-story." What happens is briefly this:

Aphrodite, having fallen in love with Anchises, disguises herself as a mortal maiden, and comes upon the object of her affection as he is wandering alone among the byres, singing to himself.

At first he takes her for a goddess, and is duly humble; but she assures him that this is not the case, but she is the daughter of the king of Phrygia, and she asserts that she has been carried by Hermes away from her home to be his (Anchises') bride. In her helpless condition, she, therefore, throws herself on his mercy, and begs him by Zeus and his parents:

> ἀδμήτην μ' ἀγαγὼν καὶ ἀπειρήτην φιλότητος
> πατρί τε σῷ δεῖξον καὶ μητέρι κέδν' εἰδυίῃ. κ.τ.λ.

His answer to this appeal to his chivalrous feelings is prompt and to the point:

"If you are really not a goddess, but only a mortal,

> οὔτις ἔπειτα θεῶν οὔτε θνητῶν ἀνθρώπων
> ἐνθάδε με σχήσει, πρὶν σῇ φιλότητι μιγῆναι
> αὐτίκα νῦν."

After this, perhaps even the last two lines of his speech are an anti-climax.

EXCURSUS C.

[P. 52.]

THE ANDROMEDA OF EURIPIDES.

OF all the plays of Euripides, the one which is generally looked upon as especially "romantic" is the *Andromeda*,[1] and it must be confessed that, at first sight, it does appear to have a certain character of its own. The common view of the story is, that Perseus, seeing Andromeda exposed, falls in love with her, and therefore rescues her. If this view is correct, this play will furnish the solitary instance in Euripides of a man's falling in love with a woman.

But how far is this view correct? A careful examination of the fragments will, perhaps, show that it requires at least to be modified.

When the play opens, Andromeda is found exposed on her rock, and after she has made due lamentations, there appears Perseus, bearing evident marks of his long journey, and generally in a deplorable condition.[2] On learning from her the state of the

---

[1] "Und wie er (Euripides) in diesen alten Heroensagen die Liebe stark in den Vordergrund gerückt hatte, so wurde namentlich das alte Märchen von Perseus und Andromeda unter seinen Händen zu einem der glänzendsten Beispiele ritterlicher Liebe, &c." Rohde, *Der griechische Roman*, p. 33.

[2] The dirtiness of his clothes, &c., is made a great point of. Cp. Hesych. περισχαδόν· τὸν ὑποκρινόμενον τόν Περσέα ὡς πτωχὸν καὶ φθισίμορφον. This too lends force to Lucian's ὠχρῶν ἁπάντων καὶ λεπτῶν τῶν ἑβδομαίων ἐκείνων τραγῳδῶν. (*De Conscr. Hist.* 1, vol. 2, p. 2. *Vide* Nauck, *Trag. Frag.* pp. 392-3.)

case, he pities her, and, say the modern critics, falls in love with her. I doubt it. This is not at all the sort of occasion on which a Greek would be likely to fall in love. Perseus is wet and dirty and hungry, and has the prospect of a dangerous encounter before him. Love, to the Greek, is essentially the child of ease and idleness;[1] to connect it with stress and struggle is entirely a modern notion. The one and only thing which a Greek in Perseus' position would be likely to do, would be to try whether he couldn't find someone—a king by preference—to lend him some new clothes;[2] and this, or something of the kind, is, in all probability, what he makes the condition of his

---

[1]
Ἔρως γὰρ ἀργὸν κἀπὶ τοῖς ἀργοῖς ἔφυ·
φιλεῖ κάτοπτρα καὶ κόμης ξανθίσματα,
φεύγει δὲ μόχθους. ἐν δέ μοι τεκμήριον·
οὐδεὶς προσαιτῶν βίοτον ἠράσθη βροτῶν,
ἐν τοῖς δ' ἔχουσιν ἡβητὴς πέφυχ' ὅδε.
                          Eur. *Fr.* 322 (*Danae*).

Cp. Athen. vi. 270 C. Similar passages are very common—in fact, the view may be said to be a universal one; it arises, of course, from that purely sensual manner of regarding love, on which so much has already been said. Indeed, those who have read the early Greek literature with any attention, need perhaps hardly be reminded of how utterly foreign to the Greek of Euripides' day is the conception of the "galante Ritter" setting out in search of ladies that want rescuing.

At the same time, it may not be amiss to emphasise a fact which, though sufficiently obvious, is yet often ignored. The fact that the *Andromeda* was looked upon as a romantic play some centuries later, even if it can be proved, is no proof that it was intended as such by its author, or so understood by its original audience. If Hermesianax could infer from the *Odyssey* that Homer was in love with Penelope, one may excuse the contemporaries of Lucian if they inferred from Euripides that Perseus was in love with Andromeda, but one need not necessarily regard their inference as a true one.

[2] One naturally thinks of Odysseus and Nausicaa, of Menelaus in the *Helena* (427 *seqq.*), &c.

saving Andromeda.[1] Then, cheered by the prospect of a warm bath and of a comfortable night's rest, he goes to face the monster.

But though he does not fall in love with Andromeda, *she falls in love with him*, and begs him, when he returns victorious,[2] to take her with him anywhere, if only as a slave. She will follow him anywhere, she says, even through the sky if he likes.[3] In the improved state of affairs,[4] Perseus is not averse to these advances; but an obstacle arises in the shape of Cepheus, who objects to the disreputable appearance of his would-be son-in-law. Perseus argues his case with considerable fervour, but apparently without success; and it is Andromeda again who, by some bold stroke, overcomes or outwits her parents, and brings off what she wishes—οὐχ εἵλετο τῷ πατρὶ συμμένειν οὐδὲ τῇ μητρί, ἀλλ' αὐθαίρετος εἰς τὸ Ἄργος ἀπῆλθε μετ' ἐκείνου εὐγενές τι φρονήσασα.[5]

In other words, the initiative in the love-affair of Perseus and Andromeda is again almost entirely on the side of the woman, and this play forms in reality no exception to the general rule in this respect.

---

[1] *Fr.* 129. The fact that this line was afterwards quoted ἐρωτικῶς (*vide* Nauck, *ad loc.*), is no proof that it had any such meaning in its original context.

[2] *Fr.* 132. There is no real objection to putting this fragment *after* his encounter with the monster, as the words τὰ ἐχόμενα (*vide Fr.* 129 Nauck) do not necessarily mean that it followed immediately after *Fr.* 129.

[3] *i.e.* πρὸς Ὄλυμπον, a very natural remark when one considers the manner of Perseus' first arrival.

[4] *Fr.* 133. ἀλλ' ἡδύ τοι σωθέντα μεμνῆσθαι πόνων.

[5] A very interesting parallel to this scene is furnished by the dream of Medea (Apoll. Rhod. iii. 625 *seqq.*); the resemblance is almost too great to be merely accidental. There too, of course, it need hardly be remarked, the initiative is on the side of the woman.

EXCURSUS D.
[P. 59.]

WHILE on the subject of the *Hippolytus*, I cannot refrain from suggesting a couple of emendations in the last scene of the play, which certainly improve the present text artistically, and, perhaps, gain some support from what we know of the two versions of the work.

The first version ended with the promise of immortality to Hippolytus as a reward for his constancy (Eur. *Fr.* 446); in the second, this feature has entirely disappeared, and the last words of the play are a lament for the dead and a complaint of the injustice of heaven. Indeed, it may be said that the injustice of heaven is the chief moral of this second version.

Read therefore in l. 1415

εἴθ' ἦν ἀραιὸν δαίμοσιν βροτῶν γένους.

"Were there but a little humanity in the gods!" Could one but

> Pierce the cold lips of God with human breath,
> And mix his immortality with death!

And, once again, in l. 1440, when Artemis leaves Hippolytus with the remark that she is very sorry, but she doesn't like death-bed scenes, he exclaims bitterly:

χαίρουσα καὶ σὺ στεῖχε, παρθέν' ὀλβία.
μακρὰν δὲ λείπεις ῥᾳδίως ὁμιλίαν.[1]

I don't much think that Euripides wrote either of these lines so, but I think it is a pity he didn't.

[1] [The reading λείπεις has considerable MS. authority, and is adopted by the majority of editors; the author is contrasting it with λείποις, the text of Dindorf, Nauck, and some others.]

EXCURSUS E.

[P. 87.]

THE SECOND BOOK OF THEOGNIS.

THE second book of Theognis consists almost entirely of love-poems addressed to boys, and might therefore be expected to furnish particularly valuable evidence in the present connection, especially as many of these poems are of a far more personal and purely erotic character than those in the first book. The date of this book is, however, disputed, and I personally am inclined to believe that it is very much later than the time of Theognis—too recent, in fact, to belong to the period we are discussing at all. This being so, I have naturally not chosen to lay stress on its contents. For the sake of completeness, however, I have added here a brief examination of its character, for the benefit of anyone who may believe in it.

The general tone of these poems, though noticeably more passionate than that of the earlier collection, is still chivalrous and dignified, and occasionally rises to a very high level indeed. That spirit of self-negation, which we have already observed to be peculiar among the early Greeks to this form of love, is in places very marked. Few passages in all classical poetry can equal the pathetic dignity of these words of resignation:

> οὐκ ἐθέλω σε κακῶς ἔρδειν, οὐδ' εἴ μοι ἄμεινον
> πρὸς θεῶν ἀθανάτων ἔσσεται, ὦ καλὲ παῖ·
> οὐ γὰρ ἁμαρτωλῇσιν ἐπὶ σμικρῇσι κάθημαι,
> τῶν δὲ καλῶν παίδων οὔτις ἔτ' οὐκ ἀδικῶν.[1] (l. 1279)

or of this farewell:

> καλὸς ἐὼν κακότητι φρενῶν δειλοῖσιν ὁμιλεῖς
> ἀνδράσι, καὶ διὰ τοῦτ' αἰσχρὸν ὄνειδος ἔχεις,
> ὦ παῖ· ἐγὼ δ' ἀέκων τῆς σῆς φιλότητος ἁμαρτών,
> ὠνήμην ἔρδων οἷά τ' ἐλεύθερος ὤν. (l. 1377)

or of this:

> οὐδαμά σ' οὐδ' ἀπιών[2] δηλήσομαι, οὐδέ με πείσει
> οὐδεὶς ἀνθρώπων ὥστε με μή σε φιλεῖν. (l. 1363)

Similarly, that fatherly attitude on the part of the older man, which we have noticed both in Theognis and in the Theocritean imitation of Alcaeus, is apparent in more than one place (*e.g.* 1351 *seqq.*). This lends a particular point to those passages which compare the lover to a horse's owner or rider (1249 *seqq.* 1267 *seqq.*)

Again, there is the same appeal to the friend's better feelings that we have noticed in Theocritus (1319 *seqq.*), the same appeal to his care for his good name (1295 *seqq.*), all marked, too, by the same consideration and courtesy (1235 *seqq.*); there is the same exhortation to constancy, the same reproof of faithlessness (1257 *seqq.*, &c.), the same warning, full of

---

[1] The MS. gives ουτοςετουταδικων (Bergk). Various readings of this have been given. The present one is mine.

[2] ἀπιών rather than ἀπεών. Cp. Prop. iii. 25, 7: *flebo ego discedens.*

earnestness, but withal full of tenderness, as to the shortness of youth (1299 *seqq.*, 1305 *seqq.*).[1]

But it is needless to go further into detail. Enough has been said to show the general character of these poems, and anyone who reads them can easily supplement these instances with others. So, whatever value one may be inclined to assign to the evidence here adduced, it must, at least, be admitted that there is nothing in it which in any way contradicts anything that has gone before.[2]

---

[1] Altogether the resemblance between these poems and the Παιδικά of Theocritus is very marked. Even in the interesting passage (1367 *seqq.*), where the love of a boy is actually contrasted with that of a woman, the great charm of the former is said to lie not in κάλλος, but in χάρις, just as in Theocr. xxx. 4. Whether this resemblance is due to anything more than the similarity of subject is a difficult question, which need not be discussed here.

[2] Similarly, I may add, if anyone cares to regard the epigrams ascribed to Plato as genuine, he will find nothing in them but confirmation of what has already been gathered from works of less questionable authenticity.

EXCURSUS F.

[P. 106.]

WOMEN IN THE MIDDLE COMEDY.

[NOTE.—A considerable part of the contents of this Excursus (originally written for the first of the two Essays in this volume) is repeated in the second Essay. The Excursus is printed here without alteration, but it should be noted that the author did not regard it as having attained its final form.]

THE fragments of the Middle Comedy, belonging, as they do, to the earlier and middle part of the fourth century—that is, to the period of transition between the two great epochs of Greek literature—might have been expected to afford very valuable evidence as to the development of the romantic feeling. Unfortunately, however, this is not the case; indeed, the information to be gathered from them is, in this respect, of so little importance, that it is hardly worth considering at all.

Various explanations suggest themselves to account for this somewhat surprising fact. In the first place, the remains of the Middle Comedy are very small compared with the enormous original bulk of this literature, and, besides this, nearly all the more important fragments that we possess are derived from Athenaeus, who generally quotes them with a view to elucidating questions of cookery, or illustrating the habits of fishmongers. But the real cause of the absence from these fragments of all traces of a romantic element is probably a less fortuitous one, and is to be found in the nature of dramatic literature in general, and of comedy in particular. A play, to be successful, must be behind the times; if it treats its subjects in an enlightened manner, it will be above the level of the mass of its audience, and they will declare it dull, or ridiculous, or both.[1] Dramatic authors know this well enough, and, for the most part, carefully refrain from insulting the spectators by telling them anything new. The writers of the Middle Comedy were no exception to this rule; and so, while their plays dealt very extensively with women, and not unfrequently, it would seem, with love-stories of a sort, the treatment of these subjects was, out of deference to their public, far more antiquated and unsympathetic than one would have been inclined to expect from writers who were often well acquainted with the works of the most enlightened thinkers of the time. Thus, therefore, strange as it may at first sight appear, in all probability those fragments which have survived furnish, on the whole, a very good general idea of the relations between men and women, as depicted in the Middle Comedy; and there is in reality little reason to believe that, even if we possessed a far larger quantity of this literature, we should be able to learn much more about this particular subject. The romantic element is absent from these fragments because it was absent

[1] With comedy this is, of course, especially the case, for comedy appeals, in the main, to a lower intellectual class than tragedy, and is therefore compelled to be even more conservative.

from the complete works to which they originally belonged.

The main features of the Middle Comedy treatment of erotic subjects (as illustrated by the fragments) are very plain. There is nowhere any trace of the romantic feeling; where "love" is praised or recommended, as is, of course, not unfrequently the case, what is understood thereby is always merely sensual gratification. Plato and "Platonic" love are stock subjects of ridicule. Marriage is invariably alluded to in terms of contempt and dislike, and the women introduced are almost always Hetaerae; but even these are hardly ever spoken of with any respect or affection, being generally described as vulgar, drunken, and stingy, and in some cases attacked with the most savage brutality. The effort which the women at Athens were making about this time to gain larger liberties, also comes in for its share of ridicule; and altogether, these comedies show a want of sympathy with every honourable ambition of the age, which throws a strange light on that cultured and artistic Athenian audience which one is generally taught to admire.

I have before me an analysis[1] of all the passages in which women are in any way referred to in this literature; but, as I have already remarked, the amount of information to be gained from them is not sufficient to warrant a lengthy discussion. A few specimens from the best-known writers will serve to illustrate what has been said, and will give a sufficiently clear idea of the nature of the rest.

[1] [Excursus G.: page 219.]

ANAXANDRIDES is described by Suidas as having been the first to introduce ἔρωτας καὶ παρθένων φθοράς,[1] and is therefore important as forming a connecting-link between Old and Middle Comedy; but there is no important example of this peculiar feature in any of the fragments of him that have survived, though passages like that in the *Gerontomania* (*ap*. Athen. xiii. 570 D), and titles of plays like *Anteron* or *Kitharistria*, serve to give a very fair idea of the nature of the "erotic element" thus introduced.[2]

ANTIPHANES again, though making frequent mention of women, yet does not tell one anything of importance about them. His opinion as to their untrustworthiness is at least emphatic,

ἐγὼ γυναικὶ δ' ἕν τι πιστεύω μόνον,
ἐπὰν ἀποθάνῃ μὴ βιώσεσθαι πάλιν,
τὰ δ' ἄλλ' ἀπιστῶ πάνθ' ἕως ἂν ἀποθάνῃ.

(*Incert.* 54.)

[1] Is it merely a coincidence that this pioneer of a love-element, of a sort, in comedy, was a native of Colophon?

[2] The view that this erotic element was in no respect romantic, but dealt purely with the sensual side of the matter, is supported by (1) its inherent probability; (2) the absence of any evidence to the contrary, not only in the fragments of this writer, but also in those of Antiphanes and Alexis, who are known to have imitated him; (3) the epithet παμμίαρος applied to Anaxandrides. (*Vide* Meineke, *Com. Fr.* i. p. 369.) Though the general sense of Suidas' words seems plain, their exact meaning is not so clear. Probably ἔρωτας refers to the introduction of ἑταῖραι and their admirers, whose mutual struggles *de nocte locanda* would then provide the action of the play. The sense of παρθένων φθοράς is even less evident; but the fact that it is mentioned specially, and after the word ἔρωτας, certainly seems to imply that the φθορά formed the climax of the action. In other words, the motive of the plot was the same as in the previous case, with the exception that the woman in question was a παρθένος instead of an ἑταίρα. If this were so, then these stories would, of course, differ *toto caelo* from those of the New Comedy, where the φθορά is an act of unpremeditated indiscretion which has taken place before the play begins, and is atoned for by the hero's subsequent behaviour.

and his invectives against marriage are occasionally humorous—

A. γεγάμηκε δήπου. B. τί σὺ λέγεις; ἀληθινῶς γεγάμηκεν, ὃν ἐγὼ ζῶντα περιπατοῦντά τε κατέλιπον; (*Philopator.*)

but, on the whole, his allusions are not very interesting.

EUBULUS was notorious as a special student and parodist of Euripides, a feature apparent in the misogyny, real or affected, in which he indulges. A good specimen of this is the passage quoted in Athen. xiii. 559 B from his *Chrysilla*. There is, besides, in the *Campylion* an interesting description of violent love for a certain κοσμία ἑταίρα, one of whose chief charms, however, seems to be that she knows how to eat decently. The same writer, in the *Nannion*, dwells on the folly of adultery, supporting his view by arguments which hardly appeal to the "romantic" sense.[1]

AMPHIS grows enthusiastic over the superiority of ἑταῖραι to γαμεταί,

ἡ μὲν νόμῳ γὰρ καταφρονοῦσ' ἔνδον μένει,
ἡ δ' οἶδεν ὅτι ἢ τοῖς τρόποις ὠνητέος
ἄνθρωπός ἐστιν ἢ πρὸς ἄλλον ἀπιτέον.
(*Athamas.*)

and in the *Dithyrambus* makes a contemptuous allusion to "Platonic" love:

τί φῄς; σὺ ταυτὶ προσδοκᾷς πείσειν ἐμέ,
ὡς ἔστ' ἐραστὴς ὅστις, ὡραῖον φιλῶν,
τρόπων ἐραστής ἐστι, τὴν ὄψιν παρείς;

---

[1] Cp. Xenarchus, *Pentathl.* 1, where the same idea is developed. When one reads such lines as these, one is tempted to agree with Aristophon, that "love had been exiled from heaven." (*Pythag. Fr.* 2.)

ἄφρων γ' ἀληθῶς. οὔτε τοῦτο πείθομαι,
οὔθ' ὡς πένης ἄνθρωπος ἐνοχλῶν πολλάκις
τοῖς εὐποροῦσιν οὐ λαβεῖν τι βούλεται.
(Dithyrambus. 2.)

EPHIPPUS gives us a pretty picture of a woman (an Hetaera, of course) coaxing away a man's trouble:

ἔπειτά γ' εἰσιόντ', ἐὰν λυπούμενος
τύχῃ τις ἡμῶν, ἐκολάκευσεν ἡδέως,
ἐφίλησεν, οὐχὶ συμπιέσασα τὸ στόμα,
ὥσπερ πολέμιον, ἀλλὰ τοῖσι στρουθίοις
χναύουσ' ὁμοίως ᾖσε, παρεμυθήσατο,
ἐποίησέ θ' ἱλαρὸν εὐθέως τ' ἀφεῖλε πᾶν
αὐτοῦ τὸ λυποῦν κἀπέδειξεν ἵλεων. (<i>Empole</i>. 1).

EPICRATES is chiefly noticeable for the brutality of his *Antilais*, a considerable fragment of which is preserved in Athen. xiii. 570 B.

XENARCHUS' best contribution to literature is, perhaps, his famous

ὅρκους ἐγὼ γυναικὸς εἰς οἶνον γράφω. (*Pentathl*. 3.)

Lastly, there is ALEXIS, who, though he extends from the Middle well into the New Comedy (388—284 are the dates—rather trying to the credulity—given for his life), yet belongs very distinctly to the former, and shows no signs of a newer spirit, unless it be in the revolt against the artificiality of the Hetaerae, of which there is a specimen in his *Isostasium*. He makes, however, a favourable allusion to "Platonic" love (*Helene*), though he does not suggest the possibility of its application to women.

For the rest, he confines himself to the ordinary topics, and his complaints against wives are, here and there, amusing, as when he argues that marriage is worse than disfranchisement:—

>   τοὺς μὲν γοῦν ἀτίμους οὐκ ἐᾷ
>   ἀρχὴν λαχόντας ὁ νόμος ἄρχειν τῶν πέλας·
>   ἐπὰν δὲ γήμῃς, οὐδὲ σαυτοῦ κύριον
>   ἔξεστιν εἶναι· τὰς γὰρ εὐθύνας μόνον
>   ἐφημερινὰς τὰς τοῦ βίου κεκτήμεθα.
>   (*Incert.* 34.)

The examination of these fragments has been very barren of any but negative results, but this very barrenness is not perhaps without a certain significance. The Middle and the New Comedy kept the stage at Athens (to the exclusion, in great part, of original tragedy) without a check during the fourth century; but at the same time, the continuity of the dramatic tradition that pervades them is by no means unbroken, and the differences between the two styles of art are very marked. Of all these differences, there is none more striking than that in the treatment of the erotic element. This, which, though introduced early enough into the Middle Comedy, yet never attained to any real development there, appears suddenly in the New Comedy as a feature of overwhelming importance. Nor is this all. The erotic element, which, from henceforward, occupies so prominent a place in comedy, differs in character *toto caelo* from that which occurs in the earlier dramas. Instead of the ἑταίρα, the New Comedy introduces us to the παρθένος; instead of marriage being the stock subject of ridicule, it becomes the hero's ideal.[1]

This change of attitude is so marked, that it seems impossible to regard the later feeling as a development of the earlier; the revolution is so violent, that it seems inevitable to admit that it came in some manner from without. And, as a matter of fact, if we consider the period from which the New Comedy dates, it is by no means difficult to conjecture what the source of this external influence may have been.

Menander brought out his first play, at a very early age, in 322; about this time, Asclepiades and Philetas were already coming into prominence; those influences which induced the Coan school to speak of women in a manner so different from that of previous writers, may well have impressed the Athenian also, and produced a body of poets who, though differing in certain important points from the "Alexandrians," were yet distinctly romantic.

To this subject of the romantic element in the New Comedy, I hope at some future time to be able to return,[2] so that I will not speak of it further here, except so far as to point out that, firstly (an obvious fact, but one that seems sometimes strangely ignored), the New Comedy is distinctly later in date than the Coan school of poets, and cannot therefore, under

---

[1] There is, of course, plenty of grumbling at marriage in the New Comedy, but there the characters who give vent to it are the old men, who belong to the previous generation, and whose relations with their wives had consequently not come under the influence of romance.

[2] [This Excursus was originally written for the first Essay; the New Comedy is discussed in the second Essay. See above p. 163.]

any circumstances, claim priority for the introduction of the romantic element into literature; while secondly, if the introduction of this element was really due, as is commonly asserted, to the influence of Euripides, it seems strange that, while so many of his views were common property at Athens from the very beginning of the fourth century, not one of the Athenian playwrights, some of whom studied him so thoroughly, should have felt this particular influence till nearly a century after his death.

EXCURSUS G.

[P. 150.]

WOMEN IN THE MIDDLE COMEDY FRAGMENTS.

(Plays in italics and marked with an asterisk are wholly lost. Of those in italics no fragment of importance is preserved.)

ANTIPHANES.

Plays named after Hetaerae:—Antea?, *Archestrata?*, Chrysis, Malthace, Melitta, Neottis, Philotis.

Plays dealing apparently with a similar class of society:—Acestria, Aleiptria, *Anterosa*, *Auletris?*, Corinthia?, Curis?, Dyserotes, Halieuomene?, Hydria, Mystis?, Neanisci.

Plays relating to erotic mythological subjects:— Aeolus, *Andromeda?*, Antea?, Arcas? *Caeneus?*, Glaucus, *Melanion* (the misogynist, cp. Aristoph. Lys. 784), *Meleager?*, Omphale?, *Phaon?*

Other plays, the titles of which suggest erotic incidents: *Acontizomene?*, Aphrodisius?, Asoti?, *Delia?*, Epiclerus?, Gamus?, *Harpazomene?*, Lemniæ, Moechi, Sappho (in the fragments the poetess merely appears as asking riddles).

Acontizomene. The drunkenness of women.
Aeolus 1. Parody of the prologue of the Canace of Euripides.
Agroecus 2. Meretrix magnum malum.

Aleiptria. The servant-girl threatens to pour hot water over some rude visitors.

Arcas 2. Mention of the Hetaera Sinope, perhaps under her nickname of Abydos.

Asclepios. An old woman induced to take medicine under the idea that it is wine.

Asoti. Mulier ducit virum.

Bacchae. The drunkenness of wives.

Boeotia. A man urges a girl to try a citron at dessert. (Copied by Eriphus, Meliboea 1. Cp. Eubulus, Campylion 5.)

Butalion. A girl (?) from the country is asked to order dinner. Cp. Acestria (where read $\phi\iota\lambda\tau\acute{a}\tau\eta$ in l. 3?), and Alexis, Homoea.

Cepurus. Mention of the Hetaera Sinope.

Chrysis. 1, 2. Description of a wealthy lover.

Coroplathus. An obscene allusion.

Drapetagogus. A woman's way of eating.

Dyspratus 1. A woman's stinginess to her slaves. (Cp. Epicrates, Dyspratus.)

Glaucus. Reference to a vesticontubernium.

Halieuomene 1. A long fragment addressed by the fish-seller to her slave (containing various puns on the names of Hetaerae and their lovers.)

Hydria 1. The praises of a true Hetaera.

Malthace. The excuses of an Hetaera.

Melitta. A merchant who boasts of his wealth.

Metragyrtes. A girl washing a man's feet.

Misoponerus. Complaints as to the trouble a baby is in the house.

Mystis 3. A man inviting a woman to drink, apparently to excess. (Cp. Athen. x. 441 C;

Eubul. Campyl. 5; Anacreont. iv. 12, μύστις νάματος ἡ Κύπρις ὑμεναίοις κροτοῦσα.)

Neanisci 2. A girl arguing with her mother on the relative values of her poor and her wealthy lover (?).

Neottis 3. Mention of Sinope.

Omphale 3. Heracles ordering his dinner of Omphale.

Philometor. Praises of a mother. (Cp. Alexis, Incert. 35.)

Philopator. Marriage compared to death.

Zacynthius. The pleasure of having one's feet washed by a woman. (Cp. Pherecrates, Thalatta, 7, and supra p. 128.)

Incert. 12. Love cannot be concealed.
13. Homœopathic cure for a wife.
51. Praise of love. (Also in Theophilus, Philaulus.)
52. Marriage the last of ills.
53. The burden of a rich wife.
54. The one thing in which you can trust a woman is, that when she is dead she will not come to life again—nothing else.
55. The one advantage of ophthalmia is that you can't see your wife.
57. To tell a secret to a woman is like telling it to the town-crier.
71. An old man must forego the pleasures of love.
95. κασωρὶς ἡ πόρνη.

ANAXANDRIDES.

The following titles of plays suggest erotic subjects:—Aeschra (name of an Hetaera), Anchises, *Anteron, Citharistria*, Helene, *Locrides?*, Melilotus?, Protesilaus.

Gerontomania 1. Two old men discuss Lais and the other ladies they used to know in their youth.
Odysseus 1. Women are attracted by good dinners.
Tereus 2. An allusion suggestive of Theocr. i. 87.
      3. A royal bride.
Theseus 2. A girl is easily pleased.
Incert. 1. The troubles of being married.
      5. A father tells his daughter that a wife should not leave her husband.
      9. Women are slaves of pleasure.
     10. Love the best schoolmaster. (Cp. Alex. Incert. 38, where, however, the image is somewhat different.)
     13. An unmarried daughter is a terrible thing. (Cp. 17.)

EUBULUS.

Plays named after Hetaerae:—Chrysilla, *Clepsydra** (so called because she used to regulate the duration of her favours by the clock), Nannion, Neottis, *Plangon*.

Plays dealing with mythological erotic subjects:—Anchises?, Echo?, Europe?, Ixion?, Nausicaa?, Pelops?, Procris?

Other plays which seem to have dealt with erotic subjects:—Astyti?, Campylion, Mylothris?, Orthane,

Pamphilus, Pannychis, Pornoboscus, *Psaltria*, Stephanopolides.

Ancylion 3.   Kisses mentioned among the prizes at a "pannychis."
Campylion.   *Vide supra*, p. 155.
Cercopes 1.   The dangerous attractions of Corinth, narrated by a traveller.
Chrysilla 1.   The folly of marrying again.
       2.   An attempted defence of women breaks down.
Nannion.   The folly of adultery. (*Vide supra*, p. 158.)
Orthane.   A party of ladies and gentlemen come together to celebrate a sacrifice to Orthane.
Pamphilus 1.   A man takes up his station at the window of an inn to watch the proceedings of a lady opposite. (Cp. Ter. *Phormio* i. 2, 38 *seqq.*)
       3.   The drinking capacities of the lady's chaperone.
Pannychis.   A description of Hetaerae, in part the same as in Nannion.
Pornoboscus 1.   A woman describes her keeper.
Sphingocarion 2.   Women anointing a man's feet.
       3.   A lady excuses her absence on the previous evening (?).
Stephanopolides 1.   A flower girl (?) ridicules the cosmetics of the professional Hetaerae.
       2.   The pleasures of love from a woman's point of view. (A very graceful passage, with an

>   allusion to the legend of Cissus
>   and Ololygon.)
>   3, 4.   The flower-girls making up and
>   selling their garlands. (Another
>   pretty passage, with perhaps
>   an allusion to the Hetaera
>   Nannion under her name of
>   Aegidion.)
> Incert. 3. Why do girls prefer old wine, but young
>   men?
>   9. A woman in a passion.
>   20. A man excuses himself and goes home.
>   25. Mention of the festival Stenia, at which
>   the Athenian women used to abuse one
>   another. (Cp. Theopompus, Aphro-
>   disia 1; *supra*, p. 148.)

ALEXIS.

Plays named after Hetaerae:—Agonis, Atthis?, Choregis, Dorcis?, Isostasium, Lampas, Meropis?, Opora, Pamphile, *Pezonice*, Polycleia, Ponera?

Plays on mythological erotic subjects:—Atalanta, Galatea, Helenes Harpage, Helenes Mnesteres, Hesione, *Iasis ?*.

Other plays apparently dealing with erotic subjects: —Achaeis?, Apocoptomenus, Bostrychus?, Brettia?, Cnidia?, Curis, Epiclerus?, Hypnus, Lemnia?, Leucadia? (can this play have dealt with the proceedings of the comic poet Nicostratus?), Mandragorizomene, Olynthia, Orchestris, Pallace, Phaedrus, Philocalus, Philusa, *Poëtria ?*, Traumatias.

Agonis. *Vide supra*, p. 156.

Apocoptomenus 1. Lovers have wings and Love has none.

Cleobuline. A mention of the Hetaera Sinope.

Curis 1, 2. A father of two sons, one highly respectable, the other less so.

Dropides. An Hetaera brings in a decanter of sweet wine during dinner.

Graphe. The story of the man who fell in love with the statue at Samos. (It would be obvious to suggest that in this play a man is introduced who falls in love with a picture. More probably, however, this passage comes from the speech of some painter who is extolling his art, possibly to some lady, in the way Ovid used to do. Cp. *Ars Amat.* iii. 397 *seqq.*, 533 *seqq.*, etc.)

Gynaecocratia. Perhaps introduced women in the theatre, like the Scenas Catalambanusae of Aristophanes.

Helene. A mock (?) Platonic view of love. (*Vide supra*, p. 161.)

Hesione 2. The heroine complains that, as soon as Heracles saw that his dinner was ready, he ceased to take any notice of her.

Homoea. A girl is asked to order dinner.

Hypnus 1. Two women asking one another riddles.

Isostasium 1. An attack on the artificiality of Hetaerae.

Lampas. The protest of an angry father at his son's extravagance. (Cp. Mnesimach. Dyscolus.)

Lyciscus 1. A mention of the Hetaera Pythionice.

Mandragorizomene 5. A lover visits his sick lady. (The whole play seems to have turned on a subject of this kind (cp. Fr. 2), and calls to mind pictures like that in Ovid, *Ars Amat.* ii. 319 *seqq.*, especially 333 *seqq.*

Manteis. The slavery of marriage.

Meropis. A lady complains of the late arrival of someone, perhaps her maid.

Olynthia 1, 2. The poor circumstances of the heroine's family.

Orchestris. All that women want is plenty of wine.

Pallace. Perhaps the answer of the husband to his indignant wife.

Pamphile. The proper food for a lover. (Cp. *Incert.* 18.)

Phaedrus 1. The nature of love.

Philocalos. A stingy man inviting ladies to dinner.

Philusa 1. The Aphrodisia.

Tarantini 5. An allusion to the Hetaera Nannion.

Thrason. A talkative woman.

Traumatias 2. Only lovers really live.

Incert. 14. A repetition of the remark of Eubulus (*Incert.* 3) on the inconsistency of women in preferring old wine and young men.

    18. The proper food for a lover. (Cp. Pamphile.)

    26. Inviting a woman to drink.

    31. The three pleasures of life.

    34. Marriage worse than disfranchisement.

    35. One's mother is deserving of the highest respect. (Cp. Antiphanes, Philometor.)

    38. Love the best tutor. (Cp. Anaxandr. *Incert.* 10, where, however, the image is slightly different.)

39. Nothing is more shameless than a woman
—as I know from my own wife.
40. Nothing is so difficult to guard as a woman.
53. The word διαπεπαρθενευκότα.

AMPHIS.

Several plays satirising women, such as the *Acco**
(the silly woman), the Gynaecocratia and the Gynaecomania.

The Scholiast of Germanicus' *Aratea* quotes the legends of Zeus and Callisto (p. 38), and of the Dog Star and Opora (p. 76) from Amphis; these legends seem to have occurred in plays now lost.[1]

Of the Sappho no important fragment is preserved.

Amphicrates. A confidential slave arguing with his young master on the folly of the latter's attachment to a certain lady.

Athamas. The inevitable superiority of the Hetaera over the wife.

Curis 1, 2. An Hetaera who deserves to be rich, more than Sinope and the others who are.

Dithyrambus 2. Ridicule of "Platonic" love.

Gynaecocratia. The liberated husband. (It is easy to imagine how the outraged wife breaks in upon this happy party, something after the manner of Cynthia in Prop. iv. 8.)

Gynaecomania. Seems to suggest a similar scene, if indeed, the two plays be not one and the same.

Ialemus 1. An invective against lettuces.

[1] [The author is following Meineke i. 404: the name "Amphis" is a conjectural emendation in the latter passage.]

ARAROS.

The Adonis and the Caeneus dealt with erotic legends, as is plain from Fr. 1 of the former and Fr. 4 of the latter. The same is perhaps true of the Panos Gonae (Fr. 2.) The Hymenaeus contained a description of a wedding (Fr. 2), and the *Parthenidion** may also have dealt with erotic subjects.

NICOSTRATUS.

The Pandrosus introduces (Fr. 2, 3) an elderly gentleman supping with a lady, among whose acquaintances is numbered Ocimum (Fr. 1).

Incert. 9 describes a prude.

Besides these, the titles *Anterosa*, Habra, and the corrupt *Otis*,* seem to suggest erotic subjects.

PHILETAERUS.

In the Atalanta, the fragment which it is usual to assign to a parasite might perhaps be assigned to the heroine of the piece, who would thus appear in her legendary character of the "advanced woman," something like the lady in Juvenal vi. 246 *seqq.*, 425 *seqq.*

Corinthiastes. The superiority of Hetaerae to Gametae. (He repeats the remark in Cynagis 3.)

Cynagis 1. A list of veteran Hetaerae.

2. Old age is no excuse for giving up pleasure.

Meleager. A dance not suitable for unmarried ladies.

EPHIPPUS.

Empole 1. A pretty picture of a woman (an Hetaera, of course,) coaxing away a man's trouble.

Empole 2.   The same (?) urging on a disorderly member of the party the advantages of harmony.

Ephebi 3.   Proceedings commence with the ladies having a drink all round.

Philyra (named after the Hetaera) 2.   The heroine (?) coaxing an elderly gentleman to commit what he considers an extravagance. (Fr. 3 seems to suggest that a younger lover appeared on the scene and expressed himself as jealous.)

Sappho.   How to recognise a πόρνος.

ANAXILAS.

Neottis 1.   A violent invective against the whole race of Hetaerae, mentioning various names.

        2.   The difference between an Hetaera and a Porne.

Incert. 2.   Rebuke of a jealous lover (?).

        3.   The sign of an abandoned woman.

    4, 5.   Remarks on a woman's toilet.

        6.   A system of coiffure.

ARISTOPHON.

Callonides.   The folly of marrying a second time.

Iatrus 2.   An Hetaera's door is shut to a man without money (l. 1, *leg.* διαπετεῖς *pro* διοπετεῖς).

Pythagoristes 2.   The gods have driven Love out of heaven, and clipped his wings, so that he stays on earth.

EPICRATES.

Antilais 2. A savage attack upon Lais.
3. A list of erotic writers whose poems one learns by heart.
Chorus. A man cheated by a *lena*.
Dyspratus. Women's stinginess towards slaves (cp. Antiphanes, Dyspratus). *O demens, ita servus homo est?*

CRATINUS IUNIOR.

Omphale. The heroine (?) appears dilating on the pleasures of a life of ease, with a view to seducing Heracles.

The Titanes also seems to have dealt with erotic subjects.

AXIONICUS.

Philinna. One thing, at least, you can trust a woman —that she won't drink water.

CALLICRATES.

Moschion. A mention of Sinope.

DIODORUS.

Incert. Better a well-educated wife without money than one who does not know how to behave with.

ERIPHUS.

Meliboea 1. A man giving a girl some citrons at dessert. (Cp. Antiphanes, Boeotia.) Fr. 2 seems to belong to the same scene.

HENIOCHUS.

Incert. The cities of Greece, allegorised as women are entertained and made drunk by Abulia, Democratia, and Aristocratia.

HERACLITUS.

Xenizon. Mention of a certain gluttonous Helen.

PHILISCUS.

Philargyri. A woman's powers of persuasion.

SOPHILUS.

The Paracatathece and the Syntrechontes both seem to have had erotic plots.

TIMOTHEUS.

Incert. An elaborate eulogy of Love, which does not read like the work of a comic poet.

TIMOCLES.

Epistolae 1. A lover's comic enthusiam.
Icarii 1, 2. Pythionice and her lovers.
Marathonii. The pleasures of seduction. (Cp. p. 159, note.)
Neaera 1. An unfortunate lover of Phryne.
Orestautocleides 1. Autocleides the paederast appears surrounded by Hetaerae, in the character of Orestes and the Erinnyes. (Cp. Mein. *Com. Fr.* i. 432.)

Philodicastes. Mention of a new regulation by which the γυναικονόμοι had to inspect entertainments, to see that they were respectable.

Sappho. An allusion to Misgolas (cp. *supra*, p. 157).

XENARCHUS.

Butalion. A childless house.

Hypnus. Happy cicadas, for their females are dumb.

Pentathlus 1. The folly of adultery (cp. Eubulus, Nannion).

    2, 3. Woman's power of drinking.

Priapus. An earnest drinker.

Scythae 1. The effects of a rival (?).

THEOPHILUS.

Neoptolemus 1. A young wife does not suit an old husband.

Philaulus 1. Love for a maiden (a *citharistria*) described with considerable enthusiasm. (The first four lines = Antiph. *Incert.* 51.)

    2. An anxious father (?) hopes that his son will not fall into the hands of the Hetaerae.

EXCURSUS H.

[P. 163.]

WOMEN IN THE FRAGMENTS OF THE EARLY NEW COMEDY.

In the case of Menander, only the more important allusions are chronicled. In the case of the other writers, everything that bears on the subject is mentioned.

MENANDER.

Adelphi 1. The happiness of never marrying. (Adapted by Terence in his *Adelphi*.)
Andria 1. Love makes blind. (Adapted by Terence in his *Andria*.)
Androgynus 2. An allusion to a wedding ceremony.
Anepsii 1. Love is, by nature, deaf to advice.
      2. A daughter is a troublesome thing.
Aphrodisia 1. Love makes fools of men.
      2. A girl, while delirious, lets out unfortunate secrets.
Arrephorus 1. The dangers of marriage.
      3. A talkative woman.
Carchedonius. (Adapted by Plautus in his *Poenulus?*)
Chalceia 3. Youth is the time for love.
Colax 4. A list of various well-known Hetaerae. (Adapted by Terence in his *Eunuchus*.)

Cybernetae 2. The man who is counted lucky in public, but tyrannised over at home.

Dactylius 1. The obstinate father who refuses his daughter.
    2. A bridegroom who wants no dowry. (For the plot cp. Ter. *Hecyra*.)

Didymae 1. The Cynic Crates' wife. (Cp. Apul. *Florid.* xiv.)

Empipramene 1. Invective against marriage.
    4. A father's joy (at the recognition of his daughter?).

Epitrepontes. (Similar in plot to the *Hecyra* of Terence.)

Eunuchus 7. The violent joy of the successful lover in Ter. *And.* v. 5, 3, is translated literally from this play. (Adapted by Terence in his *Eunuchus*.)

Georgus 6. The unpractical lover.

Halieis 6. A daughter is an awkward thing.
    10. The flight of the adulterer.

Heauton Timorumenus 3. The respectable girl's home. (Adapted by Terence in his *Heauton Timorumenus*.)

Heros 1. Love is omnipotent.

Hiereia 2. A respectable woman should not leave the house. (The plot deals with a married woman who follows the priests of Cybele about the streets.)

Hypobolimaeus 4. The husband should rule the wife.
    8. μέγιστον θηρίον γυνή.

Leucadia 1. Sappho's leap.

Misogynes 1. The advantages of a wife.
   2, 3, 4, 5. The expense of keeping a wife.
   4, 5. A woman's superstitions.
   9. The husband seeks refuge with an Hetaera. (The plot is concerned with a man who marries a woman, and then conceives a most violent hatred for her.)
Misumenus 3. The slavery of love.
   5. Platonic love.
   6. The lover's misery.
   7. The lover in his lady's absence.
   8. An unsympathetic listener.
   10. The lover cannot sleep.
   12. Jealousy.
      (The plot deals with a Miles Gloriosus, who is in love with a slave girl of his, but will not touch her because she does not love him.)
Nauclerus 4. A lover is always easily led.
Olynthia 4. Artificial hair.
Orge 5. An adulterer is an expensive luxury.
Paedion 2. A man who goes round offering amulets to men when they get married.
Periceiromene. (The soldier who, in a fit of jealousy, cuts off the hair of his slave girl, and afterwards repents.)
Perinthia. (Adapted by Terence in his *Andria*, especially for the first scene.)
Plocion 1. The rich, ugly, and jealous wife.
   2. The disagreeableness of the same.
   3. The results of a κωμικὴ παννυχίς.
   4. The trouble that they bring on a house.

Sicyonius. (The soldier who buys a girl, and then treats her as if she were a free woman.)

Synaristosae 1, 2. The strange behaviour of some women (Hetaerae?) at dinner.

    4. Love makes one perjure oneself.

Thais 1. The ideal Hetaera, faithful to none.

Thesaurus 1. Love is a severe god, especially to the old.
    2. Music is the food of love.
    3. The lover must be bold.

(In order to estimate at its true value the prominence of misogyny in the following passages, it is well to remember that a large proportion of the *Fragmenta Incerta* of Menander are found in Christian collections of apophthegms.)

Incert. 1. If you have once married, then you must put up with it.

    3. A man ought to be allowed the chance of getting to know his wife before marriage; for every woman is an evil, but then one could choose the least. (Cp. 102.)

    6. Invective against Prometheus for creating women.

    7. The sudden effects of a kiss.

    8. The polygamous habits of the Thracians.

    14. Of the nature of love.

    16. Women are afraid of death, and seek comfort for trouble in tears.

    27. Women have no gratitude.

    32. A girl's wooing. (Transl. in Plaut. *Cist.* i. 1, 91.)

36. The advantages of a πόρνη over a respectable woman.

πλείονα κακουργεῖ, πλεῖον' οἶδ', αἰσχύνεται
οὐδέν, κολακεύει μᾶλλον.

54, 55, 57. One should not marry money.
58. The man who contemplates marriage must consider whether he prefers beauty or worth.
73. A man stands up for his wife.
99. Virtue doubles the value of beauty.
100. A woman must try to lead her husband, not drive him.
101. None are so closely related as man and wife.
102. A man who marries, may count it as a great good if his wife is only a slight evil.
103. The troubles of a family man.
104. Advice against marriage.
105. Marriage is a necessary evil.
106. A woman's fair words are most to be feared. (Cp. 197.)
107. An Hetaera cannot be expected to be good, for she makes her living out of mischief.
112. A mother loves her children more than a father.
114. The unmarried daughter in the house.
117. A lover's threats are not serious.
133. A respectable woman does not dye her hair.

154. Educating a woman is like giving poison to a viper.
155. The dangers of beauty.
156. Your wife will be nasty without being taught.
185. A bit of the marriage ceremony.
196. Love cannot be controlled by reason.
198. Women are consistent liars.
199. Night is the time for love.
241. An Hetaera's dress.
256. One must not trust a woman.
258. It is safer to stir up a dog than an old woman.
259. Women are irritable. (Cp. 499.)
294. The behaviour of a low woman.
346. Stupid women.
469. An oath to a woman is not binding.

I have added an analysis of the *Gnomae Monostichi*, for the sake of completeness. No one will, of course, attach any importance to the views expressed in this nondescript collection. [Cp. Kock, *Com. Att. Fr.* vol. iii. praef.]

56. The happiness of being unmarried. (Cp. 78, 437, 468, 595.)
77. The expensiveness of wives.
83. Women are the better for being silent.
84. The ideal woman is the good housekeeper.
85. A woman may save or ruin a house.
86. Do not trust a woman. (Cp. 633.)
87. Women consider nothing but their own wishes.
90. There is nothing so wretched as an old man in love.

91. The man who wants to marry changes his mind.
92. Virtue, not gold, adorns a woman.
93. A good wife saves a man's position.
94. It is not easy to find a good woman.
95. It is better to bury a woman than to marry her.
97. A wife is an expensive luxury.
98. Marry your wife, not her money.
99. A good wife is the helm of a household.
100. A woman cannot rule; it is against nature.
102. Marriage is an evil men bring on themselves.
103. When about to marry you should consider your neighbours.
106. Women are bad counsellors.
109. All women are alike.
134. Woman is the source of every ill. (Cp. 541, 623.)
156. Love cannot withstand poverty. (Cp. 159.)
160. Some women are virtuous.
161. Women are faithless. (Cp. 560.)
181. Women are a cause of ruin.
195. A woman's jealousy.
197. A married man is a slave.
199. Try and get a woman as your ally.
211. Don't marry mere money.
215. A man must rule his wife.
231. Women are as dangerous as sea and fire.
233. A bad woman is a treasure-house of evil.
248. Women are fiercer than beasts.
260. A woman should stay at home.
261. A bad woman is like poison.
264. Woman is like the sea.

267. Woman is as fierce as a lioness.
304. Woman is a necessary evil.
324. A wife is a constant cause of grief.
327. A woman is worse to live with than a lion.
333. A woman's virtue is worth more than her beauty.
334. A woman is full of evil.
353. Never abuse or advise a woman.
355. Never let a woman into your counsels.
361. Never waste anything good on a woman.
382. Marriage is slavery.
410. A lover's anger is short-lived.
413. There is nothing worse than a pretty woman.
426. A harlot's weeping is like a lawyer's.
469. A woman is dirt silvered over.
493. Woman is a pleasant ill.
540. A bad woman is like a storm in the house.
575. A woman is like a fire.
600. Women flatter with an object.
634. The value of a good wife. (Cp. 675.)
684. May my friends never marry.
700. Women ruin many men.
734. Pretty women are conceited.
735. Your wife is worth taking trouble for.
750. A daughter is hard to dispose of.
757. A poor man should not marry.

PHILEMON.

Adelphi 1. Praise of Solon for having introduced prostitution.
Babylonius. An Hetaera's prospects.
Pyrphorus. Greater beauty than any painter could depict.

Synephebus. An Hetaera's dress.
Incert. 31. A lady going out with a pretty servant. (Cp. Plaut. *Mercator*, ii. 3, 69.)
  32. The affections of a μῦς λευκός.
  35. The man who fell in love with the statue.
  44. A good wife obeys her husband.
  49. The growth of love.
  64. A dutiful son and his mother.
  76. Where women meet, there is sure to be mischief.
  77. Worth is better than beauty.
  78. There is no need to teach a woman mischief.
  85. The folly of taking counsel with a woman.
  95. A conceited woman.
  103. Woman is an immortal necessary evil.
  105, 106. Advice not to marry.
  124. A city of beautiful women.

DIPHILUS.

Pallace. A woman's ornament.
Synoris 1, 2, 3. A parasite and an Hetaera playing dice.
Theseus 2. A Samian lady's riddle.
Zographus 1. An Hetaera entertains lavishly.
Incert. 2. An outburst against the trade of the πορνοβοσκός.
  6. An ugly girl, from whom even a dog won't take a piece of bread.
  16. The oath of an Hetaera is not to be believed.

33. It is hard to find a good woman.
34. A virgin is a treasure that it is not easy to guard.
47. A woman described as a carcase.

ARCHEDICUS.

Dihamartanon. A dishonest Hetaera.

The fragments of HIPPARCHUS, LYNCEUS, and APOLLODORUS GELOUS contain no allusions to women.

EXCURSUS I.

[P. 163.]

THE QUESTION OF WOMEN'S RIGHTS IN THE MIDDLE COMEDY.

IT is usual to assume that there was, during the earlier part of the fourth century, a strong agitation at Athens in favour of "women's rights." The social status of the Theban, as well as of the Lacedaemonian, women, had been brought, owing to political events, under the notice of even the most consistent Athenian, and advantage is supposed to have been taken of this fact by the advocates of female liberty at Athens, to endeavour to obtain for the women there some of those privileges which notoriously belonged to their neighbours. This being so, it will be interesting to consider in how far, if at all, this movement is reflected in the literature of the period.

The general treatment of women in the Middle Comedy being such as it is, there would be every reason to expect to find plays in which these efforts of women to obtain more general recognition from men, would be made the subject of more or less contemptuous ridicule. The fashion started by Aristophanes in the *Ecclesiazusae* must have been, one would have thought, too fascinating to be abandoned.

The fact, however, remains that, in such portions of the Middle Comedy as still exist, there is practically no trace of anything of the kind. There are, it is true, one or two titles of plays which seem at first sight suggestive, but further investigation generally reveals little. Thus the *Gynaecocratia* and the *Gynaecomania* of Amphis both seem aimed, not at the tyranny of women in general, but at the tyranny of wives.[1]

As for the *Gynaecocratia* of Alexis, all that can be gathered from the fragments is that it seems to have had certain features in common with the *Scenas Catalambanusae* of Aristophanes; as to its tone or tendency, there is no clue in the two short passages that remain.

The suggestion made above (p. 228) as to the meaning of the fragment of the *Atalanta* of Philetaerus is, of course, purely conjectural, and cannot, therefore, bear evidence either way.

And that is all. This almost entire absence from the Middle Comedy of plays dealing with the question of "women's rights," would seem to justify a certain hesitation in accepting the common view that this question was at the time a burning one. So general a silence on the point, in a literature which deals exhaustively with every other phase of contemporary life, seems not unreasonably to suggest that the extent and influence of the movement have been exaggerated, and that, as far as it existed at all, it was confined to a small body of enthusiasts, and was well-nigh without effect on the body of the nation at large.

[1] Cp. *supra*, p. 227. This feeling is, of course, common enough; cp. Alexis, *Manteis*, γυναιξὶ δοῦλοι ζῶμεν ἀντ' ἐλευθέρων, κ.τ.λ.

EXCURSUS K.

[P. 187.]

SOME FURTHER NOTES ON FAMILY RELATIONS AS TREATED IN MIDDLE AND NEW COMEDY.

THOUGH it has nothing to do with our immediate subject, it may be interesting to notice briefly the attitude of the New Comedy towards that description of family problems which the *Canace* of Euripides and similar works had made popular among certain classes of art-lovers. That such works had ever any great hold over the public at large is neither proved nor probable.

In the first place, we may notice the unpleasant accident by which, in the *Curculio*, the soldier is made unconsciously to buy his sister as his mistress. Here, however (Plaut. *Curc.* v. 2, 55 *seqq.*), as soon as the recognition takes place, Planesium is at once given in marriage by her brother to her lover—as soon, that is to say, as her consent has been obtained to this course (*ibid.* 73). In the Middle Comedy *Epidicus*, where a similar incident occurs, the behaviour of Stratippocles is somewhat less correct (Plaut. *Epid.* v. 1, 42 *seqq.*), though here, too, the side of propriety is at once championed by the slave, and prevails without any real delay. That incidents of this kind were not uncommon in New Comedy seems probable from the nature of that class of drama, but there is no reason to suppose that they ever had any other conclusion than that which occurs in the cases quoted above. Cases of rivalry between father and son, such as occur in the *Casina* and the *Mercator*, belong to a class of drama which has nothing to do with romantic New Comedy. The *dénouements* of the *Asinaria* and the *Bacchides*, which are so little sympathetic to modern ideas, are both to some extent apologised for by their authors,[1] and also, as will be observed, occur in plays which have Hetaerae for their heroines.

A certain lack of regard for decency on the part of the father in the son's presence, and *vice versâ*, (which is rather startling to the modern reader in such passages as Plaut. *Asin.* v. 2, 30 *seqq.*, Ter. *Heaut. Timor.* iii. 3, 1, and elsewhere,) is probably most simply explained by *autres temps autres moeurs*. Altogether, it would seem that the privacy which is to modern ideas somewhat of an essential in these matters, was at a considerable discount at this period of society. Cp. Plaut. *Bacch.* iii. 3, 73 *seqq.*, *Curc.* i. 3, 16 *seqq.*, etc.

Lastly, attention may be called to Hanno's rather remarkable method of searching for his lost daughters. (Plaut. *Poen.* prolog. 106 *seqq.*). Whether this is intended for a realistic study of Semitic habits, can be left to others to decide.

---

[1] Plaut. *Asin.* i. 1, 53 *seqq.* (patres ut consueverunt, ego mitto omnia haec, l. 64); *Bacch.* v. 2, 89 *seqq.* (hi senes, nisi fuissent nihil iam inde a adulescentia, non hodie hoc *tantum flagitium* facerent canis capitibus, etc.) Of course, if anyone prefers to believe that these apologies are due to the *Latin* author, no one can very well contradict him.

INDEX

A. OF AUTHORS AND SUBJECTS REFERRED TO.

[The references are to pages throughout. Where the discussion of a subject is continued over several pages, only the first page is here given. Plays are usually cited under their authors' names.]

Achilles, and Briseis, 9; and Patroclus, 40, 76; and Iphigeneia, 63.
Achilles Tatius, 13, 78, 109.
Actaeon, 33.
Admetus, and Apollo, 13, 31, 90, 99.
Aeschylus, 41; and Stesichorus, 42; *Myrmidones* of, 40, 82, 92.
Ajax, and Teucer, 76, 90, 99; of Sophocles, compared to the *Antigone*, 99.
Alcaeus, the comic poet, 149.
Alcaeus, the lyric poet, 83.
Alcestis, 57, 99.
Alciphron, 146, 148.
Alcman, 22; and Megalostrate, 23; love-poems to boys, 24; Parthenia, 24.
Alexander and the wife of Darius, 181.
Alexandrian poetry, distinctive feature of, 1, 69.
Alexis, *Agonis* of, 156; *Helene* of, 161; on marriage, 162; on women, 224.
Ameipsias, 147.
Amphis on women, 227.
Anacreon, 26, 27, 86; love-poems to women, 27; importance for history of the romantic element, 28; character of poems to boys, 86.
Anaxandrides, 154, 162; on women, 213, 222.
Andromache, in the Iliad, 10; as the ideal wife, 55, 64.
Antiphanes on women, 213, 219; retort to Alexander, 152.

Antimachus 5, 107; and Plato, 111; and Catullus, 111; influence on Asclepiades, 113, 197; influence on Philetas, 113 (*vide s.v.* LYDE).
Aphrodite, and Anchises, 202; as the rival of Artemis, 59; treatment of Phaedra, 47.
Apuleius, 189.
Archilochus, 19, 82; true motive of his satires, 21; and Catullus, 22.
Archippus, *Ichthys* of, 147.
Ariadne, 12, 14.
Aristophanes, 129; weddings in, 132; views on women, 134; *Cocalus* of, 135; *Æolosicon* of, 143.
Asclepiades, 69; Meleager's criticism on, 73; eulogy of Antimachus, 113; probable influence on Menander, 196.
Aspasia, 127.

Bacchylides, 36.
Battis, 70.
Boy-love, in classical Greek literature, 74; as an element of classical Greek society, 77; as a military institution, 77; as an emblem of liberty, 77; purity of, 78; development of, 79; decay of, 79, 102; permanent influence on literature, 80; in the Anthology, 81; in Archilochus, 82; in Alcman, 24; in Alcaeus, 83; illustrated by Sappho, 85; in Anacreon, 86; in Theognis, 87, 207; in the *Scolia*, 89; in Attic tragedy, 91; in Alexandrian poetry, 102; in Meleager, 103.
Brother and sister, in Attic tragedy, 48, 101; in the New Comedy, 245.

Callias, 147.
Catullus, 81.
Chionides, 122.
Clytemnestra, 42.
Corinna, 36.
Crates, 126, 128.
Cratinus, 126.
Cratinus junior, *Theramenes* of, 151.

Daphnis, 14, 34.
Deianira, 43.
Diphilus on women, 241; belongs really to Middle Comedy, 188.
Diphilus and Gnathaena, 128.

Epicharmus, 122.
Epicrates, *Antilais* of, 73, 151.

Eubulus, on women, 214, 222; *Campylion* of, 155; *Nannion* of, 158.
Eumathius, 199.
Euripides, services to art, 50; female characters, 50; admiration for women, 51; view of love, 52; striking absence of love-element in, 52, 62, 63, 66; why E. was not a "romantic" writer, 66; E. and the Alexandrians, 53; his misogyny, 51; *Aeolus* of, 38, 52; *Andromeda* of, 140, 203; *Antigone* of, 38; *Chrysippus* of, 93; *Electra* of, 65; *Iphigeneia* of, 63; *Medea* of, 66; *Meleager* of, 38; *Phoenix* of, 38; *Protesilaus* of, 57; *Stheneboea* of, 38.

Ganymede, 13.
Goddesses, preponderance of, in Greek Pantheon, 7; in love with mortals, 13.

Haemon, motives for suicide, 44.
Helen of Himera, 33.
Helen of Troy, in the *Iliad*, 10; in Stesichorus, 33; and Theseus, 161.
Hermesianax, 14, 26, 110.
Hesiod, women in, 8; Catalogus of, 12.
Hetaera, in early times, 19; in Bacchylides, 36; in Early Comedy, 128, 147, 148; in Middle Comedy, 151, 215, 219; treated as superior to a wife, 158; in New Comedy, 175.
Hippolytus, defence of, 61.

Ibycus, 35.
Iphigeneia, 63.

Jealousy, Attic view as to, 43, 55.

Lafaye, *Catulle et ses modèles*, 20, 22.
Lesbian Poets, 83.
Licymnius, 36.
Love, early Greek views as to, 12, 17, 55, 64; in Middle Comedy, 160; in New Comedy, 169, 185; in Menander, 184; in Sophocles, 46; in Euripides, 52.
Love-element, in the *Iliad*, 75; in *Hymn. Hom.* iv. 201; in Sappho, 85; in choral poetry, 35; in Attic Tragedy, 38, 91; in Sophocles, 46; in Euripides, 50; in Eur. *Andromeda*, 203; in classical Greek poetry in general, 67; in Middle Comedy, 150; in New Comedy, 163; in Asclepiades, 70.
Lyde of Antimachus, 107; importance of, 108; characteristic tone of, 110.
Lyric poetry, subjective, 17; choral, 31.

Magnes, 122.
Mahaffy, *Classical Greek Literature*, 20, 63.
Marriage, in Comedy, 109, 212, 216 (*vide s. v.* **Middle Comedy, New Comedy**); Sophocles' view of, 43; in Greek romance, 109; in Menander, 170.
Maximus Tyrius, distinction between ancient and modern love, 54; on Achilles and Patroclus, 76; on Sappho and Socrates, 85; on Anacreon, 87.
Medea, 12, 14, 66.
Meleager, criticism of Asclepiades, 73; poem to Charidemus, 103.
Menalcas, 14.
Menander, 2; great merit of, 164; wrote plays belonging to Middle Comedy, 193; introduced the romantic element into comedy, 188; marriage characteristic of, 170; view of love, 184; father and children in, 185; why elderly married men are treated by M. as unhappy, 173; on women, 233; *Leucadia* of, 146; *Misogynes* of, 174; *Misumenus* of, 178; *Sicyonius* of, 180; *Thais* of, 177.
Middle Comedy, main features of, 150; difference from Old Comedy, 125; difference from New Comedy, 163; women in, 210, 219; women's rights in, 243; dislike of marriage, 158; ridicules Platonic love, 160; ridicules family life, 161; parodies mythological erotic stories, 161.
Miles Gloriosus as the chivalrous lover, 180.
Mimnermus, 25; and Nanno, 26; mentioned by Roman poets, 27.
Minos and Zeus, 13.
Morychis, law of, 125.
Myrtis, 36.

Nanno, 26.
Nausicaa, 10.
New Comedy, 109; ideal character of, 119; difference from Middle Comedy, 163; two common types of plot in, 165; the married state described as a happy one, 171; condemns adultery, 174; only slaves ridicule Platonic love in, 185; legal obligation to marry not urged in, 137; women in, 233.

Orestes and Pylades, 101.
Ovid, 109.

Pandora, legend of, 8.
Parthenius, 15.
Penelope, 8; and Odysseus, 10.

Phaedra, of Sophocles, 46; illustrated from the Homeric Hymn to Aphrodite, 201; of Euripides, 59.

Pherecrates, 125, 128.

Philemon, 142; wrote plays belonging to Middle Comedy, 193; more old-fashioned than Menander, 189; on women, 240; *Hypobolimaeus* of, 144.

Philetas, 69; influenced by Antimachus, 113.

Philoxenus, 36.

Phocion on marriage, 133.

Phocylides, 19.

Pindar, erotic legends in, 67.

Plato, 6; in the *Hedychares* of Theopompus, 149.

Plato comicus, 145.

Plautus, as imitating Middle Comedy, 157; as illustrating New Comedy, 187; and Menander, 234, 236; *Captivi* of, 155; *Epidicus* of, 183; *Poenulus* of, 185; *Stichus* of, 187.

Poseidippus, 26, 110.

Reitzenstein, *Epigramm und Skolion*, 25, 29, 34, 59.

Rhadina, 34.

Rhianus, poem to Dexionicus, 103.

Rohde, *der griechische Roman*, 75, 203.

Romantic Element, characteristic feature of, 4; mistaken ideas as to, 2, 40, 106; sudden appearance in literature, 69; ditto, explained, 104; origin among the Greeks, 105; nature of in Greece, 108; ditto, contrasted with mediaeval romance, 109; in the Latin elegiac poets, 109.

Sacred Band of Epaminondas, 77.

Sappho, 85, 160; and Phaon, 146; and Sophocles, 45; and Aeschylus, 45; and Socrates, 85.

Scolia, 31, 89.

Scylla, legend of, 14.

Simonides Amorginus, 18; and Hesiod, 18.

Sophocles, 43; and Sappho, 45; views on marriage, 45; view of love, 46; *Antigone* of, 47; *Cholcides* of, 38; *Niobe* of, 93; *Oenomaus* of, 38; *Phaedra* of, 38.

Sparta, 6, 24, 77.

Stesichorus, 33; and Aeschylus, 42.

Strato, 81.

Strattis, 147.

Susario, 68.

Telestes, 37.

Terence, as illustrating New Comedy, 187; and Menander, 233; *Hecyra* of, 170, 175.

Theocritus, poems to boys, 81, 83; illustrative of Alcaeus, 83; and Theognis, 208.

Theognis, 29, 87; Book II., 207; and Theocritus, 208.

Theopompus, 148; *Hedychares* of, 149.

Theseus, and Helen, 161.

Wife, Sophoclean ideal, 44; Euripidean ideal, 55; compared with Hetaera in Middle Comedy, 158; ditto in New Comedy, 176; tyranny of wives in Middle Comedy, 244.

Women, primitive position of, 7; in the Homeric poems, 8; in Hesiod, 8; in the early legends, 11; in the stories of Parthenius, 15; early literary ideal of, 17; in Simonides, 18; in Phocylides, 19; in Theognis, 29, 199; in the *Scolia*, 31; in Stesichorus, 33; in Ibycus, 35; in the later choral poets, 36; in Attic tragedy, 40; in Aeschylus, 41; in Sophocles, 43; in Euripides, 50; in the early Alexandrians, 69; in Asclepiades, 71; in Greek comedy, 118; in the Middle Comedy, 219; in early New Comedy, 233; better position in Asia, 182; freemasonry among in Euripides, 58; might be attacked openly by name, 151; women's rights in the Middle Comedy, 243.

B. OF PASSAGES EMENDED OR DISCUSSED.

Aeschylus, *Fr.* 135, 136 (92).

Alexis, *Graphe* (225).

Anth. Pal. V. 164, 4 (73).

Antiphanes, *Acestria*, 3 (220).

Archilochus, *Fr.* 100 *seqq.* (20).

Aristophon, *Iatrus*, *Fr.* 2 (229).

Eubulus, *Campylion* (155).

Euripides, *Hippol.* 1415, 1440 (206), *Fr.* 132 (205).

Hesiod, *Op.* 702 (19).

Martial XIV. 187 (177).

Mimnermus, *Fr.* 1 (25).

Philetaerus, *Atalanta* (228).

Propertius II. 6, 3 (177).

Sophocles, *Ant.* 781 (46), 909 (49); *Fr.* 855, 13 (201).

Theognis, 261 *seqq.* (199), 1282, 1363 (208).

Theopompus, *Nemea* 8 (148).

TABLE OF COMIC FRAGMENTS

In the text the fragments of the comedians are cited from Meineke's *Fragmenta Comicorum Graecorum* (5 vols., 1839–57). In the following table the corresponding numbers are given from Kock's *Comicorum Atticorum Fragmenta* (3 vols., 1880–88). The fragments referred to which do not appear in the table, can be found without difficulty in Kock's edition from Meineke's numbers.

Author.	Meineke.		Kock.	Author.	Meineke.		Kock.
Alexis.	Agonis	1	3	Anaxandrides.	Incert.	13	78
		2	2			17	68
		3	4		Odysseus	1	33
		4	5		Tereus	2	47
	Incert.	14	282			3	46
		18	279	Anaxilas.	Incert.	2	34
		26	293			3	36
		31	271			4	35
		34	262			5	37
		35	267			6	38
		38	289		Neottis	1	22
		39	302			2	21
		40	339	Antiphanes.	Acestria	1	20
		53	314		Aeolus	1	18
	Isostas.	1	98		Agroecus	2	2
	Mandragor.	2	142		Arcas	2	41
		5	144		Dyspratus	1	89
	Olynthia	1	162		Incert.	12	235
		2	159			13	300
	Tarantini	5	223			51	324
	Traumatias	2	234			52	292
Amphis.	Dithyramb.	2	15			53	329
Anaxandrides.	Incert.	1	52			54	251
		5	56			55	252
		9	60			57	253
		10	61			71	239

Table of Comic Fragments.

Author.	Meineke.	Kock	Author.	Meineke.	Kock
Antiphanes.	Incert. 95	320	**Eriphus.**	Meliboea 1	2
	Mystis 3	165		2	7
	Neanisci 2	167	**Eubulus.**	Cercopes 1	54
	Neottis 3	170		Campyl. 1	44
	Omphale 3	178		2	43
Araros.	Caeneus 4	5		3	41
Aristophanes.	Cocal. 2	347		4	42
	3	346		5	45
	4	348		6	46
	5	349		Incert. 3	125
	6	351		9	127
	7	350		20	133
	10	354		25	148
	12	355		Sphingocar. 2	108
	Daed. 3	187		3	106
	Geras 5	141		Stephanopol. 1	98
	6	140		2	104
	7	142		3	105
	Pelargi 1	438		4	99
	Polyid. 2	453	**Eupolis.**	Autolycus 10	44
	Scen. Cat. 1	472	**Menander.**	Andria 1	48
	2	864		Androgynus 2	57
	3	862		Arrephorus 3	66
	Thesmoph. B. 26	338 / 907		Chalceia 3	509
				Eunuchus 7	190
Aristophon.	Iatrus 2	3		Georgus 6	100
	Pythagor. 2	11		Halieis 6	18
Crates.	Incert. 3	Cratinus 302		10	16
	4	40		Hiereia 2	546
Cratinus.	Seriph. 12	216		Incert. 1	654
Diphilus.	Incert. 2	87		3	532
	6	91		6	535
	16	101		7	536
	33	115		8	547-8
	34	136		14	541
	47	129		16	599
	Zographus 1	44		27	564-5
Ephippus.	Philyra 2	21		32	558
	3	23		36	566
				54	582

Table of Comic Fragments.

Author.	Meineke.	Kock.	Author.	Meineke.	Kock.
Menander.	*Incert.* 55	585	**Menander.**	*Misogynes* 2	332
	57	583		3	333
	58	584		4	601
	59	586		5	326
	73	608		9	329
	99	645		*Misumenus* 3	338
	100	646		5	336
	101	647		6	337
	102	648		7	335
	103	649		8	345
	104	650		10	341
	105	651		11	342
	106	652		12	343
	107	653		*Nauclerus* 4	352
	108	662		*Orge* 5	366
	109	603		*Plocion* 1	402
	112	657		2	403
	113	659		3	404
	114	658		4	404
	115	660		*Sicyonius* 3	438
	117	661		*Synaristosae* 1	450
	133	610		2	451
	154	702		4	449
	155	703		*Thesaurus* 1	235
	156	704		2	237
	185	720		3	236
	196	798	**Nicostratus.**	*Pandrosus* 1	21
	197	745		2	19
	198	746		3	20
	199	739	**Pherecrates.**	*Thalatta* 2	56
	241	727		3	52
	256	800		4	51
	258	802		5	54
	259	803		7	53
	294	879	**Philemon.**	*Incert.* 3	89
	346	955		4	88
	469	687		8	93
	499	754		31	124
	Leucadia 1	312		32	126
	Misogynes 1	325		35	139

Author.	Meineke.		Kock.	Author.	Meineke.		Kock.
Philemon.	*Incert.*	44	132	Plato.	*Phaon*	4	178
		49	138			10	179
		64	156	Strattis.	*Maced.*	5	26
		76	169	Theophilus.	*Philaul.*	1	12
		77	170			2	11
		78	171	Theopompus.	*Capelid.*	3	26
		85	177			4	28
		95	190			5	27
		103	196		*Hedychares*	3	14
		105	198			4	16
		106	239		*Odysseus*	1	35
		124	218		*Medus*	2	29
Philetaerus.	*Cynagis*	1	9	Timocles.	*Epist.*	1	10
		2	6, 7		*Icarii*	1	17
		3	8			2	14
Plato.	*Phaon*	2	174	Xenarchus.	*Scythae*	1	12
		3	175				

www.ingramcontent.com/pod-product-compliance
Lightning Source LLC
Chambersburg PA
CBHW032142230426
43672CB00011B/2425